A Short History of
English Literature

Second Edition

A Short History of English Literature

Second Edition

by

Robert Barnard

BLACKWELL
Oxford UK & Cambridge USA

First edition published in association with Universitetsforlaget, Oslo, Norway, 1984
Second edition 1994
Reprinted 1994, 1995, 1996, 1998

Blackwell Publishers Ltd
108 Cowley Road
Oxford OX4 1JF, UK

Blackwell Publishers Inc.
350 Main Street
Malden, Massachusetts 02148, USA

British Library Cataloguing in Publication Data
A CIP catalogue record for this book is available from the British Library

Library of Congress Cataloging in Publication Data
Barnard, Robert.
A short history of English literature/by Robert Barnard. — 2nd ed.
p. cm.
Includes index.
ISBN 0–631–19088–0
1. English literature — History and criticism. I. Title.
PR83.B27 1994 820.9 — dc20 93–43242 CIP

Typeset in 11 on 13pt Garamond 3 by Pure Tech India Ltd.,Pondicherry, India
Printed and bound in Great Britain by MPG Books Ltd, Bodmin, Cornwall

Contents

Preface to the Second Edition   vi

Preface to the First Edition   vii

1   The Age of Chaucer   1

2   Sixteenth-century Poetry and Prose   7

3   The Beginnings of Drama   14

4   Shakespeare   22

5   Stuart Drama   35

6   Poetry – Donne to Milton   41

7   The Restoration   52

8   The Eighteenth Century   64

9   The Rise of the Novel   74

10   The Birth of Romanticism   85

11   Romantics and Anti-Romantics   98

12   The Early Victorian Novelists   110

13   The Early Victorian Poets   123

14   The Late Victorians   132

15   The Birth of Modern Poetry   145

16   The Birth of the Modern Novel   156

17   Depression and War   171

18   Twentieth-century Drama   185

19   From the Fifties to the Nineties   201

Index   227

Preface to the Second Edition

For this revised and updated edition the body of the text has been left largely as it was: I have had no letters from readers or teachers pointing out gross errors; this may indicate lethargy, but I have preferred to take it that there are none. There will be those who will wish I had changed my selection of more recent authors (for example, included A. S. Byatt) but I have preferred to stand by my choices.

The chapter on twentieth-century drama and the last chapter have been thoroughly revised and updated. The choice of recent writers and works presents as always particular difficulties, and the criteria I have used are whether I myself enjoy the writer, and whether I think it likely they will be taught at university level. This second one was particularly difficult to formulate judgments on, and I am conscious there is a lack of women among the novelists who emerged in the eighties treated here. I can only say that none of those whom I considered seemed unequivocally to demand a place in my final pages. That situation will almost certainly change if this book is revised again.

R. B.

Preface to the First Edition

This short history of English literature has been written to meet the needs of students in English at the outset of their courses, both in England and overseas. I hope, though, that it will also prove of interest to the general reader who feels that his reading would be enriched by a history that puts the main outlines clearly before him.

My proposed audience has dictated the proportions and the procedures adopted in this history. Firstly, I have divided the space so that by far the greatest weight falls on the last two centuries (where most of the reading of the beginning student and the general reader is likely to be). Secondly, many minor figures who would normally be expected to put in an appearance in a literary history are quietly forgotten, so that attention can be focused on the major figures. Similarly, only writers whose literary career was centred on Britain are treated. To slip in a few 'token' Commonwealth writers seemed to me more insulting than helpful; moreover, it is time Australian writers, for example, were treated in the context of Australian literature, not as appendages to English literature. Thirdly, in treating these major writers, I have tried to concentrate on a few works, the ones that are most likely to be read. I hope, in this way, to increase the usefulness of the work to the student, but I hope, too, that this plan may give to the general reader a better grasp of the major writers through their most important works.

In writing a book of this kind, in intention an introduction to English literature as a whole, my main aim has been to acquaint the reader with what is the generally accepted view of the authors and periods under discussion. It has been no part of my aim to serve up currently fashionable views, or to provide startling new insights; indeed, if an original idea is to be found anywhere in this book, it has got in by mistake and is almost certainly wrong.

In various smaller ways, too, I have tried to keep in mind the needs of my audience. In quoting from earlier texts I have cautiously modernized and revised the punctuation to make them more readily comprehensible. I have made various departures from regular scholarly practice (for example, I have italicized all titles of poems) where I felt that to follow it might be productive of confusion. To keep the period under discussion constantly before the reader I have quoted birth and death dates of all the major writers in the text. Those for the minor figures will be found in the index. Where dates are quoted for monarchs, these are the dates of their reigns.

I am grateful to several generations of students at the Universities of New England, Bergen and Tromsø for many ideas and perspectives, and (I hope) for some insight into those areas of English literature which are of most general interest.

I am indebted to my wife, Louise Barnard, for constructing the index, and for typing the final draft, in which she saved me from many errors, some of which would have been humiliating. For any that remain I am alone responsible. I acknowledge gratefully a grant from the Norwegian Humanities Research Council which enabled this book to be completed on schedule, and the help of many teachers in tertiary institutions in Norway and Sweden, who have contributed suggestions and corrections.

R. B.

1

The Age of Chaucer

England in the mid-fourteenth century, the England in which Chaucer, Langland and the author of *Gawain* grew up, was to all appearances a country cresting a wave of success. In Edward III it had a glamorous, efficient king, and one who appreciated the value of the outward show of monarchy – pageantry, honours, patronage. His court was a centre of culture and chivalry renowned over Europe. With the French monarchy relatively weak, England was losing its status as a dim little off-shore island and attaining the rank of European power. Its seamen were forging links all over Europe and North Africa; its merchants were prospering, forming the beginnings of a solid middle-class. It was a confident, exuberant age. The king had just founded the greatest order of English chivalry, the Order of the Garter, basing it on a celebrated act of chivalry performed by the king towards the Countess of Salisbury.

The reality was rather different – just as the reality behind the garter incident was rather different (according to one account the Countess was wife of the king's best friend, and he raped her). The Black Death of 1348, and subsequent plagues only slightly less terrible, had undermined the whole basis of feudal society, and the Peasants' Revolt of 1381 and the civil wars of the next century were evidence of the decline and ultimate collapse of the traditional medieval class structure. Edward's French wars in pursuit of a dubious claim to the French crown overstretched English resources and proved a chimera which was to delude English kings and impoverish their country for a century. Edward's England, then, was a glorious structure built on dangerously flimsy foundations – a thriving, exciting, fluid age, which finds brilliant expression in the work of its greatest poet.

Geoffrey Chaucer (?1340–1400) is the first English writer whom we today can read with anything like ease and he is one who speaks with particular directness to the modern reader. He was a servant of the court and on occasion its emissary abroad, yet he was born into the middle class which was then so rapidly consolidating its position. Thus his contacts ranged from the highest to the lowest in this changing, threatened, feudal society, and with his extraordinary appetite for all manifestations of human aspiration and human folly he was able to capture the essence of fourteenth-century life in a way no contemporary, in Britain or on the Continent, could rival.

The plan of Chaucer's last and greatest work, *The Canterbury Tales*, was not original: to gather together a heterogeneous collection of people and have them tell a series of stories – moral stories, romantic stories, bawdy stories, fables. It is Chaucer's genius for characterization and his feeling for social relationships, for the personal, moral and class tensions between people, that give his work a warmth and depth that other similar medieval collections lack. The people on his pilgrimage are described in the masterly 'General Prologue,' they frequently speak for themselves in the prologues to the 'Tales,' they reveal – often unconsciously – further aspects of their natures in their choice of tale and manner of telling it, and in the conversations, disputes and fights that occur between the tales we get a further sense of medieval humanity at its most unzipped and outrageous.

The pictures of the pilgrims in the 'General Prologue' are little masterpieces of characterization in which what seems at first sight to be a mere accumulation of detail, often quite haphazard, turns out on closer reading to be full of sly innuendo and subtle juxtapositions. If the Prioress wears a brooch with the inscription *Amor Vincit Omnia* (Love Conquers All), is it love of God or of man that is referred to? What exactly does it mean when we are told that the Shipman, if he took prisoners by sea, 'by water he sent them home to every land'? (It means he threw them into the water to drown). What precisely does Chaucer mean to imply when he says that the Wife of Bath (for whom the pilgrimage was a combination of package tour and husband-hunt) was very good at 'wandering by the way'? Two lines, placed together, will illuminate a character and his profession. The excellence of the Cook's creamed chicken is placed next to a description of the foul ulcer on his shin; the description of the worldly monk as a fine prelate comes next to a description of his gourmet taste in food; in the portrait of the Wife of Bath we get this:

She was a worthy woman all her live:
Husbands at churchè door she haddè five . . .

Sometimes these characters speak with a naturalness or an intensity that like a trumpet brings down the walls of the centuries between us and them. 'Alas, alas, that ever love was sin!' cries the Wife of Bath — who apart from the five husbands has enjoyed 'other company in youth,' so she clearly hasn't been unduly inhibited. 'Let Austin have his swink to him reserved!' ('Let Saint Augustine do his own bl— work!') expostulates the Monk, when he is reminded that the founder of his religious order included hard work among the daily tasks of the monks.

In the tales these people tell, too, we have a wonderful picture of all sides of medieval life, but there is also that tang of modernity that makes our heart stop as we realize our kinship with them. The Pardoner tells his story of the riotous group of young men who decide to seek out and kill Death — and we recognize the teenage rowdies in our own streets. The Nun's Priest tells an animal fable about a chicken run — about Chauntecleer who with his six wives, his parade of learning, and his overwhelming conceit is the perfect male chauvinist cock — and even in these days we recognize pale shadows of his type. The bawdy tales of the Miller and the Reeve are funny today precisely because of the swift, economical, humane delineation of characters we can recognize: the story of someone getting branded on the bare behind may be funny on first reading, but it is only funny on second reading if you are interested in the man behind the behind.

Every sort of story is here, and every technique of story-telling in its most modern form. The Wife of Bath's Prologue (longer and better than her actual Tale) tells in shameless detail how she gained the mastery over one after another of her husbands, and one gropes towards Joyce's Molly Bloom for comparisons; the Reeve's Tale tells a story of complicated changings of bed-partners which reminds us of nothing so much as a modern French farce. At one point in the Nun's Priest's Tale Chauntecleer, who has dreamed he has been seized by a fox, launches into an enormously long disquisition on the theory of dreams, their meaning in history and literature, intended to put down his silly wives who have pooh-poohed the prophetic significance of his dream. So long and rambling is it that we are about to say how medieval and dated this all is when suddenly Chauntecleer ends his lecture and is so puffed up with his learning and his debating victory over his wives that he forgets the point of the whole thing, jumps down into the hen-run – and is seized by a fox. The long disquisition has been an example of Chaucer's mastery of one of the gifts of a great story-teller – that of timing.

The Canterbury Tales were unfinished at Chaucer's death. The greatest long poem he completed was the slightly earlier *Troilus and Criseyde*, a superb re-working of one of the most popular medieval accretions to the legends of Troy. The framework is superficially a courtly love story – of how Prince Troilus courts the lovely widow Criseyde, how she is sent to join her father in the Grecian camp, and is there unfaithful to him. But Chaucer's treatment of this simple story is wholly modern in tone, particularly in its treatment of the central characters. Criseyde is the first depiction in depth of a woman in our literature, and still one of the finest. She is a widow, contented in her solitude and independence:

> I am myn ownė woman, well at easė . . .
> Shal noon housbondė seyn to me 'checkmate!'
> For either they ben full of jealousye,
> Or masterful, or loven novelryė.   (novelty)

Chaucer's sympathy with Criseyde shows itself in the way he meticulously details the considerations that drive her into Troilus's arms: since her father's defection to the Greeks she is alone in a hostile city; flattered by the attentions of a Prince, she feels the stars are ordaining that she fall to him; she is pestered by her cousin Pandarus, who acts as pimp for his friend Troilus. From being the prototype of the faithless woman, as she is in much of medieval literature, Chaucer transforms Criseyde into the tragic symbol of war's effects on human relationships and fates.

The unknown author of *Sir Gawain and the Green Knight*, writing at around the same time as Chaucer, seems at first sight more remote from the present-day reader: his alliterative verse form was old-fashioned even in his own day; his dialect, that of North-West England, is much more difficult for us; and his subject-matter does not immediately call on us to claim kinship with medieval man, as Chaucer's does in his best tales. *Sir Gawain* is a story of King Arthur's knights, but the courtly romance is married to archetypal folk myths and to religion: the knights are challenged at Christmas by a green knight – who is beheaded, yet speaks on and issues a challenge for the succeeding Christmas. But there is in fact nothing primitive in this story-teller's art: behind the odd mixture of the courtly, the Christian and the mythic is a delicate morality about man's duty – as knight, as lover, as Christian. By involving Sir Gawain in a supernatural challenge the author nullifies many of his attributes as perfect knight; and when he has him sexually tempted by his host's wife he involves him in delicate questions of conscience concerning his duty as knight and his duty to his host – questions that can be resolved only by marrying courtly and Christian codes. Through both these plot elements he succeeded in relating the idealized world of Arthur with the real world he knew. If *Gawain* demands more of us, as readers, than Chaucer does, we are ultimately convinced we are in the presence of as great an artist. This feeling is augmented by the other poems probably by him bound into the same single surviving manuscript – particularly *Pearl*, a lament for the loss of his daughter that goes some way towards negativing Barbara Tuchman's judgment that medieval man was uninterested in children, and that 'emotion in relation to them rarely appears in art or literature.'

The other major work of the age of Chaucer, *The Vision of Piers Plowman*, is also written in the alliterative verse style of *Gawain*, but it displays a very different kind of mind. Its author – William Langland – is a name to us only, but he is usually conjectured to be a rural priest, and one agonized by the social abuses of his time. Using the framework of a dream – a favourite medieval device – the poem covers a wide spectrum from social satire to religious allegory, as the author puts forward his notion of what a truly Christian community would be, and how sadly far the England he knows falls short of it. His hatred of pride, greed and ostentation, his almost 'nonconformist' conscience, ally him with later writers in the puritan tradition such as the Milton of *Lycidas* and John Bunyan. And like Bunyan he retained his popularity with ordinary readers long after his own time – at least until the Elizabethan age.

After this inexplicably rich harvest of literary genius the fifteenth century is a sad, barren period. The splendour of Edward's court gave way to popular discontent, factional strife and the desolating futility of the Wars of the Roses, with two factions of noble thugs disputing a crown that increasingly seemed not worth the winning. In England, in spite of the establishment of Caxton's printing press, literary activity was at its lowest ebb – at best imitative, uncertain of aim, fleeing from the disagreeable present into nostalgia. Even Sir Thomas Malory's *Morte D'Arthur* – a collection and retelling of the early French and English legends of King Arthur – while a superb example of the potential of English prose, nevertheless at times seems enervated and lacking in conviction, as if the knightly ideal the author was celebrating seemed even to himself remote and impossible in a country torn apart by its own nobility.

The richest poetic harvest was late in the century in Scotland. This kingdom, enjoying unusual stability under a succession of talented Stuart kings, produced several poets of consequence, notably Robert Henryson (?1430–?1506) and William Dunbar (?1460–?1513). Henryson's *Testament of Cresseid* is a sort of sequel to Chaucer's poem in which the faithless Cresseid contracts leprosy. Its dialect (and perhaps its subject) will always prevent its enjoying the wide popularity of Chaucer's poem, yet it can be mentioned in the same breath without bathos, which is more than can be said of most fifteenth century poems inspired by Chaucer. And Dunbar's famous 'Lament for the Makaris' (or poets), with its haunting, disturbing refrain *Timor mortis conturbat me* (I am troubled by the fear of death) may be taken as a requiem for a sad, confused, barren century:

> The state of man does change and vary
> Now sound, now sick, now blith, now sary   (sorry)
> Now dansand merry, now like to die;
> > *Timor mortis conturbat me . . .*
> He takis the knichtis in to field
> Enarmit under helm and shield,
> Victor he is at all mellie   (battles)
> > *Timor mortis conturbat me.*

2
Sixteenth-century Poetry and Prose

The Wars of the Roses were ended in 1485 by the military victory of Henry VII, and the establishment of the Tudor dynasty – strong, brilliant, subtle, tending to the tyrannical, but strongly rooted in national life and national impulses. A good part of its strength flowed from the decimation of the old aristocratic class during the civil wars, and the need to create a new nobility of thrusting, yet dependent, newcomers. Its weakness was its inability to produce heirs, and it lasted no more than three generations.

It was not until the reign of Elizabeth I (1558–1603), the last of the Tudors, that England began once more to play the sort of role in international affairs it had done in Chaucer's time. However, the earlier reigns saw impulses from the European Renaissance seeping into English intellectual and artistic life, often taking a form rather different from that it took in more Latin countries. The rediscovery of the classical writers proceeded apace, with English humanists such as More and Colet in close touch with continental humanists such as Erasmus. Highly influential, too, was Castiglione's *The Courtier*, with its ideal of an educated, artistic, wise courtier, true adviser and support of his prince. The influence of Renaissance ideas on English education was very great, and as luck would have it Roger Ascham, one of the foremost educationists of the day, was tutor to the young Princess Elizabeth, producing in time one of the most cultivated, widely-read and multi-lingual sovereigns of her age (as she was careful to have generally acknowledged). The Renaissance absorption in man, his potential, the fascination of his mental and physical make-up, finds expression in the exuberant hedonism of the poet-dramatist Marlowe; but more typically it is modified by the very English caution, piety and sobriety of an Edmund Spenser.

The Reformation is the other crucial influence in the period, but it crept cautiously in through the back door, and by and large England was spared the internecine theological and physical struggles that ripped through central and southern Europe. Henry VIII was a conspicuously faithful son of the Catholic Church, named 'Defender of the Faith' by the Pope, and only his need of a male heir, and hence a new wife (or, as it turned out, several), led him to cut ties with Rome. The Church of England thus established gradually Protestantized itself, with the brief hic-cup of the Catholic Mary's reign (by no means so bloody as later propaganda suggested). By the middle of Elizabeth's reign a balance between Catholic and Protestant elements in the Church had been established which has persisted more or less to this day.

When one reads the first notable poet of the Tudor period, John Skelton (?1460–1529) it is impossible not to feel how much had been lost since the days of Chaucer – how much of sophistication, subtle humour, delicate feeling. Direct Skelton is: rumbustious, bawdy, up-roarious, with a biting, bully-boy kind of wit. But, remembering that Skelton was apparently poet-laureate of the universities of Oxford and Cambridge, one can only conjecture just how much extended pleasure the learned gentlemen derived from verse such as this:

> Her loathly lere   (complexion)
> Is nothing clear,
> But ugly of cheer,
> Droopy and drowsy,
> Scurvy and lowsy,
> Her face all bowsy,
> Comely crinkléd,
> Woundrously wrinkléd,
> Like a roast pig's ear,
> Bristléd with hair.

There is, admittedly, a sense of an urgent, almost brutal talking voice behind Skelton's verse. Many things, no doubt, could be done in metres such as his, but they were not things that the new Renaissance men around the court much wanted to do.

The two foremost poets of Henry VIII's age, acknowledged as path-blazers by the greater poets of his daughter's reign, were Sir Thomas Wyatt and the Earl of Surrey. Both were men of the Court, men of public affairs, frequently in trouble, occasionally in favour. Wyatt (?1503–1542) seems to have been universally liked, and to have had the King's trust, in spite of his possibly having enjoyed the favours of Anne Boleyn before she caught the eye of the King and became his second queen:

> *Noli me tangere*, for Caesar's I am   (do not touch me)
> And wild for to hold, though I seem tame

Wyatt wrote in one of his translations of Petrarch which may have been chosen for its application to himself and the King's favourite. Vigorous, bluff, forthright, Wyatt stands before us vividly from the historical records, and it is tempting to read personal experiences into many of his poems. The fact is, most of his verse was written within the subject-conventions of the time, but those subjects were living and unstale because they were still close to the poet's experience. Thus, if Wyatt or Spenser wrote about the artificiality and hypocrisy of court life, they wrote with a strong tradition of such complaints behind them, but also with personal and bitter experience to back it up. If Wyatt's favourite poetic voice is that of the complaining, forsaken lover, each poem is not to be taken as personal experience (no one, and certainly not Wyatt, could be that often forsaken), but his love life presented enough examples to give personal spice to that particular convention. His greatest poem is a vivid miniature drama, in which he envisages such a situation: the male is angry, jealous, bitter, affronted in his maleness, and his mood is sharpened by the tingling memories of past pleasures:

> They flee from me, that sometime did me seek,
> With naked foot stalking in my chamber. . . .
> Thankéd be fortune it hath been otherwise,
> Twenty times better; but once in special,
> In thin array, after a pleasant guise,
> When her loose gown from her shoulders did fall,
> And she caught me in her arms long and small,   (slender)
> And therewithall sweetly did me kiss
> And softly said, 'Dear heart, how like you this?'

Where Wyatt is often rough, experimental, immediate, his poetic disciple the Earl of Surrey (1517–1547) is musical, regular, traditional – in former times he was counted much the greater of the two for this reason; in our own he tends to be denigrated as facile. Surrey was indisputably a noble (unlike Wyatt), and though he aimed at Castiglione's ideal of the courtier, as a man of action and of learning, his life was punctuated by quarrels and scandals, and he ended on the executioner's block in 1547, only one week before that syphilitic old ruin his king himself departed this life.

Superficial many of Surrey's poems may be, but his claims as an innovator are impressive. Wyatt introduced the sonnet form to England, but the form which has been so constant an inspiration throughout English poetry was Surrey's invention – that is, three quatrains (rhyming abab, cdcd, efef) followed by a clinching couplet (gg). He it was, too, who established the blank verse form that Milton, Wordsworth, Tennyson and others were to use in many of their major poems. In his translations of parts of Virgil's *Æneid* his use of the form he himself devised is flexible and impressive:

> The Carthage lords did there the queen await;
> The trampling steed, with gold and purple decked,
> Chawing the foamy bit, there fiercely stood.
> Then issued she, backed with a great rout,
> Clad in a cloak of Tyre, embroidered rich. . . .

Wyatt and Surrey are fascinating and lively poets in themselves, but part of their importance lies in the fact that they re-established English as a vivid and flexible medium for poetry. The prose writers of the time were more ambiguous in their attitude: for example, the saintly humanist Sir Thomas More wrote his *History of King Richard III* (a work of Tudor history-cum-propaganda) in English, but his masterpiece *Utopia* in Latin. Many intellectuals of the day agonized over this problem, but a number of important works came to be written in English, especially later in the century. Among them were Elyot's *The Governor*, a treatise on the education of the man of public affairs, and Roger Ascham's book on archery, *Toxophilus*. As tutor to Princess Elizabeth Ascham no doubt influenced her own admirably direct style in her correspondence and her speeches:

> I know I have the body of a weak and feeble woman, but I have the heart and stomach of a king, and of a king of England too; and think foul scorn that Parma or Spain, or any prince of Europe, should dare to invade the borders of my realm.

She was, in fact, one of the few English leaders (Churchill, for better or worse, was another) who could sum up the temper of the times and kindle with words the national spirit.

The great ornament of Elizabeth's court, during his brief life, was Sir Philip Sidney (1554–1586), who seemed to his contemporaries to epitomize all the qualities of the ideal courtier, and to add to them a sober yet steadfast Protestant spirit. Like Surrey, he was both soldier and poet, yet unlike him he was genuinely no man's enemy, and was a solicitous patron of artists, including artists greater than himself. In poetry Sidney's claim to distinction is that he wrote the first English sonnet sequence – to form a sort of story, or emotional progression. Though the sequence, *Astrophel and Stella*, frequently deals with the familiar stuff of the sonneteer and love-sick courtier (conventions inherited from the courtly love tradition), it does so in language that is fresh, direct, and frequently even colloquial (no mean feat within the sonnet form):

> Because I breathe not love to every one,
>   Nor do not use set colours for to wear,
>   Nor nourish special locks of vowéd hair,
>   Nor give each speech a full point of a groan,
> The courtly nymphs, acquainted with the moan
>   Of them who in their lips Love's standard bear,
>   'What, he!' say they of me, 'Now I dare swear
>   He cannot love; no, no, let him alone . . .'

Even in literature Sidney was the perfect all-round man, for he wrote the most ambitious prose romance of the time – the pastoral *Arcadia*, interspersed with songs – and the finest piece of extended criticism, his *Apology for Poetry*, a vigorous and humane refutation of a narrow Puritan attack on the art.

One evidence of Sidney's generosity of mind, and of purse, was his patronage of the greatest poet of his generation, Edmund Spenser (1552–1599). Spenser, like so many of the great Elizabethan writers, was born into the class of skilled tradesmen – his education was gained on a scholarship for the sons of such, and he later went to Cambridge and (unlike many nobler university undergraduates) took the degrees of BA and MA. His talent was undeniable and recognized, and he looked to the Court for future patronage, both because this was natural for aspiring members of his class, and because, with his sense of history and tradition, the Court was a sort of emotional lodestone. He was, by and large, disappointed. Patrons he had, including Sidney, whom he clearly loved and admired. Much of his life, however, was spent in Ireland, where he was Secretary to the Lord Deputy, the effective ruler of the country – no mean position, but one he seems to have regarded as a bitter exile. After Tyrone's rebellion of 1598 he lost his estates there, and escaped to England with his family. He died, acknowledged as England's greatest poet, apparently in poverty. But the Earl of Essex gave him a splendid funeral.

Spenser carried a stage further the concern of the Tudor poets to establish English as a suitable medium for poetry. He looked back to Chaucer as his inspiration, using in his poems many words and forms which had since fallen out of use in educated circles. This deliberate archaism was condemned by many at the time ('He writ no language' said Ben Jonson), and indeed was a dangerous precedent that few followed. But it was all of a piece with Spenser's temper of mind, which was romantic and backward-looking, seeking to revive an idealized past. In *The Faerie Queene*, for example, he recreated the world of King Arthur's knights, as it was filtered through his own intensely moral, even Puritan, cast of mind (Tennyson was later to do something similar). Such a subject was of natural appeal to the Elizabethans: chivalric sports were being revived at court, as part of the romantic exaltation of the Sovereign, of 'Gloriana.' Spenser's poem was a long, sometimes almost dreamlike, series of heroic adventures, each centred on the virtues necessary to the perfect knight or gentleman. Prince Arthur makes periodic appearances, and the poem (which was to be twice as long as it is now – some nine hundred pages) was to culminate in his appearance at the court of the Faerie Queen, Gloriana. The heroic, amorous, grotesque episodes pass, like splendidly coloured sections in a tapestry, but each one is layered deep with allegorical significance – political, moral, religious.

So dazzling is Spenser's technique, proclaiming him at once the first great English poet since Chaucer, that the great episodes of the poem are still unquestionably among the treasures of our literature. Yet it must be said that, taken as a whole, *The Faerie Queene* is no longer admired as it was for centuries. Spenser's sort of allegory seems foreign to us, his conception of the poet as one removed from the dust and sweat of life is uncongenial, and even his earnest, thoughtful moralism does him no service. We prefer poetry where the jagged edge of life is more vividly revealed to us, for example the poetry of John Donne. *The Shepheardes*

Calender is difficult and remote in a slightly different way: Spenser uses the pastoral convention (as later Milton, Shelley and others were to) for his own ends, to comment on current preoccupations, and on moral questions close to his heart. The poem is rich in metrical experiment, and was interspersed with songs. Some of his occasional verses, such as the lovely *Prothalamion*, with its haunting refrain of 'Sweet Thames, run softly, till I end my song,' are further evidence of his superb technical gifts. It is sad that Spenser, always known as 'the poet's poet,' has been largely deserted by poets in our century, and thus has lost his natural audience.

3

The Beginnings of Drama

Drama begins in ritual. The mass and other ceremonial observances of the Christian Church contain many of the basic elements of drama: colour, movement, costume, props, audience involvement. When, in order to bring biblical stories to a largely illiterate congregation, the Church began to use dumb-show enactments of scenes from the Passion, or popular Old Testament stories, it aroused a thirst that could not for long be contained within the four walls of the churches themselves. Thus the Christian Church, which had been largely instrumental in suppressing the gross and decadent Roman drama in the sixth century, was ironically the motive force behind its rebirth: it is the step-mother of the modern drama, and, as in the fairy-tales, the relationship has been frequently difficult, sometimes actively hostile.

When the drama broke out of the confines of the church (perhaps because the dramatizations became too elaborate, perhaps because they were thought hardly seemly) the spectacles were still largely religious, and were thus called 'mystery' or 'miracle' plays, but the production and acting of them passed to the guilds, or unions of skilled craftsmen. Often one set of craftsmen would be responsible for one biblical story, perhaps for a story which seemed particularly relevant for their skills: thus at York the Shipwrights undertook 'The Building of the Ark;' the Fishers and Mariners 'Noah and the Flood;' and the Bakers 'The Last Supper.' The York cycle consists of nearly fifty playlets, and would provide the spectator with a very fair selection of Old and New Testament stories. These would be performed on a series of raised platforms, or sometimes on a succession of carts which could be pulled round to various parts of the city, at each of which the representation would begin anew.

I said that the spectacles were 'largely' religious, because the fact is that cheerfulness of a rather unbiblical kind would keep breaking in. The biblical characters, naturally enough, became very like English townspeople and rustics, and thus they began to break free of their religious moorings: Noah gets drunk; Noah's wife is a shrew, who refuses to board the ark unless she can bring all her fellow 'gossips' along for the trip. In the 'Second Shepherd's Play' in the Towneley cycle of miracle plays, the adoration of Christ by the shepherds is preceded by a comic action which ironically prefigures it: Mak steals a sheep from the shepherds, and when they come after him, he and his wife put it in the cradle and pretend it is their latest baby.

The medieval dramatic scene was completed by the jugglers, dancers and mimes, travelling entertainers on the fringe of society. By the period of the early Morality plays, the later fifteenth century, we begin to get evidence of small 'companies' of players, some attached to great families or prominent men of state, some travelling.

The Moralities at first sight seem a small step forwards in the gradual liberation of the drama from its religious and didactic straightjacket. They convey moral and spiritual instruction through dialogues between actors who represent abstract qualities rather than characters – Pride, Sensuality, and so on. In the best known, *Everyman*, the central figure, Everyman, travels towards Death, and in the end is left with nothing but Good Deeds to plead for him. In fact these abstractions left the dramatist – for we must now begin to think in terms of individuals writing the plays – considerable room for vivid characterization, just as the divorce of these plays from specifically biblical topics gave them much more scope in plotting and action. Gradually the dramatists and players emancipated themselves from too narrow a didacticism and began writing pieces – usually called Interludes – with stronger plots of an exclusively secular kind. Such pieces were popular in the great houses of the time, and even such a man as the saintly humanist Sir Thomas More delighted in them. John Rastell's *Calisto and Melebea* (?1530) is a love story with strong moral overtones. In Heywood's *The Play of the Wether* Jupiter gets fed up with the general dissatisfaction with the weather, and summons people to tell him what they would really like; since every trade desires a different kind of weather, he resolves to go on giving them a bit of everything, as before. It is a very English subject.

It is important to remember that there was no smooth progression from Miracle plays via Morality and Interlude to the drama as we know and still perform it. All kinds existed side by side; the Miracle plays survived the Reformation, and were still being played in the 1580s, when Marlowe was writing his first plays.

It is in the 1550s that we sense the transition to a kind of drama which we can perceive as genuinely modern, in spite of crudities and absurdities. Renaissance learning had resulted in a rediscovery of classical (especially Roman) models, and Terence and Seneca were strong, perhaps too strong, influences on the new dramatists. In addition, the earlier history of England was being re-discovered and re-interpreted – part of a general mood of recovered national self-confidence. Around 1553 were performed *Ralph Roister Doister*, a comedy of intrigue, full of stereotyped characters that were to be, in essence, repeated over and over in later comedies, and *Gammer Gurton's Needle*, a rustic comedy, broad but well-constructed. In the 1540s John Bale had written *Kyng Johan* – a half-Morality, half-history play, which contains both personified virtues and vices and also historical characters, all intended to elevate the unsavoury King John (1199–1216) into some sort of proto-Protestant hero. By 1562 *Gorboduc*, a tragedy with roots in the more mythical areas of British history, sought to dramatize, for the new Queen Elizabeth and her subjects, the dangers of a disputed succession, showing the way more clearly forward to the History Play which is one of the great glories of the later Elizabethan stage. If none of these plays is seriously stage-worthy today, in all of them we can discern the evolution of new forms and the enunciation of themes which later dramatists were to develop.

But before the great uprush of activity that characterized the last years of Elizabeth's reign could come about, something permanent in the way of a theatre had to emerge. The first such structure, called simply The Theatre, was built in 1576; within months it had a rival, The Curtain, and by the 1590s there were three or four theatres in London, all of them in the suburbs, outside the jurisdiction of the Lord Mayor.

Their construction was at once simple and convenient, and no doubt was influenced by the open courtyards inside inns, where up and down the country the actors had been accustomed to set up a simple platform and perform their plays. The typical Elizabethan theatre consisted of a three-story circular (or octagonal) building, surrounding a central acting area open to the sky. The built-in part comprised covered galleries, for the better off; in the open area, in front of the stage, stood the 'groundlings,' or poorer spectators. The stage was a large, bare platform, roofed over against the elements. Here, without scenery, was acted out the major portions of the play. There might also be a curtained-off inner stage (though this is a matter of dispute among scholars) for certain scenes, and also the upper balconies behind the stage might be used for certain sorts of scene (the balcony scene in *Romeo and Juliet* is an obvious example, and one notes scenes in which persons from beseiged towns appear on the walls); alternatively it might be used for musicians. This is all well explained, from a member of the audience's point of view, by Thomas Platter, from Basle, in 1599, after a visit to The Curtain:

> The places are built in such a way that they act on a raised scaffold, and everyone can well see everything. However, there are separate galleries and places where one sits more pleasantly and better, therefore also pays more. For he who remains standing below pays only one English penny, but if he wants to sit he is let in at another door, where he gives a further penny; but if he desires to sit on cushions in the pleasantest place, where he not only sees everything well but can also be seen, then he pays at a further door another English penny. And during the play food and drink is carried around among the people, so that one can also refresh oneself for one's money.

Though it is estimated the theatres could hold up to two or three thousand people, – economically a vital fact, allowing the managers to employ large numbers of actors – the theatres themselves were not large, and the distance from actor to spectator was never very great. Later, Jacobean dramatists were very satirical on the subject of bellowing, ranting actors, and it may be that a large, declamatory style was adopted in the early days of the theatres, but that later it was found that more subtle techniques were possible even in this open-air theatre, due to the intimate contact between actor and audience.

The acting of the women's parts in these companies was invariably entrusted to boys. It is a tribute to their skill that dramatists were not inhibited from creating full-scale female characters, such as Cleopatra or Lady Macbeth. Though from the modern theatre-goer's point of view the lack of scenery might seem a deprivation, it must be remembered that it was this that gave great flexibility of staging and speed of action to the plays. Modern Shakespeare production, in fact, tries constantly to re-create that speed and flexibility. And if scenery was lacking, spectacle was not: costume could be extremely lavish – often having belonged to a dead nobleman, or been filched by servants from a living one – and banners and pennants could add a touch of pageantry.

The companies of actors who performed at these theatres usually attached themselves to noblemen and courtiers, and were thus known as the Earl of Leicester's men, the Lord Chamberlain's men, and so on. Being technically part of the nobleman's household, they could not be arrested as 'vagabonds,' as might otherwise have been the case (vagabondage was very severely punished in Elizabethan England). But the protection of the nobleman had the additional advantage of giving them a powerful spokesman at court, an influential friend very necessary in turbulent times. The Queen herself was a lover of the new drama, but a woman who could stay on her progresses round the country with Catholic families and have them arrested for their religion when it was time for her to leave was not likely to tolerate nonsense even from her favoured players. Her Council was particularly concerned about plays with possible contemporary relevance: as long as the plays confined themselves to a general vainglorious patriotism that was fine, but if they treated such subjects as the deposition or murder of a sovereign they could be in trouble – as Shakespeare's company, the Lord Chamberlain's men, found when they revived *Richard II* at the time of the Earl of Essex's rebellion.

The authorities of the City of London were suspicious of the new theatres for different reasons: the vast crowds attending them encouraged the spread of plague; apprentices were seduced from their work by the day-time performances; there was drunkenness and disorder in and around the theatres (as at modern football matches). And many of the city authorities disliked the theatre for 'religious' reasons: Puritanism had already made considerable progress in London. So the companies of players walked a tightrope, and frequently found performances forbidden for one reason or another – in which case they often went off to tour major centres outside London.

The plays which these companies presented in the last two decades of Elizabeth's reign were of many kinds: chronicle plays of English or foreign history, especially on topics of an anti-Catholic nature, or ones that emphasized English triumphs; tragedies, frequently very bloody, often with a strong 'revenge' theme; comedies of intrigue; farcical, bucolic comedies. Kyd's *Spanish Tragedy* is a fair specimen of what audiences enjoyed in the serious vein: it begins as a love intrigue, but after the murder of one of the central figures by his supposed friends, it develops into a bloodthirsty tragedy of revenge. The murder, and the corpse-strewn finale, were among the most popular scenes in Elizabethan drama.

One should not look, at this stage, for too much subtlety of theme or character; the stage-direction in Shakespeare's *Titus Andronicus* (ca. 1590) 'Enter . . . Lavinia, ravished, her hands cut off and her tongue cut out' is symptomatic of one kind of sensationalism; that in Marlowe's *Tamburlaine the Great* 'Enter Tamburlaine, drawn in his chariot by the Kings of Trebizon and Soria with bits in their mouths' of another. But extravagant, stilted, absurd though these early Elizabethan plays often were, they have a vigour, a directness, a daring which gradually is lost in the more subtle imaginings of the Jacobean and Caroline dramatists. As, in the history of the film, much was lost as well as gained with the coming of sound, so with the early stage greater sophistication was not an unmixed blessing.

The greatest of Shakespeare's predecessors was in fact his exact contemporary, Christopher Marlowe (1564–1593). He was the son of a shoemaker, but was much better educated than Shakespeare, taking his degree at Cambridge. His scholarship there was meant for those intending to take holy orders, but one who at the end of his life was apparently giving it as his opinion that Jesus Christ and St John were lovers was clearly not someone likely to fit easily into the framework of the established Church. His life was short but riotous, and he became notorious for his atheism, his homosexuality, his drinking and brawling. He was held in the deepest suspicion in his last years by the Queen's Council, and it was possibly by a government spy that he was killed, in a tavern fight in the London suburb of Deptford. His entire life was both murky and lurid, yet it is clear that his exuberance and extravagance – which indelibly mark his plays – deeply affected his contemporaries.

Both his poetic talent and his dramatic flair were prodigious. Often the one has to come to the aid of the other: *Tamburlaine* would be a collection of ludicrous extravagances were it not that its verse – for all its bombast and its manic reaching for superlatives – so often seems to convey strange truths about the wilder extremes of human personality and ambitions. *Doctor Faustus* is dramatically a mess (though we cannot be sure the text as we have it is as Marlowe left it), yet the opening and closing scenes have overwhelming poetic power, and capture as powerfully as anything in Shakespeare the desperate human urge for power over one's fate, for a limitless knowledge:

O, what a world of profit and delight,
Of power, of honour, of omnipotence,

Is promised to the studious artisan!
All things that move between the quiet poles
Shall be at my command: emperors and kings
Are but obeyed in their several provinces,
Nor can they raise the wind, or rend the clouds,
But his dominion that exceeds in this,
Stretcheth as far as doth the mind of man;
A sound magician is a demi-god . . .

Few of the texts of Marlowe's works are reliable indicators of how his works were played in his lifetime, so it is hardly possible to say whether he was a 'golden boy' who was unlikely to discipline his prodigious talents, or whether the seeds of true maturity were there. However, his *Edward II*, probably written in the last year of his life, seems to display a firmer dramatic grip than the earlier plays, a willingness to sacrifice the passing beauty to a more consistent dramatic pulse. The theme may have been suggested by his treatment in *The Massacre at Paris* of contemporary events on the continent: the St Bartholomew Day massacre of Protestants, and the subsequent reign of Henri III, a homosexual in the power of his mother and his favourites. The nearest English equivalent was the fourteenth century Edward II, a king neither successful nor loved, and one who was deposed and murdered. It is typical of Marlowe that, having recently written a propaganda play in *Massacre*, which is rabidly anti-Catholic and pro-English, he should go on to write a piece which on every count was likely to cause unease in governing circles.

There is nothing heroic about Marlowe's Edward, and very little that is glorious or defiant in his homosexuality. He is besotted with the vain, untrustworthy Gaveston, and on his death transfers his affections to the hardly more admirable Spenser. He is a hopeless ruler, an impossible husband, a pathetic wreck of a man. And yet we are involved in Edward's slow and painful decline from power: Marlowe emphasizes the trappings of regal splendour, and counterpoints them with the pitiful, trivial nature of the man's obsession, and the increasingly brutal nature of the nobles' opposition. Edward's end is terrible enough – though less so than in real life. We do not get a sense, as we do in Shakespearean tragedy, of a man of potential greatness, brought down by character faults or an unkind destiny. Marlowe's Edward could never have been much, yet the analysis of his inadequacies and failures produces in us, to the fullest degree, pity, understanding, and a kind of respect.

In *Edward II*, and in the finer pages of *Doctor Faustus* and *Tamburlaine* we have an achievement of some magnitude. It is at least possible that, but for the knife in the ribs in the sordid Deptford tavern, Elizabethan drama might have boasted two pillars of equal strength and grandeur. As it is, it is difficult to think of Marlowe other than as the predecessor of William Shakespeare.

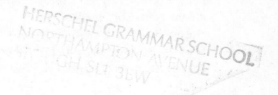

4

Shakespeare

What we know – really know, as opposed to what we conjecture or what we hope – about Shakespeare is almost nothing. Even the birthdate, 23 April 1564, is a guess complicated by patriotism, for that day is also St George's Day. His father was a glover, a man of some substance in the midlands town of Stratford-on-Avon, though his fortunes seem to have waxed and waned – being decidedly precarious during the period of Shakespeare's adolescence. He almost certainly attended the Stratford Grammar School, and when only eighteen he married Anne Hathaway, several years his senior, and already pregnant. By her he had a daughter, and a twin boy and girl, of whom the boy died at the age of eleven. Then we lose sight of Shakespeare for some years, but he reappears in London in 1592, arousing the jealousy of Robert Greene ('he . . . is in his own conceit the only Shake-scene in a country') and, apparently, the admiration of the printer and literary hack Henry Chettle ('divers of worship have reported his uprightness of dealing . . . and his facetious grace in writing'). He both acted (small parts) and wrote for the Lord Chamberlain's company, later known as the King's Men, and by 1598 he was hailed by Francis Meres as 'the most excellent in both kinds [comedy and tragedy] for the stage,' as well as the author of 'sugared sonnets among his private friends.' Around 1611 he seems to have gone into semi-retirement at Stratford, returning to his wife and family. He died on his supposed birthday in 1616. In his will he left his wife 'my second-best bed,' a fact which has afforded more scope for fun (and conjecture) than all the rest of his shadowy life.

Any biography of Shakespeare – even so brief a summary as the above – is of necessity rich in 'must have's and 'almost certainly's. The sparse, bare facts are filled out with political, social and theatrical history. The fact that we know so little of Shakespeare has meant that he has been 'taken over' by men of all professions and opinions: he is a Catholic, a puritan, a soldier, a sailor, a proto-Socialist, a Fascist. In fact, we gain from the record *no* sense of Shakespeare's personality, and no evidence of his opinions. We may *guess* from the plays that – for example – he was suspicious of 'democracy,' contemptuous of 'the mob,' in favour of strong, centralized government and in love with the mystique of monarchy. But plays are not political manifestos. Speeches in plays are expressions of the character who speaks them. Plays are written for certain audiences and (in Shakespeare's time) to catch the ear of possible patrons. Shakespeare the man is a blank, a mystery. Our sense of the 'character' of the author may fill out and complicate our response to his works (as it does in the case of Shakespeare's contemporaries Marlowe and Jonson). Not so with Shakespeare. We are left with the plays.

The dramatic works with which the provincial upstart tried to shake the scenes of London around the year 1590 – these were the years of the Spanish Armada and its aftermath – were the plays of a young man, as they also were the plays of a young theatre: they were fiery, uneven, grand, absurd; they tried everything except playing safe. Within a single scene we may encounter superb rhetoric and ludicrous fustian, a brilliant dramatic stroke and a catastrophic piece of contrivance. In the past commentators have often tried to slough off the fustian and the dramatic disasters by explaining that these plays were collaborations – the plums all by Shakespeare, the plum-stones by his work-mates. Sometimes, perhaps, this was the case. But few people today would wish to see Shakespeare as the dramatic equivalent of Dickens's Young Smallweed, born wearing a top-hat and morning coat. Like any other artist he needed his apprenticeship, he needed to test his powers and the theatre that was to employ them, and he needed to press both beyond their limits. Thus, if *Titus Andronicus* is a bloodthirsty mess of a play, it was perhaps a mess necessary for a man who was eventually to achieve the controlled horror of *Macbeth* and *King Lear*. And the grand-guignol exaggerations and cardboard-cut-out history of *Henry VI* lead us directly to the apotheosis of the Machiavellian villain in the early and brilliant *Richard III*.

In this play Shakespeare took the bogey-man figure of Richard III as he was presented in Tudor times (he has more recently been whitewashed by enthusiastic amateur historians, and turned into a conscientious bourgeois statesman of the Stanley Baldwin type), and created a dramatic figure of unsurpassed vitality and fascination: crooked of body, crafty of mind, delighted with his own villainy, he magnetizes those around to give up their will to his and wades through slaughter to his throne, smiling his friendship as he plunges in the knife. He is the archetype of the modern politician whom nobody trusts and everybody votes for. Shakespeare's verse technique suddenly takes on a new variety and eloquence, and, most important, it gains individuality and becomes the means of presenting a thoroughly-imagined character. Richard's verse, with its subtle changes of mood, its spurts of outrageous cheek, its misanthropy, its sudden mockery, its self-love, *is* the man, and could be spoken by no other. This outrageous tone is already caught in Richard's initial self-analysis:

> But I, – that am not shaped for sportive tricks,
> Nor made to court an amorous looking-glass;
> I, that am rudely stamp'd, and want love's majesty
> To strut before a wanton, ambling nymph;
> I that am curtail'd of this fair proportion,
> Cheated of feature by dissembling nature,
> Deform'd, unfinished, sent before my time
> Into this breathing world scarce half made up,
> And that so lamely and unfashionably
> That dogs bark at me as I halt by them . . .
> I am determined to prove the villain.

Richard III is a triumph of bravura style; in the later histories (virtually all written before the turn of the century) we find greater depth in his human as well as his social understanding. *Richard II* certainly looks backwards to Marlowe's *Edward II*, but – more notably – it looks forwards as well to Shakespeare's own great tragedies. The king, petulant, self-dramatizing and unwise, yet with a constant, vivid and poetic apprehension of the drama of kingship and his own central place in it, is a role of great human complexity and dramatic sophistication: the king's self-consciousness both involves us in his plight, yet distances us from any too facile spectator-identification. Already Shakespeare is expert at conveying the business of government, the political cross-currents, the constant intrigue behind the professions of loyalty, the ebb and flow of fortunes. Such a play is no celebration of patriotic wishful-thinking, but an investigation into the foundations of English nationhood. In the famous death-bed speech of John of Gaunt, memorized by generations of school-children, the dream-world nationalism of the opening

> This royal throne of kings, this sceptr'd isle
> This earth of majesty, this seat of Mars,
> This other Eden, demi-paradise

swiftly modulates into the savage disgust of

> Is now leas'd out – I die pronouncing it, –
> Like to a tenement or pelting farm:
> England, bound in with the triumphant sea,
> Whose rocky shore beats back the envious siege
> Of watery Neptune, is now bound in with shame,
> With inky blots, and rotten parchment bonds:
> That England, that was wont to conquer others,
> Hath made a shameful conquest of itself.

The speech seems to sum up twin impulses which run through English politics and literature: the tendency to national glorification, and the tendency towards agonized and pessimistic analysis of the State of the Nation.

In the two parts of *King Henry IV* Shakespeare's scope widens: the nature of kingship is still a major preoccupation, but it is set in its true context by the national panorama which was lacking in the earlier plays. Through Henry's son, Prince Hal, and his friend the boozing, boasting, lying Sir John Falstaff, one of the greatest comic creations in our literature, we gain an entry into a classless world of thieves, layabouts and whores. The agonizing political problems of the monarch are given perspective by this backcloth of wenching, drinking, soldiering. The histories begin to be Shakespeare's vision not of the nation's rulers, but of the nation itself.

In comedy too, Shakespeare's art made enormous strides in his first decade as a playwright. The early comedies tend towards rumbustious farce, splendidly playable, but hardly advancing the boundaries of comedy as such. In *The Taming of the Shrew*, for example, verve and energy have to go a long way to compensate for a subject which many will find distasteful – the taming of a 'shrew' into total wifely submission. The most artificial of these early comedies, *Love's Labours Lost*, is nevertheless the one that points most interestingly forward: it is the work of a young man in love with language and its possibilities (as he always was), and the intricate verbal beauty of its celebration of the pains and pleasures of love looks ahead partly to his superb sequence of sonnets, but also to the more viably dramatic beauties of the mature comedies.

The three comedies that most securely hold the stage today are *As You Like It*, *Twelfth Night* and *Much Ado About Nothing* — all written within two or three years, each one subtly different from the others in its exploitation of comic modes. *Much Ado* looks forward to the Restoration comedies of manners: we have the 'witty couple,' whose intellectual sparring leads them inexorably towards marriage, contrasted with the more serious, more 'romantic' lovers, whose love is crossed by mistrust or misunderstanding. *As You Like It* exploits the perennial appeal of the pastoral mode — the impulse to escape from life's complexities and involvements to a simpler mode of existence in rural surroundings. The Forest of Arden, where most of the play takes place, and to which almost all the characters at one time or another come, is shelter and spring-time, pasture and nurture, the ideal setting for the pleasures, pains and delightful mix-ups of young love. But lest escapist fantasy should cloy, we have the melancholy and cynicism of the courtier Jaques to put it in perspective, as well as the grating wit of the clown, Touchstone.

Most subtle of all in its interweaving of different modes of comedy and farce is *Twelfth Night*. Like *As You Like It*, the play has as its starting point a girl disguising herself as a boy — a comic ploy that is only half-realized on the modern stage: at Shakespeare's Globe Theatre, with a boy playing a girl disguised as a boy, the possibilities for farce, innuendo and parody of sexual roles must have been infinite. Disguise always serves as some kind of mask, often one from behind which truth may be told, but it is worth remembering that when the disguise involves a woman dressing up as a man, audiences of the time would have had particular fun from the fact that the female character is utter-ing truths that normally a woman would have had to keep to herself.

Viola, then, disguised as a boy, goes into the service of the Duke Orsino, and there she finds others whose real natures are also disguised, less to deceive others than to deceive themselves. The Duke is in love with Lady Olivia — poetically, passionately, hopelessly in love. We soon suspect that he is not in love with Olivia so much as he is in love with love, and in love with the hopeless spectacle of his own love. The fact that he feels an odd attraction for his 'page' Viola adds an interesting gloss and opens the way for much ambiguous humour. Olivia is another cultivator of emotions, though she certainly has no desire to cultivate a love for Orsino. She is luxuriating in her grief at her brother's death, and has forsworn the world to nourish her sense of loss. Like most such self-immolators and misanthropes in comedy (and, indeed, in such a serious book as *Wuthering Heights*) her artificially-cultivated rejection of the world quickly wears thin, and her defensive wall collapses at the first suggestion of a siege. Viola, as messenger of the Duke, arouses her barely suppressed romantic longings, and the scenes between them catch fire into a breathless poetry, both beautiful yet (in the circumstances) comic. The pattern of the play is still further complicated by the fact that Viola has fallen in love with her master, so that the central plot of the play is a comic chain: the Duke Orsino loves Olivia who loves Viola who loves the Duke.

The 'high' comedy of the main story of the play is complemented by the lower comedy of the scenes in the less exalted regions of Olivia's house. Her relation Sir Toby Belch is a Lord of Misrule, a minor Falstaff, drinking, wenching and concocting elaborate japes. With his henchmen, the gull Sir Andrew Aguecheek, the clown Feste and the maid Maria he persuades Olivia's steward Malvolio that his mistress is in love with him. Malvolio is honourable, humourless, egotistical and puritanical. The Americanism 'uptight' might have been invented for him. Because he takes no enjoyment from the pleasures of the flesh, he is all too willing to prevent other people from indulging in them. 'Dost thou think, because thou art virtuous, there shall be no more cakes and ale?' demands Sir Toby, the classic rebuke to the joy-denying Puritan. Yet as he is 'gulled' (fooled and discomfited) by Sir Toby and his gang, as he first makes himself ludicrous at the supposed command of Olivia, and eventually lands up in the madhouse, Malvolio gains a certain painful dignity. As in the case of Shylock in *The Merchant of Venice*, we may dislike and disapprove of what he does and what he stands for, but we recognize in him a potential, even a certain grandeur, which sets him apart from his tormentors. Sir Toby and the rest assert the legitimacy of pleasure, but Malvolio as a man contains possibilities beyond and higher than pleasure. It is this balance, and psychological insights of this kind, that mark off these plays as among the supreme achievements in the comic vein.

The first years of the seventeenth century were the crowning ones in Shakespeare's career – above all the period of the great tragedies. Shakespeare's first mature tragedy, *Romeo and Juliet*, had been written around

1596. This is less a tragedy of character – passionate and pathetic as the two lovers are – than one of fate and social circumstance. The two adolescents are caught up in the petty, blood-thirsty politics of Renaissance Italy, and the fate which at first seems to smile on their love, later changes aspect. Their death is the result of accident; in later tragedies Shakespeare prefers to trace the effect of a particular character's involvement in a particular situation, the interaction leading to catastrophe.

Julius Caesar (1599) is a tragedy that never receives its due praise, perhaps because generations of school-children have had to study it for examinations. The play catches remarkably the spirit of the classical world – not that it is ponderous or stiff, as in so many modern recreations of antiquity, but that it shows the positive virtues of restraint, order, self-control, and sees too the reverse side of the coin – the coldness, the ruthlessness, the power-seeking. Such breadth of understanding is remarkable in one who enjoyed only a rudimentary classical education. The tragic hero of the play is not Caesar himself but Brutus, the reluctant conspirator who sees Caesar, with his desire to be crowned Emperor, as so grave a threat to Roman 'democracy' – the rule of his own class – that only assassination can restore the purity and ideals of the state. Brutus is indeed, as he proclaims, selfless, noble, inspired by the highest motives. As he half realizes, he is a survival from a greater age, surrounded by lesser men. But Brutus is also rigid, unable to see points of view other than his own, unable to compromise. When disagreements arise among the conspirators, it is his judgment that settles the question, almost as if it were he not Caesar who aspired to imperial powers. He is noble, but he is much too fond of proclaiming his own nobility. When he settles questions, he is almost invariably wrong, due to his own lack of human insight, as well as his lack of a politician's ruthlessness. When he allows Mark Antony to speak at Caesar's funeral, his reasons are complex: such a thing is 'right,' the proper thing; he basically despises Antony as a playboy; he has no understanding of the Roman 'mob;' above all he believes that his own rational arguments will settle the question beyond all possibility of dissent. It is a fatal error, springing from the tragic flaw, or complex of flaws, that is at the heart of Shakespearean tragedy. Brutus, in his nobility, his slightly inhuman, self-regarding nobility, is the first of Shakespeare's great tragic heroes.

The first of the great tragedies was *Hamlet*, probably written around 1601. Generally agreed to be the peak of modern tragedy, so much has been written about the play that it has almost sunk beneath the weight of commentary. Only the reinterpretation of the title part every decade or so by a new major actor proves the play still to be living, controversial, open to fresh insight. Shakespeare takes the bare outlines of Revenge Tragedy (such as had been used by Kyd among others), but what he adds is infinitely more interesting than what he adopts. Hamlet's father, King of Denmark, has been murdered by his brother, who has then taken over both his throne and his widow. Spurred on by his father's ghost, Hamlet seeks revenge, but he has none of the single-minded blood lust of the earlier revengers. He is not incapable of action, but the cast of his mind is speculative, questioning, contemplative – so much so that action, when it finally comes, seems almost like defeat, seems to diminish rather than add to the stature of the hero. Through the long drawn out strategies and skirmishes which lead to the final catastrophe, action is punctuated by a series of questioning monologues for Hamlet, speeches of surpassing power and insight which have survived centuries of being torn from their context. But our interest is not only in Hamlet the tragic hero, for this play is also Shakespeare's most detailed evocation of a court – the power-seeking, the jostling for place, the hidden motives, the courteous superficialities that veil lust and guilt. *Hamlet*, even more than the other tragedies, is a play whose heights each generation must scale for itself.

The power of *Othello* is of a very different kind. Far from being a scholar or philosopher, Othello is a man of action – a negro in the service of the state of Venice, a man foreign to this sophisticated environment, yet accustomed to command on land and at sea. It is when he marries the white, aristocratic Desdemona that he both achieves the summit of his happiness and puts himself in a position of unusual peril. Iago, one of his military subordinates, has been passed over for promotion, and bears a grudge against him. On the surface Iago is the typical middle-rank soldier: bluff, hearty, open. 'Honest Iago' he is called, over and over. Beneath that companionable surface there lurks one of the vilest natures in all Shakespeare: jealous, cynical, corrupt, and sexually obsessed. Against such a type Othello has no chance, not when he is off the field of battle, in the strange, unaccustomed situation of being a civilian, one of a tiny coloured minority, and newly married. His nature is simple, open, self-confident – he has none of the sophisticated man's false modesty, insincere evasions, civilized shows. In the first part of the play Othello's language is like himself – grand, confident, wide-ranging:

> O my soul's joy!
> If after every tempest come such calms,
> May the winds blow till they have waken'd death!

Iago's, on the other hand, is brutal, obsessed, littered with images of low animals and copulation:

> Even now, now, very now, an old black ram
> Is tupping your white ewe.

Even in Shakespeare's day, the language of racialist abuse was beginning to establish itself.

Such distinguishing of characters by their imagery, by the nature and quality of their word-music, was not unusual in Shakespeare. What is most impressive here, and most terrible, is that in the great Act III, scene III – perhaps the greatest single scene in all Shakespeare – we are enabled to watch the take-over of one mind by another. Iago first mutters – audibly, of course – his supposed doubts about Desdemona's faithfulness; then he questions Othello, in a roundabout way, but one full of meaning, about her relations with his handsome lieutenant Cassio; then he counsels him against jealousy, thus making sure that he starts to look for reasons for jealousy: soon he is giving him details of an (imaginary) erotic dream of Cassio's, about Desdemona. By the end of the scene, and until the murder of Desdemona is accomplished, Othello is a man possessed: his innate simplicity and nobility of mind make only occasional, poignant reappearances; for the most part he is in the grip of the 'green-eyed monster' jealousy, and as he bellows his foul abuse of her the very imagery he uses – obsessively sexual, full of animality – shows that Iago has taken possession of his mind. He speaks of Desdemona as 'a cistern for foul toads / To knot and gender in;' to her hope that he believes her honest, his reply is: 'O ay, as summer flies are in the shambles, / That quicken even with blowing.' We have a terrifying sense of hearing the voice of Iago from the body of Othello.

Othello is a superbly constructed piece, fast, clean of line, free of all irrelevance. Perhaps this is because it is the least political, the least social of the tragedies. Here we are concerned not with the health and proper functioning of the state, but with the health and proper functioning of a marriage. Because it is the most domestic of the tragedies, it is (to my mind) also the most involving on a personal level, the most immediate.

So total is Othello's overthrow, so brief the moment of self-realization and restoration allowed him at the end, that it is also the most fearful, the one that speaks most terrifyingly about ourselves. At the end of the tragedies of state, a new generation may pick up the pieces and make a new start. With the murder of Desdemona and the suicide of Othello there is total desolation, without hope of any new beginning.

Though *Macbeth*, too, has a marriage at its centre, it is in every other way poles apart from *Othello* – a tragedy of state, a tragedy in which eternal forces engage. It was written as a sort of compliment to the new king, James VI of Scotland who had in 1603 become James I of England: not only is his ancestry hailed, his special interest in witchcraft (he caused the persecution and death of a great many innocent old ladies in the course of his reign) is doubtless the cause of the dramatic stroke which begins the play – the appearance of three witches, amid thunder and lightning, and their assignation with Macbeth (whose name thus takes on demonic overtones).

Macbeth is a very different kind of tragic hero to Othello. The 'tragic flaw' which mars most Shakespearean heroes and wreaks their downfall is in Macbeth more basic, more cancerous – is undoubtedly an evil rather than a weakness. Macbeth at the beginning of the play has just fought loyally (but brutally) in support of his king; he is near enough to the throne to be ambitious, yet his ambition is checked by a politician's hesitations, a fear of consequences, an unwillingness to take the irrevocable step. That step is the murder of King Duncan while he is on a visit to Macbeth's castle of Glamis – a doubly damned treachery, since not only the duty of a subject but also the duties of a host cry out against it. To accomplish it, Macbeth needs his courage screwed to the sticking place by the prophecies of the witches and the taunts of his terrible wife. But once the deed is done, Macbeth gains a fearsome confidence from the success and plunges from covert to open slaughter. The crown has been an end, not a means to him: he has aimed to be king, not to do anything with his kingship. He can only flail about him, killing suspected as well as real enemies, in an attempt to make his throne secure for himself and for the heirs he will never have. As he progresses towards a total atrophy of feeling, his wife, who has deliberately suppressed all compassion and compunction, finds herself, in her sleep, hag-ridden by horror and remorse.

A terrible pair, certainly. It might be asked what is tragic in Macbeth's downfall, since one of the emotions the spectator feels at the end of the play is exultation at a tyrant's downfall. Yet in that first half of the play, for all Macbeth's shuffling ruthlessness, one is conscious of another side of him. His imagination is that of a poet – and to the objection that this is hardly surprising in a poetic drama, one should reply that by no means all Shakespeare's tragic heroes have poetic minds: Coriolanus and Brutus assuredly do not. Macbeth has an imagination which ranges beyond the sordid greed of the immediate crime; it comprehends a limitless universe which shrieks with outrage at the deed in prospect. The as-tounding flexibility of Shakespeare's dramatic language here mirrors the mind of one who can affrightedly contemplate the wrath of God at his crime, the universal order that it wounds, at the very moment of com-mitting it:

> this Duncan
> Hath borne his faculties so meek, hath been
> So clear in his great office, that his virtues
> Will plead like angels trumpet-tongued, against
> The deep damnation of his taking-off;
> And Pity, like a naked new-born babe,
> Striding the blast, or heaven's cherubim, horsed
> Upon the sightless couriers of the air,
> Shall blow the horrid deed in every eye,
> That tears shall drown the wind . . .

If Brutus was noble, but enjoyed contemplating his own nobility, Mac-beth is evil and, horror-stricken, contemplates from a God-like vantage-point the monstrousness of his own conduct. We are struck by the terrible paradox of a sordid deed committed by a great mind, and it is the dulling of this poetic apprehension of himself that reduces Mac-beth to a common tyrant in the latter half of the play. It is the brief revival of this mental range in the monologue 'Tomorrow and tomorrow' at the end of the play that ensures that among our emotions at Mac-beth's downfall will be a sense of waste, of fine qualities dissipated and destroyed.

But *Macbeth* is also a play about Scotland, about the bond of trust between ruler and ruled, the ties which knit together the commonwealth into a fruitful, mutually dependent unity. The bonds are ragged even at the beginning of the play: it is typical of Macbeth that he should take advantage of another's rebellion, rather than initiate one himself. By his murder of Duncan he destroys all equilibrium in the kingdom: Nature itself protests, in storms and unnatural happenings, for the king is the anointed of God. The God-ordained nature of the institution of kingship is stressed in the scene (dramatically expendable but thematically vital) in which we hear of King Edward the Confessor's 'touching' the sick, acting – like Christ – as the healing emissary of God. But Macbeth is not clothed in the lurid glamour of Milton's or Byron's rebels against God, and as we watch the increasing monstrousness of his deeds, we also become conscious that those very deeds are ensuring that forces will combine as a reaction against this terrible reign, that the social and spiritual health of the kingdom will be restored under the dead king's son, Malcolm.

The tragedies looked at briefly here (together with *Antony and Cleopatra* and *King Lear*, sprawling masterpieces that respond even less well to any abbreviated treatment) are the peaks of Shakespeare's achievement, the inexhaustible masterpieces that compel each generation to re-examine and re-appraise them. During this same period Shakespeare was also writing a series of plays, comedies at least in name, that have only really won wholehearted recognition in our own century, perhaps because their rather bitter taste chimes in with the cynicism and despair of today's world. *Measure for Measure* is typical of them all in its obsession with the sexual, its undertone of disgust. The Duke of Vienna proclaims unchastity a capital offence – and then leaves the city, to return in disguise and watch the effects of his proclamation. The play touches on problems of government as well as sexual behaviour and the role of women. Sex is no longer a matter of springtime love or Elysian frolics: it is about disease, bastards, frustration, death. More bitter still is *Troilus and Cressida*, a play which even the first editors of Shakespeare found difficult to classify. Its subjects are war and love, as in Chaucer's poem on the subject, but the balance here has shifted. Troilus and Cressida are in love, certainly, but her love is light, changeable, a whimsical vanity. As she is traded from the Trojans to the Greeks, she shows herself an all-too-willing spoil of war. Around this central subject we see – at great length – the war itself, and the political arguments on both sides of the futile struggle. The characters involved – Helen, the witless cause, Paris, the trivial-minded seducer, the soldiers, the kings, the statesmen – all are bitterly satirized: as the arguments and rivalries develop we see only vanity, pompous blundering, bully-boy tactics, vainglory. The diseased cynic Thersites acts as a commentary on the play, and he is the bitterest character in all Shakespeare: 'all the argument is a cuckold and a whore: a good quarrel to draw emulous factions and bleed to death on. Now the dry serpigo on the subject! and war and lechery confound all!' The comedy of the play is so bitter as hardly to arouse laughter at all; there is no tragic purging at the end – Hector is dead, but the war will go on. A tragic end would have suggested that war *settled* something. Shakespeare's point is that it does not and cannot: undertaken in levity, vanity and bellicosity, it lays waste nations, kills the pride of the men, reduces the women to harlots, beats two peoples to exhaustion. In war there are only greater and lesser losers.

These bitter, or 'problem' comedies were not Shakespeare's last word in the comic field. His last plays, the product of his Indian summer as a playwright (1608–1612), stress reconciliation, harmonization of warring opposites, forgiveness and benison. In the most notable and magical of these plays, *The Tempest*, Prospero – who with his daughter has been exiled from his dukedom, and found refuge on an island – is fortuitously offered revenge on his usurper brother and his court, but he puts it aside in favour of forgiveness and reconciliation, symbolized by the marriage of his daughter and his enemy's son. Prospero is a figure half-human, half-God, the philosopher possessed of magic powers. When in the course of his play he meditates on his magic, and finally forswears his powers, it is difficult not to read into his words a personal meaning:

> Our revels now are ended: these our actors,
> As I foretold you, were all spirits, and
> Are melted into air, into thin air:
> And, like the baseless fabric of this vision
> The cloud-capped towers, the gorgeous palaces,
> The solemn temples, the great globe itself,
> Yea, all which it inherit, shall dissolve,
> And, like this insubstantial pageant faded,
> Leave not a rack behind: We are such stuff
> As dreams are made on, and our little life
> Is rounded with a sleep.

It is impossible to imagine a more beautiful or more serene farewell – to his art, his theatre (the Globe itself), to the world of his imagination, to life.

5
Stuart Drama

It was in the reign of James I that English drama began to change in character, becoming at once less popular, more rarefied and more obsessive in its themes and treatments. This change is often taken to be a 'turn for the worse,' but we should perhaps avoid such judgments; for all the loss of vigour and directness, a great deal of highly effective drama – brilliant yet perverse, in a mode that appeals to our century – was produced in these years.

And the change was perhaps inevitable: the theatre could not have remained the popular, socially unifying force it had been in the Elizabethan years. Coming as it did under increasing attack from puritans and moralists, it began to acquire the aura of bootleg liquor under Prohibition. In James and his queen, Anne of Denmark, the dramatists found patrons as enthusiastic as Elizabeth, and rather more generous. At court there developed the entertainments known as masques, supervised by the great Inigo Jones, in which drama combined with song, dance and elaborate settings to produce an entertainment fit for a king – splendid, but slightly witless. The story of these entertainments belongs more to the history of opera than to that of drama.

With the dramatists looking more and more to court, both for patronage and even protection, it was inevitable that the plays would become more specialist in their appeal, and that some theatres would become more exclusive, the preserve of various elites. More plays began to be performed in the 'private' theatres, which were roofed in, with smaller audience areas – and therefore higher charges. Though in other respects the stages did not change greatly, experiments began to be made with scenery and 'effects.' Very tentatively moves were made that were to culminate in the Restoration theatre – a theatre that was regrettably exclusive and cliquish, but which nevertheless held the seeds of modern performing conventions.

One can hardly perceive any diminution of vigour in the plays of Ben Jonson (1572–1637). Energetic, combative, opinionated, he bestrode the Stuart drama world as a personality and as a theorist, in a way that Shakespeare, presumably, had no desire to do. His birth was low; he had been a bricklayer and a soldier – had killed men, in fact, both on and off the battlefield. Yet somewhere he had picked up a formidable learning, which he made no effort to conceal. He said of Shakespeare that he had 'small Latin, and less Greek,' and seemed to think it mattered. His classical bias affected his dramatic theory and practice, not always for the good. But in the best of his comedies the combination of a learned and powerful mind with a wide experience of low life is unique and irresistible.

We associate Jonson with the comedy of humours – that is, the sort of characterization which aims, in broad strokes, to delineate the dominating features of a man's character. Dickens is always quoted in this context, but the comparison should not be taken too far, for though Dickens loved the plays of Jonson his own practice was different. There is a gusto and joy in Dickens's characters that spreads itself even over the villains: we would love to meet Pecksniff or Quilp, horrible though they are. We would certainly not wish to meet Corbaccio or Corvino – and the fact is that almost all Jonson's characters *are* villains. Thus the satiric tone of most of Jonson's plays is strenuous, permeated by disgust, and it may alienate the audience. 'I knew this play would be dull,' complained Lord Melbourne, Queen Victoria's first Prime Minister, watching Dickens performing in *Every Man in his Humour*, 'but that it would be so damnably dull as this I did not suppose!' Modern audiences have benefited from slightly more frequent revivals of Jonson's plays, but though they have not usually found him dull, equally they have never taken him to their hearts. He is too rigorous, too unbending for modern tastes. He is a dramatist for a particular mood, rather than (like Shakespeare) one whose emotional richness brings response in any mood.

It is not surprising that in the burgeoning capitalism of Jacobean England, with a mercantile class flourishing and making their interests and opinions felt, Jonson should direct his satiric offensive most often in the direction of those hungry for money and power. The central figure in *Volpone* is certainly greedy for both. He is the typical rascal-figure of comedy who by his wits gulls those stupider than himself. He pretends to be on the point of death, and would-be inheritors gather round him like birds of prey, bringing rich gifts in the hope of becoming his heirs. The brilliant deception is orchestrated by his servant Mosca, who at one point seems about to out-deceive the deceiver. Our sympathies are in any case seldom with the duped, for they are if anything more corrupt than Volpone, and much less entertaining. Volpone himself, though assuredly not lovable, has a certain rich extravagance of ambition that makes him subtly fascinating:

> Good morning to the day; and next, my gold! –
> Open the shrine, that I may see my saint. . . .
> Hail the world's soul, and mine! More glad than is
> The teeming earth to see the long'd-for sun
> Peep through the horns of the celestial Ram,
> Am I, to view thy splendour darkening his;
> That lying here, amongst my other hoards,
> Show'st like a flame by night; or like the day
> Struck out of chaos, when all darkness fled
> Unto the centre . . .

The totality of Volpone's own obsession lays him open to the machinations of Mosca, and the whole action suggests a Darwinian struggle in which it is the quickest-witted and most ruthless who survive. When Justice intervenes it is both quick and merciless, but it is impossible to feel satisfaction that Right has triumphed. If, in a detective story, murder is an interruption in a settled state of order, in *Volpone* justice seems an interruption in a settled state of roguery. We leave the theatre entertained, mentally stimulated, uncomfortable.

What Ben Jonson, in many of his comedies, brings to the front of the stage is the teeming, uproarious life of the London streets – the fighting, japing, copulating mixture of middle and lower classes, which can quite easily become that feared entity 'the mob.' In Shakespeare the people tend to be a footnote to the doings of the great, except in a few of the history plays. His only bourgeois play, *The Merry Wives of Windsor*, is one of his weakest. Jonson was no democrat, but his birth gave him a unique insight into the pulsing life of the London sidestreets and alleyways, and the hectic, flowing exuberance of such plays as *Bartholomew Fair* and *Every Man in his Humour* owes much to this. In them we seem to see the Jacobean ordinary man, not sentimentalized, but speaking directly to us, speaking for himself.

Nor was Jonson alone in this. Several plays have come down to us in which the citizen of London finds his voice – though he is seldom flattered, and as often as not is ridiculed. In, for example, *The Shoemaker's Holiday* and *The Knight of the Burning Pestle* we find the world of merchants, craftsmen and their apprentices (those apprentices whose playgoing habits were so much criticized by Puritan worthies) opened up to us in a spirit more free and generous than we find in Jonson. The former play, by Thomas Dekker, is so genial in tone it seems to point forward to the sentimental drama of the next century, or even to Dickens. In the latter Beaumont is more satirical, but effectively contrasts the mercantile spirit with the extremes of heroic drama and the courtly ideal which Spenser had re-animated. If there is a good deal of class satire in the play, there is much warm good fun as well.

'Bards of passion and of mirth' Keats called Beaumont and Fletcher, whose most notable work was done in collaboration. His words remind us how much the rediscovery of the early drama meant to the Romantic poets, but we cannot, perhaps, be so wholeheartedly enthusiastic about this pair as he was. They were, indeed, reliable practitioners in several fields – almost, one might say, journeymen-craftsmen. What was wanted, they could skilfully deliver. Such writers, it may be felt, survive on the wave of talent that the theatre of the time threw up. *The Maid's Tragedy* is perhaps the height of the collaboration, and it has a splendidly effective plot that was to be oft-reworked in the centuries to come, right up to the time of nineteenth century romantic opera. The king marries off his mistress to an unsuspicious courtier, who realizes too late the role assigned to him. The mistress, her conscience aroused, kills the king in a perverse, vastly effective bed scene, and the play ends with corpses littered round the stage as plentifully as in the last scene of *Hamlet*. The difference is that only in a totally incompetent performance does the ending of *Hamlet* arouse mirth, whereas *The Maid's Tragedy* needs playing of virtuoso range and sensitivity to bring it off. For it is not underpinned by any Shakespearean seriousness or passion: well-wrought though it is, the motive force seems merely to provide effective scenes, thrilling or titillating situations. This it certainly does, but the lack of overall structure or moral vision provides as good an illustration as any of the gap between Shakespeare and his rivals.

John Webster (?1580–?1625) survives more confidently in the modern theatre, for frequent revivals of *The Duchess of Malfi* have demonstrated its power and vitality. Webster's best plays are broadly in the 'revenge' tradition, and like most Jacobean writers he revels in the Italian or Spanish settings which such plays traditionally had. Italy, for Webster, was a land of subtle intrigue, insinuating violence, of perverse passions and totally amoral abandonment to them. His poetry is the poetry of the bed-chamber, the dungeon, or the graveyard; his plays leave a memory of gorgeous colours seen by flickering torchlight. He is sometimes accused of writing plays that have moments of intensity which are an end in themselves, brilliant details in defective structures. Such is hardly the case with *The Duchess of Malfi*. The motivation of the play is the determination of her brothers that the widowed Duchess should not remarry, and, when she does, and marries beneath her, their long-drawn-out, pitiless revenge. Greed, social pride and perhaps incestuous lust lie behind their torment of her. The positives in the play are the Duchess herself, and her second husband: their scenes together have a tenderness and a frank warmth which contrasts with the hothouse passions and twisted ambitions of those around them. Through all the Gothic horrors of her persecution and murder, the Duchess maintains her dignity and integrity, and an independence rare in the female characters of the time. She is also wonderfully moving:

> I know death hath ten thousand several doors
> For men to take their exits; and 'tis found
> They go on such strange geometrical hinges,
> You may open them both ways: any way, for heaven sake,
> So I were out of your whispering. Tell my brothers
> That I perceive death, now I am well awake,
> Best gift is they can give, or I can take.
> I would fain put off my last woman's fault,
> I'd not be tedious to you . . .

The fascination of Webster with the amoral, ruthless codes and courts of Renaissance Italy was symptomatic of the growing involvement of dramatists with court life, and the ambivalent feelings they had towards it. For example, when, at the opening of *Malfi*, the Duchess's husband-to-be expatiates on the excellence of the French king's rule and his sharp way with 'flattering sycophants,' Webster seems to be both paying a sincere compliment to Henri IV and offering an implied criticism of court life under the Stuarts, where James I was notoriously prone to be guided by his handsome favourites, with all the inevitable jockeying for position around the favourite that followed. This obsession with the intricate relationships and involved dependencies of court life, with the Machiavellian intrigues that resulted, increased during the reign of James I, as did the dramatists' use of horrors with perverse undertones. Tourneur's *The Revenger's Tragedy*, with its fascinated rendering of nearly every crime in the book, its poetic relishing of horror, is not untypical of the period. Though the dramatists are both fascinated by and critical of the court, their fantasticated Mediterranean settings, their involuted intrigues and frequent blood-lettings, are so extreme and grotesque as to make their relevance to the British reality rather tenuous. More effective, perhaps, are some of the plays in which there is no shrinking from blood and horror in moderation, but where the characters bear some relation to a moral reality that its audiences could recognize: Middleton's *The Changeling* is one such play, Heywood's *A Woman Killed with Kindness* another.

The theatres were closed on the outbreak of civil war (1642), and did not legally reopen until after the death of Cromwell and the restoration of Charles II. That there was a degree of surreptitious or semi-private theatrical activity is now clear, but it was always 'fringe' activity – on the run, reviving past glories of the stage in a moral climate quite antagonistic to it. That the period of the British stage's greatest glory should be succeeded by one in which it could only exist in such a hole-and-corner way is entirely consonant with the love-hate relationship the British have always had with the stage. When the theatre resumed activity, it was a new kind of theatre, presenting a new kind of play, for a new kind of spectator.

6

Poetry – Donne to Milton

The generation that grew to maturity in the 1590s, the post-Armada generation, was in some ways a typical *fin-de-siècle* one: witty, questioning, questing, cynical. With their victory over what had seemed the greatest nation in Europe the English had proved themselves, made an indelible impression on international power politics. Yet one couldn't go on indefinitely penning pæans to the national greatness, still less endless devotional hymns of praise to Gloriana, England's saviour, the bald and toothless Elizabeth I. The young wits, at any rate, did not think so. The first thirty years of Elizabeth's reign had been a time of consolidation, stabilization, respect for tradition – at least in poetry. Now was a time for daring, novelty, adventure. The age produced John Donne.

John Donne (1572–1631) was born a Catholic, lapsed while in his twenties, and eventually took Anglican orders and became the most popular preacher of his time. With the exception of the years after his runaway marriage, when he was in disgrace, he lived much of his life on the fringes of the court, and his natural audience was an educated, sophisticated, aristocratic one. His verse, significantly enough, circulated in manuscript during his lifetime, and was only published after his death. Both then and in the centuries after he was emphatically a minority taste, yet in our own time Donne has become a prime influence on modern poets, and an immensely popular classic to boot. Metaphysical poetry, of which he was the great ornament, has progressed from being considered an oddity, a crank taste, to being seen as one of the great periods of our poetry. Why does Donne seem to speak so directly to our time? To answer that question, we need to have some idea of what was special and new about Metaphysical verse.

The first thing we notice about Metaphysical poetry is the immediacy of the contact between the poet and us. Coming between the high, self-conscious seriousness of Spenser and Milton, Donne seems (unlike them) to talk to us as if we were his friend – or his lover, his enemy, his critic: the reader occupies a series of secondary but vital roles in a collection of vivid miniature dramas. We are in the room – sometimes in the bed – with the poet, as he addresses us in his various tones of voice:

> I wonder, by my troth, what thou and I
> Did, till we loved

he will say, with the intimate wonder of a lover. Or, by contrast, 'When by thy scorn, O murderess, I am dead' he will hurl at us, with the angry humiliation of the rejected suitor. The tone will change as the poem progresses, but all the basic emotions of human relationships – tenderness, cajolery, protest, scorn – will be there.

But we soon see that the immediacy and intensity of the emotional appeal to us does not rule out intellectual subtlety. In fact, Donne and his followers present tough intellectual challenges as part of the staple content of their poems: as we hear the man talking we sense the mind working – and it is as subtle, brilliant and well-stored a mind as any in his generation. Donne's intellect does not stand apart from his emotional life: the two constantly enmesh and cohere. Perhaps that is why our own time, in which many fine critics have conscientiously tried to recapture the contours of Elizabethan thought and belief, has been best equipped to rediscover the originality of Donne.

A metaphysical poem, then, is as often as not an *argument*, and one in which the whole panoply of knowledge of an Elizabethan intellectual is called into play. Scholasticism, popular superstition, classical learning, modern geographical or astronomical discoveries – are all grist to the metaphysical poet's mill. But all are used with a lightness, a playfulness, that means that the tone of the poem seldom becomes heavy, or the content a matter of mere display.

At the heart of the metaphysicals' poetic practice is the conceit – or rather their distinguishing mark is a special sort of conceit, used in a special way, for the conceit is no more than a comparison, of which Shakespeare's 'All the world's a stage' speech in *As You Like It* is an extended but fairly conventional example. The metaphysicals' conceits were intended to shock or surprise by their unexpected nature – the reader's initial sense of the unlikeness of the things compared was to give way to an assent to the likenesses the poet discovers. The conceit was often prolonged over several lines, or even through the entire poem, and the concentration and abrupt strength of the poetic style gives the metaphysicals' conceits a sort of strikingness very different from the effect produced by the average Elizabethan poet's conceits. For example, in Donne's *Holy Sonnet* number XIV, the one that begins with an anguished cry to God to take him by force — 'Batter my heart, three personed God' — we find that the sonnet develops an analogy between the poet's heart and a city under the control of an usurper, besieged by its rightful lord:

> I, like an usurp'd town, to another due,
> Labour to admit you, but Oh, to no end,
> Reason, your viceroy in me, me should defend,
> But is captiv'd, and proves weak and untrue . . .

Or, in the 'Elegie: Going to Bed,' as his mistress undresses Donne indulges in various geographical, celestial and astronomical images before, as he commences love play, he cries: 'Oh, my America, my new-found-land . . .'

Some of the characteristic features of tone and content in Donne's poetry may be illustrated from a poem — *The Sun Rising* — which has one of his most famous opening lines:

> Busy old fool, unruly sun,
> Why dost thou thus,
> Through windows and through curtains call on us?

On first reading one is taken by the sheer cheekiness of this: the sun, traditionally the revered source of warmth, promoter of fertility, is here reduced to the status of a busy-body and voyeur, peering in on lovers through their windows and insisting on reminding them of their worldly obligations. But if he is a 'saucy, pedantic wretch,' apparently confined within rigid schedules, he is also 'unruly' — which means that he intrudes where he has no rights (into the lovers' privacy, for example), but may also include a glance at the Copernican revolution, which has displaced the sun from its old, earth-encircling position — it is 'unruly' because it is no longer susceptible to the old confident laws.

After several lines in which Donne bids the sun go attend on the normal rounds of conventional people, engaged in everyday, time-serving occupations – 'Go tell court huntsmen that the king will ride' – and after a typical piece of metaphysical bravado, in which the power of the sun's beams is denied because 'I could eclipse and cloud them with a wink,' Donne brings his poem to a climax with the confident spareness of

> She is all states, and all princes I,
> Nothing else is.

But this (comparatively conventional) statement of the primacy, the all-sufficiency, the exclusiveness of love is taken, stretched if you will, to its furthest limits: if they, on their bed, are the only reality, if they include the whole world, then 'Princes do but play us,' and the sun, which must be old and tired – 'Thine age asks ease' – will, by shining on them, do its work of warming and illuminating the entire world:

> Shine here to us, and thou art everywhere;
> This bed thy centre is, these walls, thy sphere.

The poetry of Donne – more so than that of most of the metaphysicals – is so individual, so strong-lined, so sharp of tang, that it is not altogether surprising that it provoked equally forceful reaction later in the century, and for centuries to come. Still, when Dryden complained that Donne 'perplexes the minds of the fair sex with nice speculations of philosophy, when he should engage their hearts and entertain them with the softnesses of love,' he told us more about his own attitude to women than provided a reasoned criticism of Donne's love poetry. Might not some women prefer to have their minds stimulated by witty and erudite argument to being compared to a red, red rose or some other horticultural specimen? And, of course, love poetry is only part of Donne's output. His *Holy Sonnets* are equally complex, equally erudite, but Dryden presumably sheered off opining that God's mind was not to be perplexed with nice speculations of philosophy. In fact, almost all of Donne's best qualities told against him in the age of neo-classicism – his 'roughness,' his colloquial tone, his inclination to punch in the solar plexus. Yet it is his brusque, staccato utterance which gives many of his poems their telling immediacy, which gives us the illusion that we are hearing the very voice of the poet, unpremeditated, and therefore truthful to the experience of the moment. The neglect of him not only deprived readers of some of the great glories of English poetry; it diminished the possibilities of poetry itself.

Donne, in spite of his faith, which was sincere, even fervent, always seems to resemble one of the great Renaissance prelates – not corrupt, yet imposing, dramatic, demanding to be painted in brilliant reds. George Herbert (1593–1633) was a clergyman in a very different tradition, the epitome of humble piety, the model of the good shepherd: it is a line that stretches from Langland's and Chaucer's priests, through Bunyan and Trollope, to some of the Catholic priests of Graham Greene in our own day. Herbert's place in the Metaphysical tradition is second only to Donne's, but his use of metaphysical devices is very different from his master's. His conceits are unexpected, they give rise to a thread of argument that may run through an entire poem, yet they are most often drawn from everyday life, from the domestic minutiæ around him, or from the natural world, observed with wonder yet scientific precision:

> Only a sweet and virtuous soul,
> Like seasoned timber, never gives;
> But though the whole world turn to coal,
>   Then chiefly lives.

Like Donne, Herbert has his struggles with God, his moments of rebellion, for his faith, though firm, is not a mere torpid acceptance. But if a poem begins in rebellion against the social restrictions of his faith:

> I struck the board, and cried 'No more.
>   I will abroad.
> What? shall I ever sigh and pine?
> My lines and life are free; free as the road,
>   Loose as the wind, as large as store'

the reader still knows, instinctively, that the moment of rebellion is destined to end in acquiescence:

> But as I raved and grew more fierce and wild
>   At every word
> Me thoughts I heard one calling, *Child!*
>   And I replied: *My Lord*.

Religion also dominates the poetry of Richard Crashaw (?1612–1649) and Henry Vaughan (1622–1695). Crashaw was Catholic, a lover of the baroque, the fantastic, the stylized, and his poems often carry their conceits beyond the reader's threshold of acceptance. Vaughan is more direct, more down-to-earth, at times even humdrum, but his interest in the supernatural and the occult gives his poems a rather different flavour from that of his mentor Herbert. By the time these poets were at the height of their powers, the 1640s and 50s, the climate of poetry was very different from what it had been in Donne's heyday. Metaphysical poetry, always something of a brilliant sideshow, had by mid-century come to seem decidedly stale and peculiar. The so-called Cavalier poets – smooth, easy, cultivated lyricists like Lovelace and Suckling – had come and (like their king) gone. The central figures on the poetic scene, as on the political stage, were sober, serious, religious men, essentially Puritan. In particular the mid-century was dominated by the towering and controversial figure of Milton.

John Milton (1608–1674) bestrides these middle years – lonely, magnificent, uncompromising, and (according to some modern critics) regrettable. He seems to have seen his vocation as poetry from a very early age, and his dedication was enthusiastically seconded by his family who, though not aristocratic, were wealthy enough to ensure that he could devote himself single-mindedly to his art, and to his self-conscious preparation for mastery of it. There was, to be sure, talk of Milton's entering the church, to which he would have been as great an ornament as his older contemporaries Donne and Herbert. But the state of the Church of England under Archbishop Laud, with its authoritarian and Anglo-Catholic tendencies, and its intolerance of dissent, made such a move impossible for one of Milton's religious persuasion. When the Civil War broke out (1642) Milton put his pen for many years to the service of the Parliamentary cause, and later of the Commonwealth. He also in those years wrote notable pamphlets on divorce and the freedom of the press. At the time of the Restoration, 1660, he was largely left in peace, which was much to the credit of the new government, since he had written in support of the execution of Charles I. It was in the first years of Charles II's reign, which was in spirit and morality anathema to all he had stood and worked for, that he wrote his greatest works, *Paradise Lost*, *Paradise Regained* and *Samson Agonistes*, all works whose inspiration is biblical.

The early poems of Milton, successful and impressive in themselves, sometimes have the flavour of conscious apprenticeship, of being deliberate preparations for the large works that Milton knew would one day be within his grasp. All of them are marked by immense learning — Milton was one of the most widely-read Europeans of his time — and by a fastidious attempt to explore new modes and metres. In *L'Allegro* and *Il Penseroso* he produces brilliant exercises defining the cheerful and the pensive man, the extrovert and the introvert as we might call them today. In *Comus*, a masque written for performance by the younger members of a noble family at their country seat on the Welsh border, Milton uses some of the features of the masque, so popular at the Stuart court, but in his hands it becomes a dramatized debate on chastity versus permissiveness. One hopes it was more popular with the children who were its first actors than it has been with schoolchildren ever since. In *Lycidas* Milton wrote an elegy for his friend (or acquaintance, for the poem is not informed with much personal feeling) Edward King, an elegy couched in the pastoral mode, which allowed him to generalize the tragedy of King's drowning and comment on other matters close to his heart, including the vocation of poetry and the state of the English Church. Its beautiful (and usually misquoted) end seems a conscious acknowledgement that the time of poetic apprenticeship is over:

And now the Sun had stretched out all the hills,
And now was dropped into the Western bay;
At last he rose, and twitched his mantle blue;
Tomorrow to fresh woods, and pastures new.

But it was not until twenty years later that Milton was in fact able to take up his work on his long-meditated epic, and those twenty years of turmoil and debate, largely ended by his going blind, left their mark on *Paradise Lost*. Earlier he had had thoughts of a national epic drawn from the legends of King Arthur — another *Faerie Queene*, in fact. Now it was clear that no subject less majestic than a biblical one could match his powers or fit the turbulence, the massive struggles on issues of conscience, that his mature years had witnessed and participated in. *Paradise Lost* opens with a vision of Hell so terrible, yet so majestic in its horror, that no one reading the first two books can doubt that Milton had, indeed, found his subject, or that the mighty periods of his blank verse — Latinate, convoluted, grand — were the only suitable style to render it in. The grandeur of the descriptions of the fire, the lurid light, the perpetual torment, is highlighted by those moments of simplicity, of quiet directness, of which Milton is also capable. Thus, after the opening picture of Hell, of

> sights of woe
> Regions of sorrow, doleful shades . . . a fiery deluge, fed
> With ever burning sulphur unconsumed

Milton comes in with the understated comment:

> O how unlike the place from whence they fell!

The flexibility of Milton's style, the range of his responses to his mighty material, prevent boredom over the epic length of his poem.

The figure of Satan that we see against this Stygian background is undoubtedly impressive, powerful, immense. He has about him, at this point, the last flickers of heavenly radiance, the traces of his ruined greatness. There is undoubtedly something thrilling as he summons up his defeated powers, collects together the scattered legions of the lost angels, addresses them with words of defiance of God, and draws forth a response of militaristic assent as his troops

> Clashed on their sounding shields the din of war,
> Hurling defiance toward the vault of heaven.

But the thrill we feel, the sense of the heroic, is not a sense of human fellow-feeling; it is more like the emotions aroused by, say, a Nuremburg rally – an irrational blood urge. The more we examine Satan's speech, the more attention we pay to its content rather than its thrilling style, the more we distance ourselves from his magnificent egotism. Everything is seen in nakedly personal terms, nothing in terms of principle. Even the splendour of 'Better to reign in hell, than serve in heaven' pales when we realize that he himself is the only one who is actually going to reign in hell. There is even the petulance of the born loser in his complaint that God

> still his strength concealed,
> Which tempted our attempt, and wrought our fall.

It is hardly an heroic posture to say, in effect, 'you should have told me you were a good fighter, then I wouldn't have taken you on.' And indeed, the closer we look at it, the more the attempt of Satan to defeat the Almighty becomes not something heroic, but something absurd.

The problem with *Paradise Lost* is that its figures have to function both on a human and on a mythical level. Lord David Cecil tells a story of an ancestress who, during a church service, heard the clergyman read the Genesis story that is the central matter of *Paradise Lost*; when he came to the words of excuse that Adam made to God – 'The woman . . . gave me of the tree, and I did eat' – she snorted contemptuously: 'Shabby fellow indeed!' We should not bring to great myths the sort of judgment we would make on John Smith and Sally Brown, but it is Milton's job to enforce another standard of judgment. To a large degree he is successful in doing so. God, to be sure, is a problem, but then He always is. In the case of Adam and Eve, Milton does manage to assert both their mythic function and their humanity, at least if we can accept a pretty horrendous male bias. The scene (one uses the word advisedly, for the conception is dramatic) between Eve and the serpent in Book IX is both psychologically convincing in an elementary way, and yet full of a sense of grand mythic issues depending on her choice. One sees the point of the similar temptation scenes in *Comus* now, but here the climax is the failure of the woman's resolution:

> So saying, her rash hand in evil hour
> Forth reaching to the Fruit, she plucked, she ate;
> Earth felt the wound, and Nature from her seat
> Sighing through all her works gave signs of woe,
> That all was lost.

The scene immediately following, between Eve and Adam, is similarly convincing on a human level, though marred slightly by Milton's determination to underline, in a niggling way, the fact that Adam was 'not deceived, / But fondly overcome with Female charm.' From this point the poem moves majestically to its conclusion, in which Adam and Eve take on the burden of their fall, assume the load of pain, sin, fallibility which are the lot of common humanity. The poem, which began with a titanic vision of Hell and the monstrous angel/devil figure wallowing in its flames, ends on a note of quiet recognition, of strength and resolution, as Eve and Adam make their way out of Paradise into the world of fallen man:

> The World was all before them, where to choose
> Their place of rest, and Providence their guide:
> They hand in hand with wandering steps and slow,
> Through Eden took their solitary way.

There is no ducking the difficulties of Milton for the modern reader: the weight of his learning, the length and complexity of his sentences, the latinate constructions, the gravity of his mind. Milton had no gift for simplification, he made nothing easy, for himself or for his reader. Even the ambition stated at the end of his invocation which begins Book I of the poem:

> What in me is dark
> Illumine, what is low raise and support;
> That to the height of this great argument
> I may assert Eternal Providence,
> And justify the ways of God to men

is one that may seem irrelevant, or comically portentous, to the modern reader. Long ago A. E. Housman's Shropshire Lad declared mischievously that 'Malt [i.e. beer] does more than Milton can / To justify God's ways to man.' But when we have once begun to get his measure, as thinker and poet, accepted that his high seriousness is nothing remotely like pretentiousness, gone some way at least with his theological pre-occupations, we see that in scale, vision, dramatic sweep, *Paradise Lost* has no parallel in our literature outside Shakespeare.

One of the friends and associates who seems to have saved Milton from retribution at the time of the Restoration – and thus to have preserved him to write not only most of *Paradise Lost*, but also its successors *Paradise Regained* and the 'closet drama' *Samson Agonistes* – was his one-time assistant Andrew Marvell (1621–1678). Marvell's own verse was then little known, and indeed it has made its way in the world slowly. Its wit and sprightliness look back to the high days of the Metaphysicals, but there is about Marvell a balance, a judgment, a grave rightness which suggests contrary impulses from John Milton. In his *Horatian Ode Upon Cromwell's Return from Ireland* his lines seem the inevitable summing up of his country's then leader, of the achievements and limitations of his rule; but it manages to be also a worthy requiem for Charles I, the man Cromwell had had executed:

> He nothing common did or mean
> Upon that memorable scene:
>> But with his keener eye
>> The axe's edge did try:

> Nor called the Gods with vulgar spite
> To vindicate his helpless Right,
>> But bowed his comely head
>> Down as upon a bed.

This balance and inevitability characterize much of his poetry — the splendid *Bermudas*, where the Puritan exiles from 'prelate's rage' in England praise the Lord for the abundance and beauty of the New World; the poem *To His Coy Mistress*, one of the great treatments of the theme of passing, ravaging time; his celebration of withdrawal from the hurly-burly and perils of public life in *The Garden*. Marvell's poetic production is small, but whatever he did he did with accomplishment and style. His poetry forms a pleasant, satisfying coda to the age of Donne and Milton.

7

The Restoration

In the popular English imagination, the Restoration of 1660 is one of those watersheds of history, a period when the whole atmosphere changed from that of a gloomy prayer-meeting to one of licence, ribaldry and unashamed pleasure. No doubt the popular view is nonsense as far as the vast majority of the inhabitants of the British Isles were concerned: the average villager (and Britain was still very much a rural civilization) would doubtless have registered that church services had regained a little of their old ceremony, that country pastimes such as maypole-dancing were no longer to be regarded as works of the devil, but there would have been no great change otherwise in their lives. It needed more than a new regime in Whitehall to change the patterns of existence in Little Totham by the Wold.

But in so far as the king set the tone for metropolitan life and the life of the gentry in general there is a grain of truth in the popular myth. The new ruling class – many of whom, like the King, had spent formative years in exile on the Continent – looked to France for their culture and their manners; the dominant tone of the Court and of upper-class London life in general was gay, cynical and permissive. The King himself – in every way the opposite of his virtuous, domestic and unwise father – used all his considerable political skills to avoid 'going on his travels again'; he was gregarious, democratic in his habits, unashamedly promiscuous. London gossip fed delightedly on the doings of his mistresses, from the flagrant Duchess of Castlemaine, busty, greedy and vicious, to the charming and earthy Nell Gwynne. It was all very different from Oliver Cromwell's time.

One inevitable consequence of Charles II's jubilant and acclaimed return was the reopening of the theatres: the thirst for drama was such that he had hardly set foot on English soil before troupes of actors were being formed and the old plays dusted down. Nevertheless, when things settled down, the new theatres were physically and spiritually very different from the old. For a start, the theatre confirmed the trend of the pre-Commonwealth stage: it moved entirely indoors. It was roofed in, lit by artificial lighting, with scenery, and the stage area divided off from the audience by the proscenium arch (though in early years there was an 'apron' out into the audience, one tiny relic of Elizabethan customs). In addition, the female roles were now played by women, as on the Continent – an innovation which was made, according to Charles, 'in the interests of morality,' though the reverse might have been a more honest justification. All these changes marked great gains for the theatre as a place of illusion, though many of them involved a loss of that speed, vigour and free play of the imagination which had characterized Elizabethan theatre at its best.

Charles was no more anxious than the city worthies of Elizabethan times that the theatre (though it provided him, in one way or another, with his main forms of entertainment) should blossom in an unrestricted manner. Performances in London were licensed, and restricted to two companies. Perhaps the most significant fact about Restoration drama is this: until the end of the century two theatres, and often only one, supplied the needs of play-going London; yet even so, plays were seldom performed more than five or six times, the performances frequently being little better than shambles. Nothing could more vividly illustrate the contraction of the audience for drama than this. The theatre may have attracted a fair cross-section of the nation, but it was a very tiny segment, and in the middle and lower reaches the theatre-goers were only typical of the more 'liberated' members (the diarist Samuel Pepys is a good example). The theatre was no longer the mirror of the nation, but was dominated by a small, like-minded clique, who looked to the theatre to confirm its prejudices, cynicisms and aristocratic illusions.

One sees this very clearly in the comedies of the time: the principal characters are generally drawn from the charmed circle of aristocratic life in the metropolis, and anyone outside that circle is a booby, a villain or a butt. The city businessman or the rural squire is equally to be ridiculed and deceived. There are, to be sure, fools within the charmed circle: elegance overdone becomes foppery, and is mocked; amorousness in women is admirable until the lady becomes middle-aged, then it is depicted as a ravening fever close to nymphomania. But as a whole the characters display the qualities that were admired: balance, judgment and cool, cynical sense. The dramatists, in other words, turned a blind eye to the uglier sides of aristocratic life under Charles – to the violence, the disease, the exhaustion of excess. The court wanted to see themselves as an exquisitely refined elite, as the witty custodians of civilized values. And that, for the most part, was how they were shown.

One of the few playwrights who was a partial exception to this rule was William Wycherley (?1640–1716). He was himself a fringe member of the Court circle (he was one of the many lovers of the Duchess of Castlemaine, which argued a strong constitution rather than a delicate stomach), yet he seems to have been as much repelled as attracted by it. There is no doubt he perceived the heartlessness and hypocrisy behind the elegance and charm. He seems to have been a tormented, uncomfortable, bitter man, a moralist and a libertine, a strange mixture of old values and new. The contradictions find expression in his plays. *The Country Wife*, the most famous of them, was for two centuries unperformable in its original version, though in our own more lax time it is perhaps the most frequently revived Restoration comedy. It has two concurrent, intersecting plots. In one Horner, a London gallant, has the rumour spread through town that – as a result of an unsuccessful operation for the pox – he is now impotent. The result is that whereas once he was the terror of all husbands, they now rush to offer their wives to him, seeing him as a harmless companion for them while they, the husbands, go about their own business. The wives, once the secret has been revealed to them, enthusiastically play along, for they are voracious harpies to a woman. The second plot concerns Pinchwife, an elderly roué, who has married a 'country wife' much younger than himself. Much of the action concerns his attempts, inevitably vain, to keep her faithful to him, and culminates with Horner both cuckolding Pinchwife yet managing to keep his secret safe.

Wycherley's satiric flail cuts to left and right: sex-crazed wives, negligent husbands, reformed rakes and foolish men of fashion fall beneath its blade. Words change meaning in the mouths of these fashionable hypocrites: 'honour' – as in the phrase 'man' or 'woman of honour' – becomes synonymous with dishonour, unchastity, limitless sexual appetite; similarly with 'reputation,' which means nothing but a false front. In the famous 'China' scene, a masterpiece of elegant obscenity, Lady Fidget, who has been copulating with Horner in the next room, emerges holding a piece of his china collection, and in the ensuing dialogue 'china' gains a monstrous patina of sexual significances:

LADY FIDGET: I have been toiling and moiling for the prettiest piece of china, my dear.

HORNER: Nay, she has been too hard for me, do what I could.

MRS SQUEAMISH: Oh Lord, I'll have some china too. Good Mr Horner, don't think to give other people china and me none; come in with me too.

HORNER: Upon my honour, I have none left now.

MRS SQUEAMISH: Nay, nay, I have known you deny your china before now, but you shan't put me off so. Come.

HORNER: This lady had the last there.

LADY FIDGET: Yes, indeed, madam, to my certain knowledge he has no more left.

MRS SQUEAMISH: O, but it may be he may have some you could not find.

LADY FIDGET: What, d'ye think if he had had any left, I would not have had it too? for we women of quality never think we have china enough . . .

The elegant indirection of this is not altogether typical of Wycherley. More often his wit has a whiplash quality: the innate honesty of Wycherley's mind cuts through pretence, it shouts 'Look how things really are':

HORNER: But prithee, was not the way you were in better? Is not keeping [a mistress] better than marriage?

PINCHWIFE: A pox on't! the jades would jilt me. I could never keep a whore to myself.

HORNER: So, then you only married to keep a whore to yourself.

What modern critics find puzzling, even disturbing about Wycherley is what were his positives: they find it inconceivable that Horner the libertine should be able to waltz through the play, bedding women right, left and centre, yet should find himself at the end unexposed, quite prepared to continue with his rake's progress. Why, the man even seems to be happy! In bewilderment, critics have called him a 'horned beast,' a shell of a man unable to find real emotional fulfilment; one critic has even called the joyous seduction of the delightful Margery Pinchwife 'moving drama, the result of a realistic imagination as powerful, almost, as Ibsen's.' That is not how it seems in performance. On stage the play becomes a delighted celebration of Horner's enterprise, initiative and cunning. And I have little doubt that that was what Wycherley intended.

Most Restoration dramatists made more effort than Wycherley to cover a brutal sexual code under a cloak of elegance and wit. The typical Restoration comedy plot concerns the efforts of a gentleman of fashion to disencumber himself of stale amorous entanglements, and win the hand of the heroine, who is, typically, virtuous (for double standards prevail for almost all the dramatists except Wycherley), witty, and 'a good match' from the financial point of view. Dorimant, in Etherege's *Man of Mode*, is the archetypal Restoration hero: his attitude to women has been described by John Wain the novelist as a sort of 'fighter-pilot's mentality: he wants to get them before they get him.' After several acts in which we have seen his ruthless, contemptuous, purely accumulative attitude to women, it is not easy to get any warm, pleasurable feeling when finally he wins the charming Harriet. But perhaps we are not meant to; perhaps hoping for such a feeling is a modern sentimentalism. To most Restoration writers marriage seems to be less a matter of love than of dynastic necessity: one married to perpetuate one's line, and the honeymoon is no more than an interlude between pursuing beddable women and pursuing more beddable women. It is hard to take. At least Wycherley did not commit the hypocrisy of granting Horner a happy marriage at the end of *The Country Wife*.

The most elegant of all the Restoration writers was Congreve, (1670–1729) and it is in his work that the uglinesses of the age were transmuted into something infinitely witty, imaginative and delicate. Even his butts – the country boobies, the ageing but amorous women of fashion – express their oddities with such verbal distinction that the edge is taken off the brutality. In his masterpiece *The Way of the World* the elderly Lady Wishfort (i.e. wish-for-it, and the reader should be able to guess what she wished for) is a case in point. An absurd, posturing, amorously optimistic creature, her language removes her into a realm of artificiality and fantasy, so that she becomes almost a person of crazy distinction. She is not a butt, more an oddly misshapen vessel from a distinguished pottery firm. Her misuse of the English language is more subtle and imaginative than Sheridan's Mrs Malaprop in the next century, and less likely to bore on repetition: 'You must not attribute my yielding to any sinister appetite, or indigestion of widowhood; nor impute my complacency to any lethargy of continence. I hope you do not think me prone to any iteration of nuptials.' It is mostly when she is emotionally disturbed by the presence of a member of the opposite sex who might (with luck) have designs on her that her language becomes deranged. At other times it has a directness that is still imaginative yet precise: 'I look like an old peeled wall.'

With Congreve, in fact, we move away from comedy as social comment and towards comedy as fantasy. When Millamant, the heroine, comments that when she does her hair she always uses poetry for curl-papers, because it never will sit pleasantly with prose, we are very close indeed to the world of Oscar Wilde. This makes it difficult to see the progress of Millamant and her admirer Mirabel towards a *modus vivendi* that will enable them to endure married life as anything as serious as a 'rationalization of sex,' as some critics have called it. It is true that the high-point of the play is the scene in which both of them state their terms for matrimony, the necessary conditions which will render marriage tolerable enough for Mirabel to give up his life of promiscuous pleasure and for Millamant to (as she puts it) 'dwindle into a wife.' But since the conditions put forward by both of them *all* concern the conduct and rights of the *wife*, it is by no means easy to see the scene as a serious or impartial investigation of the state of marriage. In fact, if we bring any sort of moral code to bear on the play at all, Mirabel's actions throughout are nothing short of loathsome. It is Congreve's achievement that he persuades us to leave such codes along with our hats and coats in the cloakroom, and enter a world of high, fantastic comedy, purged of the grossness of the earlier Restoration plays.

There was good reason why the blatant crudities of Wycherley and Etherege had been refined out of Congreve's style. In the closing years of the century there had been published Jeremy Collier's *Short View of the Immorality and Profaneness of the English Stage*, in which Congreve had been singled out for attack, though for the wrong reasons. Collier, like the Elizabethan puritans before him, saw the theatre as a sink of iniquity, a place where vice was recommended and virtue ridiculed. His ire was in no way diminished by the existence of a more elevated sort of play in the Restoration theatre: the heroic tragedy. These plays, classical in conception, French in inspiration, were often full of splendid rhetorical poetry (Dryden's *All for Love* is the best known example, but Otway's *Venice*

Preserved is perhaps more theatrically viable), yet their expressions of invincible heroism and undying loves are ultimately unconvincing, and sit uneasily in the English dramatic tradition. Collier's attack was most opportunely timed: in 1698 the hectic, permissive world of the Restoration was gone; since the Glorious Revolution of 1688 which chased out the Catholic James II, a Dutchman had occupied the throne, worthily and unspectacularly; the revels were over, responsibility and dullness reigned.

Restoration comedy never really recovered from the attempts to clean it up. Perhaps it was unscrubbable. In the early years of the eighteenth century there were several lively, eminently stageworthy plays: Farquhar's *The Beaux' Stratagem* and *The Recruiting Officer* are works of no great distinction, but they can still charm audiences in performance. But when the middle-classes started trickling back to the theatres and demanding a more sentimental, more overtly moral type of comedy, the stage was set for a long period of decline in the British theatre.

If we look in vain to most Restoration dramas for firm principles, for consistent moral and social attitudes, these qualities were to be found in abundance in the greatest poet of the age. John Dryden (1631–1700). This may seem odd at first sight: Dryden began his poetic career with *Heroic Stanzas to the Glorious Memory of Cromwell* yet spent most of his life as a defender of the restored Stuart sovereigns; he wrote one long poem in defence of the Protestant religion as enshrined in the Church of England, and another, after his conversion, in praise of Catholicism. Nevertheless, the old gibes that Dryden was a turncoat and a time-server could not be further from the truth. Like many who grow up in times of social upheaval (his adolescence covered the period of the Civil War, his young manhood the dictatorship of Cromwell), his first commitment was to public order, to a strong, accepted central authority. Radical or revolutionary movements seemed to him at best to bring dubious benefits, at the cost of certain misery. Authoritarian rule which sprang from and respected the ancient traditions of the country seemed infinitely better than (what he saw as) a democracy supported by a rabble and led by power-crazed egotists. It was inevitable that Dryden should support the country's legitimate monarchs, inevitable that his religious quest should lead him finally to the Catholic Church.

It is Dryden's political ideas, and his political gut-reactions too, that give such strength and urgency to his greatest satire, *Absalom and Achitophel*. It was written to order, about a particular situation at a particular time, the 'Catholic plot' crisis of 1679–1681, and it was intended to influence that situation. In the late 1670s the joy that had greeted Charles II's Restoration had given way to scepticism and disillusion: restorations always bring disappointment, for they are expected to restore times which are gone forever. A new opposition party began grouping, consisting of members of the gentry who felt they had failed to get their just rights, puritans who had opposed the Restoration throughout, traditional Parliamentarians, and Protestants with a genuine and deep-rooted fear of the Catholic Church. The catalyst of the crisis was an exceedingly unsavoury character called Titus Oates, a man with a Catholic past, a dubious theological degree (like Dr Ian Paisley in our own day, and the comparison need not end there) and a new-found but loud devotion to the Protestant religion. It was Oates's 'revelation' of a series of Catholic plots centred on Charles's brother and heir, James, Duke of York, and involving Charles's Catholic queen, that brought this heterogeneous opposition together. Soon anti-Catholic hysteria gripped the nation in much the same way that anti-witchcraft hysteria was to grip American Salem not long afterwards. The opposition began to demand the exclusion from the succession of the Catholic Duke of York, and the adoption of Charles's illegitimate son the Duke of Monmouth (the white Protestant hope) as heir to the throne.

It was into this situation that Dryden weighed with his scoriating satire *Absalom and Achitophel*. His choice of a biblical parallel to the present situation was a stroke of genius. Charles II becomes King David from the Old Testament, and at once his profligacy takes on a new, attractive, even a spiritual look:

> In pious times, e'er priestcraft did begin,
> Before polygamy was made a sin;
> When man on many multiplied his kind,
> E'er one to one was cursedly confined,
> When nature prompted, and no law denied
> Promiscuous use of concubine and bride;
> Then Israel's monarch, after Heaven's own heart,
> His vigorous warmth did, variously, impart
> To wives and slaves: and, wide as his command,
> Scattered his Maker's image through the land.

Thus the loose-moraled Charles is transformed into David, father of his people, living in the days before monogamy was ordained, and before priests of varying religions began causing trouble and restricting natural pleasures (Dryden was no friend to priests of any religion: it is worth looking closely at the first line, with its suggestion that priests *diminish* rather than increase piety, and its wicked pun on the word 'craft'). Sexual licence becomes 'vigorous warmth' – something good and (literally and metaphorically) life-giving. Charles's habit of scattering bastards in his wake is transformed into something like largesse – a shower of gold descending on his subjects: 'scattered his maker's image through the land.'

After a no-holds-barred description of the English (called here, of course, the Jews) as 'a headstrong, moody, murmuring race,' and one that had veered from religion to religion over the last century or so ('Gods they had tried of every shape and size / That God-smiths could produce, or priests devise'), Dryden comes to the heart of his poem and his purpose. This is a series of satirical portraits of the main conspirators against Charles II. Dryden is one of the great artists of the satirical portrait, the thumbnail sketch of a man that utterly demolishes his reputation and credibility, and at the same time both establishes him as an eternal type and suggests general reflections on human nature. For example, the Earl of Shaftesbury ('Achitophel' – one of the main conspirators, and evil genius to the young Duke of Monmouth) is depicted as fiery, turbulent, cunning, the incurable and perennial conspirator, and a man 'for close designs and crooked counsels fit.' Then Dryden broadens out the picture to establish him as a type: he makes him into a crazed, over-venturesome sailor, good in high seas, but bored in calm waters:

> Pleased with the danger, when the waves went high,
> He sought the storms; but, for a calm unfit,
> Would steer too nigh the sands to boast his wit.

And then he immediately comes in with a trenchant couplet of generalized reflection that has become the classic quote to describe not only the brilliant political adventurer, but all erratic men of genius – a quote that is as relevant in our own day as in his:

> Great wits are sure to madness near allied
> And thin partitions do their bounds divide . . .

The portraits in this rogues' gallery range from the crude, contemptuous daub to the most subtle pieces of ironic brushwork. Exuberant mudslinging is good enough for the mean, slippery Sheriff of London, who 'Did wisely from expensive sins refrain, / And never broke the Sabbath but for gain.' More subtle arts of destruction were called for by the various, talented, changeable Duke of Buckingham ('Zimri'), who, according to Dryden, changed sides as he would his coat, dabbled in everything and excelled in nothing:

> Stiff in opinions, always in the wrong,
> Was everything by starts, and nothing long:
> But in the course of one revolving moon
> Was chemist, fiddler, statesman and buffoon.

The placing of those last four nouns is in itself a lesson in the techniques of satire.

If these portraits are the central achievement of the poem, Dryden shows almost equal mastery in the action of the poem, which is mainly a dialogue between Achitophel and Absalom (The Duke of Monmouth) in which, amid echoes of *Paradise Lost*, Achitophel takes on Satanic dimensions as the tempter, and Absalom becomes the weak, narcissistic pawn in a political game he barely understands (for Charles loved Monmouth, as David did Absalom, and any more culpable involvement could not be suggested). The poem is by turns subtle, vigorous, dangerous and uproarious – a triumph of suggestion, tact and sheer impish cleverness. It has claims to be the greatest satire in our language.

Dryden's other great satire is *MacFlecknoe*, in which a rival poet, Thomas Shadwell, author of some bad poetry and some lively and very dirty plays, is crowned King of Dullness by his predecessor Flecknoe (another dreadful poet):

> Shadwell alone my perfect image bears,
> Mature in dullness from his tender years;
> Shadwell alone of all my sons is he
> Who stands confirmed in full stupidity.
> The rest to some faint meaning make pretence,
> But Shadwell never deviates into sense.

But we should not forget that Dryden is not just a satirist. In fact, he can claim to be among the most various poets in our language. He was a master of the Ode, with two outstandingly brilliant Odes to St Cecilia (patron saint of music), of which the second, *Alexander's Feast* shows him still at the height of his technical powers, and still experimenting, in the last years of his life. His tributes to friends and kinsmen (for example *To the Memory of Mr Oldham*) are as positive and sober as his satire is destructive and hilarious. His occasional poems (such as that celebrating the return of Charles II from exile, or *Annus Mirabilis*, in which he depicts the year of the Great Fire of London and the Plague) are much above the average for such productions, and no doubt gained him the Poet Laureateship (he was one of the few to hold this office while still writing good poetry). His poems on serious and religious matters are restrained but often moving statements, and his translations are frequently brilliant – he made Chaucer available again after generations of neglect due to the transformation of the language since his time. We know virtually nothing of Dryden the man. If we judge him from his poetry he was versatile, trenchant, contemplative, witty, and supremely sane.

Dryden stood alone among Restoration poets: there were others with talent, notably the Earl of Rochester, whose life of daring and varied debauchery, ending in that ultimate debauch a death-bed repentance, interfered with his poetry too greatly for him ever to do justice to his talent. But there is something in the literary history of the Restoration period which is of greater significance for the future than any bouquet of minor poets: this is a vigorous crop of prose writers, forging a prose idiom to match the already established dramatic and poetic idioms. Aubrey's *Brief Lives* of his contemporaries are quirky and delightful contributions to the as yet new art of biography, and we get an even more vivid picture of notable personalities from the best diaries of the period, notably Evelyn's and Pepys's.

But of all the writers in this new and rather difficult medium of prose the one whose influence was greatest was John Bunyan (1628–1688), for his *Pilgrim's Progress* was staple reading for generations, the sort of book that is read first in childhood (as George Eliot's Maggie Tulliver reads it) and constantly returned to for delight and spiritual refreshment thereafter. Modelling his prose on the Bible (the influence of the 1611 Authorized Version of the Bible on English prose cannot be exaggerated), he describes the pilgrimage that to him life was in the form of an allegory. Christian, the principal pilgrim, travels with other like-minded people of varying degrees of determination and genuine piety through a series of perils – natural, human and supernatural – to his destined heaven. Bunyan's experience as a preacher (in and out of jail) is obvious, but so is his natural talent as a story-teller, and his feeling for language that is at once simple, forthright, homely, yet vivid.

A very different sort of narrative was that provided by Aphra Behn (1640–1689), the first woman writer to be mentioned in this survey (and, alas, it will be a century before another gains a place). Mrs Behn wrote a series of plays, notably comedies that went a good deal further in bawdy than even most male writers of the time. But what she is remembered for today is some prose narratives which are clearly stepping-stones from the Elizabethan short tale to the novel as we know it today. The best remembered of these is *Oroonoko*, the tale of a noble savage sold into slavery in Surinam. The impeccable and high-toned moral sentiments of this noble creature are not likely to appeal to the modern reader, but the believable setting and inter-racial relationships are the result of Aphra Behn's own stay in the colony. Aphra Behn created a narrative that seemed to people at the time to be not really fiction, but a documentary account of events and people that actually took place. Defoe in the next century created several such works, and they lead us directly to the novel proper.

8

The Eighteenth Century

In the Restoration period, most of the important writers took their standards from the court, and looked towards it in turn for patronage. To a large extent this was still the case in the reign of Queen Anne (1702–1714). But quite early in the eighteenth century, things began to change. Anne's successor, George I – Protestant, German, and remarkably unattractive – spoke little English, and was thus ill-fitted to be a patron of literature. His boast that 'I hate all Boets and Bainters' suggests that he had no great desire to be one either. The great minister of the age, Sir Robert Walpole, usually counted as the first Prime Minister, preferred to direct money where the power lay, in the House of Commons: 'All those men have their price,' he said, surveying his fellow members.

The literary men of the eighteenth century, therefore, began looking for support in another direction – towards the growing and greedy reading public. At its lowest this could mean 'Grub Street,' where hacks could gain a miserable and precarious living churning out what would sell. But the more enterprising booksellers could ensure for a good and popular writer a very satisfactory return for his works, thus enabling him to shake off the tyranny of the patron – the figure, usually a nobleman, whom Johnson bitterly defined in his *Dictionary* as 'a wretch who supports with insolence, and is paid with flattery.'

Politically the age was remarkably stable. The Hanoverians established themselves with surprising ease on the throne, and the Jacobite rebellions of 1715 and 1745 never presented any serious threat to their permanent tenancy of it. The age saw the consolidation of the two great political parties, the Whigs and the Tories, which had been germinating since the time of the Popish plot – or perhaps since the Civil War. The

Whigs were an amalgam of rich nobility with the mercantile and dissenting interests, and they dominated politics in the period 1714–1760. The Tories were orientated towards the smaller landed gentry and the Anglican Church; in the early part of the century they were tainted with Jacobitism, but they dominated politics in the reign of George III (1760–1820). Although that king made continuous and not unsuccessful attempts to 'be a king,' as his mother urged him, in general the period saw the monarchy shrinking in power, and the establishment of cabinet government under strong Prime Ministers, notably Walpole and the two Pitts.

The literary and spiritual temper of the eighteenth century is often summed up under such labels as The Augustan Age, or the Neo-classical Period. Such labels are ideally best avoided, because they stamp an age with a single tendency or collection of related tendencies, and the reader feels he can ignore the delicate play of contrary impulses which every age produces. In a short history of this kind, however, some degree of generalization is inevitable. Certainly the classics were widely admired, and the pioneering works of Ben Jonson, Dryden and others in the previous century reached their apogee in the first half of the eighteenth century. But Latin and Greek models never gained the sort of dominance that they had attained in France, and the 'rules' (for example the dramatic unities of time, place and action) were more honoured and discussed than they were followed. Always there was the example of great writers like Shakespeare to counterbalance the classical precepts that he had ignored, and there were no writers of consequence willing to follow Voltaire in dismissing *Hamlet* and the rest as 'barbarous' pieces. The classics were an inspiration, in form, in diction, as a source of reference, but no great writer used them as the only touchstone by which to praise or damn, or let himself be imprisoned in neo-classical theory.

The eighteenth-century writers lived in the aftermath of chaotic political disruptions and damaging religious divisions. They valued stability in political institutions, and their religion tended towards Deism, or a rational, non-miraculous style of faith. They believed that, in Pope's words, 'the proper study of mankind is Man,' and that man should be observed in his relationships with other men. Social man, rather than solitary man, engaged their attentions, and they tended easily towards generalizations that were the products of their observation and experience. When they talked about Nature, they often meant the truth about man, and the common factors in human experience.

They had a strong sense of decorum, in the literary sense, meaning what was suitable to the subject matter, hallowed by tradition, and not liable to startle or disconcert. They were very concerned to forge common standards of judgment, generally acceptable views of statecraft, philosophy or religion. They worked towards a community of minds, and believed the artist should be firmly rooted in his society. The outsider readily brought on himself the label of egotist or madman.

All this sounds, to our post-Romantic ears, rather unexciting. In fact we have an image of the eighteenth century – bewigged, beruffled, all exquisite manners and artificiality – which it is hard to dispel. Such an image easily embraces a figure like Lord Chesterfield, with his frigid prescriptions for polite behaviour ('there is nothing so illiberal and so ill-bred as audible laughter') or his stale and cynical aphorisms about people ('Women . . . are only children of a larger growth . . . for solid, reasoning good-sense, I never knew in my life one that had it'). But the image ignores the obverse side of the coin, the strain of melancholy and madness which runs right through the literature; and it does injustice to a robust, rumbustious, strong-minded century – as a look at some of its great writers will show.

The character and actions of Jonathan Swift (1667–1745) have been the subject of infinite controversy and slander. He has been seen, by Thackeray, as 'a monster gibbering shrieks, and gnashing imprecations against mankind,' and, at the other end of the scale, presented by Michael Foot as a proto-socialist. His character is an irrelevance it is best to ignore altogether; in opinions he was in fact a Tory, deeply attached to the Anglican Church, sceptical about man's nature (man was a creature, he wrote carefully, *capable of* reason), disgusted by the easy optimism of many contemporary philosophers. But he was also a doughty fighter for liberty and justice, a hater of meanness, a vigorous defender of the Irish, among whom he was born and grew up, and for whom he had a kind of exasperated tenderness.

A mind of this kind, sceptical of intellectual fashions, scornful of human pretensions, takes naturally to satire. Swift was the most perfectly equipped satirist that ever lived, and his works cover the whole gamut from gentle ridicule to swingeing contempt. Though he wrote for the government at times, he was no mere propagandist. So subtle was his way of going about things that his aim was often misunderstood. Queen Anne took the *Tale of a Tub* to be an attack on the Anglican Church, which it certainly was not. One divine announced, as if proud of his own perception, that he 'hardly believed a word' of what he took to be a travel book – *Gulliver's Travels*. In his most savage satirical pamphlet, *A Modest Proposal*, Swift suggested that the poverty and over-population of Ireland could be cured by fattening up Irish babies and killing them for food at the age of one, by which time a child is

> a most delicious, nourishing and wholesome food, whether stewed, roasted, baked, or boiled; and I make no doubt that it will equally serve in a fricasee, or ragout.

So reasonable is the tone of the pamphlet, so enticing is the incidental detail that backs up the argument, that one is almost surprised the proposal was not acted upon. But what we today cannot miss is the savage but generous indignation at the English treatment of Ireland.

The beguiling reasonableness, the apparent realism, of the surface text still bedevils discussion of Swift's greatest satire, *Gulliver's Travels*. It is a dangerous book to read part of, and it is sad that it is thus that it is generally read. The satiric stance alters from book to book, and it is only after reading and re-reading the whole, and considering it in the context of Swift's other writings, that one can come to a tentative judgment about the author's aims and attitudes. For example, the position of Gulliver at the end of the book, when he returns home after his stay among the virtuous horses, and can no longer tolerate the loathsome smell and disgusting habits of a 'Yahoo' or human being, has often been taken as an image of Swift's own relation to the human race. Yet no simple equation of Gulliver with Swift is possible. If in the first book (Lilliput) Gulliver finds himself the only honest man (the moral giant) in a nation of civilized yet scheming and treacherous politicians, in the second (Brobdignag) it is his description to the King of Brobdignag of English politics of the previous century that prompts the king to describe the English as 'the most pernicious race of little odious vermin that Nature ever suffered to crawl upon the surface of the earth;' and when Gulliver, not put down, goes on to describe gunpowder and its effects, and offers to show him how to make it, the king describes him as a grovelling insect, and forbids him to mention the subject again. 'A strange effect of narrow principles and short views!' comments the (in this Book) morally obtuse Gulliver.

In so far as there are heroes in *Gulliver*, they are in Brobdignag, not in the country of the Houyhnhnms or virtuous horses, whose limitations are cunningly suggested. Gulliver himself, well-meaning, yet easily influenced, is an observer whose eyes we use, but whom we frequently need to *see through*. The satire of *Gulliver* is subtle, balanced and profound. What everyone has noticed is the continuously entertaining surface of the book, with Swift's delighted manipulating of his splendid central idea, and the riotous satire on travel books ('we set in the lee-braces, and hauled forward by the weather-bowlings, and hauled them tight, and belayed them' etc. etc.). To penetrate below this scintillating surface, we must read with every ounce of sensitivity and subtlety at our command. If we do that, we may believe Swift when he says that 'I hate and detest that animal called man,' but we must also credit him when he goes on that 'I heartily love John, Peter, Thomas, and so forth.'

With Alexander Pope (1688–1744), it sometimes seems, the situation is reversed: about the world in general he expresses great optimism, and he has a high opinion of the capacities of man in general; but he does seem mortally to hate a large number of individuals. This impression needs to be modified on closer inspection: his most congenial mode was satire, and his satire was personal, bitter, and sometimes unduly vindictive. But the people he satirized – the people who had offended him, wittingly or unwittingly – were mostly his inferiors both intellectually and morally, and he retained the love and trust of the big people who were his friends: Swift, Bolingbroke, Gay. His optimism is easily ridiculed by quoting his more incautious aphorisms: 'whatever is, is right,' by itself, is a piece of fatuity that demanded a Voltaire to shoot it down. Yet behind the bland, accepting facade of Pope's philosophy there is loneliness and deep consciousness of pain.

Pope was a man of letters, one of the first who lived entirely by his pen. He was also, appropriately, the supremely competent technician, a poet who had exploited the infinite possibilities of his art, who achieved total and effortless control. In his hands the heroic couplet – the preferred form of most of the neo-classical writers – was a thing of enormous variety. Most characteristically he could use it, as his master Dryden had done, for purposes of satire; yet he used it too to expound his philosophy in the *Essay on Man*; to write a treatise on literature and criticism in the *Essay on Criticism* (still authoritative, funny and stimulating); and even to express passionate feeling. In *Eloisa to Abelard*, for example, the habitual authority and smoothness of the couplet breaks down, and we find something disjointed, breathless, hysterical, as the nun Heloise fails to subdue her long-ago passion for the monk Abelard:

No, fly me, fly me, far as pole from pole;
Rise Alps between us! and whole oceans roll!
Ah, come not, write not, think not once of me,
Nor share one pang of all I felt for thee.
Thy oaths I quit, thy memory resign;
Forget, renounce me, hate whate'er was mine . . .

This poem, at least, proves that Pope was not incapable of passion. But we should not fall into the trap of judging eighteenth-century poets by how far they can approach to being Romantic ones. Pope's preferred mode is satire, and his range, though narrower than Swift's, is remarkable. *The Rape of the Lock* is his single most perfect poem – a beautifully proportioned, mock-heroic treatment of a trivial incident in noble circles. *The Dunciad* is a rambling, bawdy, nightmarish farce, in which all sorts of literary pedantry, pretension and dimness are clouted with Pope's satiric club. Perhaps the cream of Pope's satiric art is contained in sections of the *Moral Essays* and the *Epistle to Dr Arbuthnot*. In the fourth Moral Essay there is a matchless description of the noble Lord who exemplifies conspicuous consumption with his monstrously heavy house: the mansion is 'a labour'd quarry above ground,' his grounds are blown up hideously out of all sensible proportion, his library consists of rare editions whose binding is prized above their content; his chapel has an obsequious Dean who 'never mentions Hell to ears polite.' In all this deadening ostentation, the only puny thing is the owner himself. Even more lethal is Pope's portrait of his former friend Addison the essayist, in the *Epistle*. He becomes the epitome of the second-rate man of letters, who aspires to be an arbiter of taste, and who is so jealous of real talent that he contrives to diminish his rivals' reputation in the most elegant yet deadly way conceivable. He will

Damn with faint praise, assent with civil leer,
And without sneering, teach the rest to sneer . . .

Pope will never again be the popular classic he was in his own century. But renewed appreciation of him in the last few decades has sharply reversed the nineteenth century's judgment that he was 'a classic of our prose.'

The undercurrent of melancholy, perversity and psychological disturbance which was the obverse of the neo-classical coin was not absent from the works of Pope and Swift. It became more noticeable in the later years of the century in the work of Gray, Thomson, Smart, Cowper and Blake. Thomas Gray (1716–1771) demands treatment, in spite of his slim output, because in the *Elegy Written in a Country Churchyard* he wrote a poem that seems to rouse sympathetic echoes in all Englishmen, so that quotations from the poem come to mind unbidden in certain moods. Especially melancholy ones. Like the later Housman, whose poems have similar qualities, he was an academic, though in his case his great distinction was never to have given a single lecture. Though he wrote the occasional energetic or playful poem, the tone of his mind was pensive, even depressive. Sometimes (as with Housman) his reactions can seem exaggeratedly gloomy, designed to 'make the flesh creep,' as with his reflections on the schoolboys of Eton:

> Alas, regardless of their doom,
>   The little victims play!
> No sense have they of ills to come,
>   Nor care beyond today . . .

But in the *Elegy* the natural cast of his mind is matched by his subject matter: his reflections on the nameless, obscure country people who lie around him in unmarked graves, or commemorated by rough peasant memorials. The poem is very eighteenth century in diction, and in its use of inverted word order, but the wistful gloom, and some of the sense for the qualities of the humble, point forward to Wordsworth. Certainly there is no question here of the formal language masking the strength of feeling:

> Let not Ambition mock their useful toil,
>   Their homely joys, and destiny obscure;
> Nor Grandeur hear with a disdainful smile
>   The short and simple annals of the poor.

If Gray wrote in a spirit of unsentimental assertion of fellow-feeling with the rustic poor, the best known poem of Oliver Goldsmith (?1730–1774) protests eloquently and indignantly at the changes which were taking place in rural life. Behind *The Deserted Village* lie the Enclosure Acts, which were removing common grazing land from the peasantry in the interests of large-scale, more scientific farming – or, sometimes, to create a large estate for the local nobleman. Historical hindsight tells us that some of Goldsmith's indignation was misplaced, but it is, nevertheless, a poem of generous passion and genuine affection for village life. He may, at times, reduce the inhabitants to something like traditional stereotypes, but this is always mitigated by his sharp eye and the undercurrent of humour. And in spite of the smoothness and flexibility of his use of the heroic couplet, Goldsmith can muster a formidable weight when possessed by the urgency of his social message:

> Ill fares the land, to hastening ills a prey,
> Where wealth accumulates, and men decay . . .

Of Irish birth, like so many of 'our' dramatists, Goldsmith played a significant part in the brief revival of original drama in the 1770s. *She Stoops to Conquer* reads haltingly, but it acts uproariously, and the central comic ploy – the mistaking of a country house for an inn – leads to a joyful series of farcical misunderstandings. At the same time Richard Brinsley Sheridan (1751–1816) was recapturing some of the wit and polish of Restoration comedy – though avoiding much of its grossness and moral brutality – in *The Rivals* and *The School for Scandal*. Both writers reacted against the prevailing intellectual disease of the age, sentimentalism, and the spirit of the comedies is admirably sharp and direct. But one has only to compare these plays with those produced by the contemporary Frenchman Beaumarchais – particularly *The Marriage of Figaro*, with its layers of social and political comment beneath the gay surface – to see that even at its best English drama had become comparatively thin, and even facile.

Samuel Johnson (1709–1784) is the writer who, in the public imagination, bestrides the later phase of the neo-classical period. Like Goldsmith he cut across literary categorizing, producing poems, a play, essays and a sort of novel, as well as works of criticism, biography and travel. But it is not his versatility that gives him his commanding position: no one reads his play *Irene*, few read his philosophical novel *Rasselas*, and fine and resonant with moral weight as his poem *The Vanity of Human Wishes* is, it has one reader for every one hundred who go gratefully and often to Gray's *Elegy*. Some of Johnson's commanding position is due to Boswell's vastly entertaining *Life* of him, the best biography in our language. But it must not be forgotten that the quality of the *Life* is in large measure due to the quality of the man it chronicles. Johnson comes

living off the page due to Boswell's art, but due also to his own individuality, which set its impress on everything he did, and particularly
on everything he said. His retorts, moralizings and generalizations are
famous; but his quality also comes across through his staunchness in
poverty, the dignity of his assertion of independence when Lord Chesterfield offered him belated patronage, the magnitude of the task he
undertook when he wrote his *Dictionary*, his bearish kindness to many
who were poor, inexperienced, or unfitted for polite society. Johnson's
retorts could be cruel, but his reflections are always the product of a
mind that is weighty, disciplined, incredibly learned – and one that
seems to have come through an agonizing spiritual struggle. No doubt
his intellectual and moral superiority to his fellows gave him no right to
play the bully, as he sometimes did, but it is this superiority which is
instinct in everything he wrote, enriching even his heavier pieces with
learning, reflection and the knowledge born of painful experience. The
breadth and humanity of his mind are perhaps seen at their best in the
Preface to his edition of Shakespeare, and in his *Lives of the Poets*, which
showed how biography could enrich our understanding of literature, and
contained criticism which is at times questionable or prejudiced, but
which is usually soundly based and magisterially argued. Our impression from the marvellous series of *obiter dicta* quoted in Boswell's *Life* is
of a mind cranky, prejudiced, but infinitely lively: his views on woman
preachers, Whigs, the Scots, the Irish ('The Irish are a fair people; they
never speak well of one another') are at once racist, sexist, even absurd,
but they tingle with personality. And who can resist a man who will
import his cantankerousness and bias even into his *Dictionary*? Johnson's
definition of the word Whig reads simply 'The name of a faction.' And
he defines 'pension' as 'An allowance made to anyone without an equivalent. In England it is generally understood to mean pay given to a state
hireling for treason to his country.'

Johnson stands in our mind for a great, apparently confident civilization that was metropolitan, conservative and based on the primacy of
reason. Yet in the decade in which he died, two poets began writing
poems which presaged a decisive shift in sensibility. Robert Burns
(1759–1796) was hailed as a child of nature, a plough-boy poet, a
peasant heaven-endowed with song. All this was hardly true, but the
very desire for such a figure was significant. Burns's poetry was lyrical,
regional, cultivating simplicity and a direct emotional appeal – though
he also wrote superb satires which look backward to the dominant

eighteenth-century mode. William Blake (1757–1827) was a still more extraordinary and individual figure, who broke more firmly with traditional neo-classical modes. True he was inspired by the supposed sagas of Ossian (one of the century's celebrated frauds), and can be compared to the earlier Christopher Smart (a poet who, like Blake, was often considered mad, though it is arguable that he merely made the mistake of taking the Christian religion seriously). But Blake's maturity was devoted to a series of long, obscure, impressive Prophetic Books, quite unimaginable from a truly neo-classical writer. Their complexity of symbolism and philosophy prevent their being treated briefly. But in the early *Songs of Innocence* (1789) and *Songs of Experience* (1794) he attained a simplicity of style and poignancy of utterance that clearly prefigures the theories of the great Romantics. The naive, childlike, accepting songs of *Innocence* give way to the dark, disturbed, threatening tones of *Experience*, in which even Love manages only to 'build a Hell in Heaven's despite,' where the rose is destroyed by the invisible worm, and where the cities of England are hells of repression, poverty and disease:

> But most thro' midnight streets I hear
> How the youthful harlot's curse
> Blasts the new-born infant's tear
> And blights with plagues the Marriage hearse.

Blake voices the individualist's cry against the tyranny and corruption of his so-confident social system. His dissatisfactions, his lonely cultivation of his extraordinary visions, are part of that revolution in outlook and sensibility which was to be articulated more publicly and directly by the first generation of Romantic poets.

9

The Rise of the Novel

In the first half of the eighteenth century there began to appear works of prose to which we today give the name of novels. The novel form has its roots in the short tales the Elizabethans enjoyed, in French romance, in the exotic prose fictions of Aphra Behn and others. But few today except literary scholars read those works for pleasure, while *Moll Flanders* and *Tom Jones* are read, and obtain still wider currency through adaptations. It is clear that social and intellectual currents in the age had combined to create something new and different. At some point 'I will tell you a story' became 'I will tell you a story about certain characters living in a certain society.' The persons carrying the action became individualized: they were analysed in all their complexity, and the social pressures on them were minutely detailed. When people began to demand to hear stories about people not too unlike themselves, in a society recognizably akin to their own, then the novel proper was born.

The rise of the novel is usually associated with the rise of the middle classes, but a bald statement of the relationship misses the point. The middle classes had been rising in importance since Chaucer's time. What is important are the circumstances and conditions of middle-class life. More and more middle-class people in the eighteenth century were acquiring an education, and the education they were acquiring was less exclusively classical in content than the education of the upper class. Women were the crucial factor in providing a readership for fiction: it no longer accorded with eighteenth-century good sense to mate with an illiterate dim-wit. Women were educated, and if they were provided with an education which was regarded as appropriate to the inferior sex, it is by no means clear today that they were the losers by this. If we compare, from the next century. Trollope's education at Harrow ('no attempt had been made to teach me anything but Latin and Greek') with Charlotte Brontë's at an obscure middle-class girls' school (History, English, grammar, geography, French, German and drawing) it is obvious that Charlotte Brontë was both the luckier and the better educated.

Better education for women coincided with a period of greater leisure for women in the middle and upper ranks. It no longer seemed lady-like for a woman to involve herself directly in the domestic duties of her household: the middle-class woman, gradually, became only a supervisor, the upper-class woman became a lady of leisure. This trend spread gradually from London to the rest of the country. Compare, in *Tom Jones*, the life of Squire Western's wife, a mere drudge, with that of his daughter, an educated, artistic girl with a mind and a moral judgment of her own. The greater leisure of women left a vacuum in their lives which demanded to be filled. Men too, educated to look a little beyond the narrow interests of locality and profession, demanded imaginative stimulus. Both the sexes were receptive to literary forms that would open up to them new worlds, but real ones, outside their immediate ken.

The proliferation of newspapers in the eighteenth century is evidence of this, and so is the popularity of periodicals such as the *Spectator* and the *Tatler*. The creation by Addison and Steele in these last-named of a series of memorable characters such as Sir Roger de Coverley showed the way the wind was blowing. In a series of essays that sometimes verge on the short story, Sir Roger and others have their individuality and their peculiarities paraded. Also significant is the thirst for travel books, both genuine and fraudulent, a thirst that was capitalized on by the authors of *Gulliver's Travels* and *Robinson Crusoe*. But perhaps most significant of all was the thirst of the reading public to learn about the manners, behaviour and circumstances of other classes and localities than their own. The germ of Richardson's *Pamela* was a plan to write a series of letters which provided examples of the correct way of proceeding in various delicate social situations. The aim was to introduce the reader to behaviour patterns in polite society. To learn how others (particularly one's 'betters') behave is a universal urge, and by providing some of the necessary expertise the novel facilitated that comparatively easy social mixing that has always been a characteristic of British life.

Nor must we forget that the novelists saw it as their duty not only to inform, but to inculcate morality. *Usefulness* was an important concept for the middle-classes, and that included moral usefulness. Many extreme puritans, it is true, condemned all fiction, on the ground that it was not true, it was lying. But the average novel reader was a believer in the Christian religion, probably with a slight bias towards evangelicalism, and he took as an essential ingredient in the pudding passages of explicit moralizing that we today find intrusive or embarrassing. Thus, as the novelists were introducing their readers to new social worlds and delineating the behaviour therein, they were also providing the moral framework within which that behaviour should be judged. This triple aim – to reveal, to educate, to stimulate moral judgments – runs right through the eighteenth- and nineteenth-century novel.

The thirst, then, was there. The men of genius were there to minister to it, as were the inevitable hordes of hacks. There remained a practical problem. The novel was involving and immediate and detailed as no earlier fiction had been, and as a consequence it was long. Being long it was also expensive. The possibility of purchasing a *lot* of novels, sufficient to beguile extended times of leisure, was out of the reach of all but the finest ladies and gentlemen. By the middle of the century circulating libraries were established; by the end of the century they were flourishing all over the country, and in the nineteenth century the work was carried down into the educated working class by means of Mechanics' Institutes and free libraries. It was a development of crucial importance, and the British have remained a nation of book borrowers. A recent survey showed them some way down the list of European countries as book *buyers*, but top of the list as book *readers*.

The great (if unconscious) pioneer of the English novel was Daniel Defoe (?1660–1731) – a businessman, politician, journalist, spy, hackwriter and (at the end of his life) the author of five or six narratives that laid the foundations for the novel proper. Of these *Robinson Crusoe* is the best known – often via adaptations and simplified versions for children. The theme of man cut off from civilization and adapting himself to an island existence is a thread running through English literature, but the bias in Defoe's narrative is significant. Crusoe's island sojourn is only an important part of a much longer narrative, in which Crusoe's adventures at sea and round the world are seen, on the one hand, as punishment for disobeying the commands of his father, and on the other as a series of transactions by which he makes his way in the world. Sums of money, quantities of goods, commercial deals play a very large part in the story. When he finds himself alone on Juan Hernandez, the interest is first on how he will survive, then on how he will establish himself and increase his stock. When Friday appears, Crusoe gains a companion, but (more important) he gains a slave. The book is a perfect picture of man as an economic being. Crusoe is practical, capable: he learns by his errors and is firm in command. As an emotional being he hardly exists at all. He may profess to be moved by the devotion of his slave Xuri, but a few pages on he is selling him for sixty pieces of eight. It is probably this obsessive practicality, this devotion to economic self-help, this distrust of the romantic, that has frequently repelled readers, particularly in the nineteenth century. But perhaps it needed such hardheaded attention to the realities of life to drag prose-narrative out of the generalized idealities of the earlier stories into the actual world of eighteenth-century living.

Moll Flanders illustrates this perhaps even better than *Robinson Crusoe*. Once again Defoe goes to great lengths to convince his readers that what he is telling is not fiction, but a true story: the confessions of a notorious seventeenth-century thief. But a life of crime is (as with Crusoe's island years) only part of the story. Moll begins life in jail, and, after a run of disastrous marriages, nearly ends it there too, but a great deal of the book is taken up with her life as a middle-class wife. Her 'marriages' and her 'husbands' are detailed one by one, and at the end of each such episode a balance sheet is drawn up by Moll of her material profit and loss. The book is often thought to be bawdy, Moll to be another Wife of Bath. Nothing could be further from the truth. We learn the *fact* that Moll goes to bed with a lot of men, but we learn very little more. True we might draw up a scale, put the husbands in order, from the least loved to the most. But Moll loves her favourite, Lancashire husband infinitely less than she loves herself, and the dominant interest in the book is her own material well-being.

Scheming, cajoling, marrying, thieving, Moll may not be *the* complete woman, but she is *a* complete one, the first in our fiction. And because of her rampant materialism, because of the prosaic nature of Defoe's imagination, we learn an enormous amount about (almost feel we experience) eighteenth-century life, particularly the aspects historians overlook. And Defoe's contemporaries learned too, as they were meant to, from Moll's story. They learned how to protect themselves against pick-pockets and shoplifters; they learned about conditions in the American colonies; they learned the prudent method of contracting a marriage; they learned how to board out inconvenient children; what items were most profitable to thieve, what loot most easily got rid of. In one extraordinary passage they learned in detail how much a woman should expect to pay if she has to retire into lodgings to give birth secretly to a child. A great heap of highly miscellaneous information is here, both for the law-abiding and the lawless, and it is held together by the character and the narrative voice of Moll herself.

Moll tells her own story, and the manner is that of the confessional autobiography (still so popular in English Sunday newspapers). So heterogeneous a mass of material needed the immediacy of the first person and a convincing unity of tone in the narrative voice. Moll boasts as she confesses, relishes as she beats her breast. We never quite believe in her repentance: it is a jail-house, shadow-of-the-gallows repentance, and it is too stridently proclaimed. But luckily we don't have to believe in it: the Preface tells us that Moll was at the end of her life 'not so extraordinary a penitent as she was at first,' and, if we will, we can imagine her on her death bed, with a good clergyman bending over her – and as she mutters her prayers Moll's tired, experienced old hands relieve the reverend gentleman of his watch.

The importance of Defoe's achievement was not immediately appreciated. Defoe himself was despised by the arbiters of taste as a hack, a sensationalist, and something less than a gentleman. The novel, it should be remembered, never completely gained respectability as a literary form until our own century. It was left to a member of Defoe's own class, Samuel Richardson (1689–1761) another small tradesman, to advance on his brilliant beginnings.

It is difficult not to see something almost accidental in Richardson's career as a novelist. Would he, if he had not been asked to compile the model letters already mentioned, have discovered in himself the brilliant dramatic sense which is the great contribution *Pamela* makes to the early history of the novel? *Moll Flanders*, however lively and engaging, is the record of a career recollected in old age. But *Pamela*, where possible, was the record of events just past, of feelings rendered in the white heat of experiencing them. The bulk of the novel consists of letters from Pamela to her parents. Few interpolations from the author himself are allowed to distance the narrative. Frequently Richardson contrives to have a crisis in the narrative anticipated by a breathless coda to a letter: 'But mum! Here he comes, I believe – I am &c.' It is easy to see the appeal of such a narrative: the reader is totally involved with the situation: he is there quivering with Pamela in her bedroom as she hears rapacious footsteps approaching along the corridor. Nay – he *is* Pamela herself.

Once one has accepted the conventions of the epistolary narrative, no very great difficulty, the gains in drama, immediacy, verisimilitude are enormous.

Yet it cannot be denied that, even today, when his critical reputation stands very high, Richardson is not a living classic in the way that Fielding is, in spite of the comparative remoteness of Fielding's narrative methods. We are in fact still troubled by the things that caused controversy in Richardson's own day: we doubt the healthiness of the proclaimed morality, we feel queasy at the tone, we dislike the mind behind the books. *Pamela* concerns the efforts of a virtuous servant girl to avoid seduction or rape at the hands of her young master Mr B. Half-way through the novel she marries him, and the rest of the novel celebrates her virtues, her happiness and (not least) her growing social acceptance in her new position. Richardson himself handed a weapon to his critics when he subtitled the book *Virtue Rewarded*. It is not just modern critics who have seen Pamela as a calculating prude who uses her virginity as a means of keeping her gentleman hot. The Puritan notion that virtue *brings rewards* is distasteful to us, as it was to Fielding. We can say that Pamela is both virtuous and calculating, that she sets a high price on her freedom to choose her partner, yet is strongly influenced in her choice by worldly considerations. This is all true enough, but it implies a complex evaluation of Pamela's religious and moral notions that Richardson never comes close to attempting.

Clarissa Harlowe is a much greater book, and perhaps it is mainly its length (2000-odd pages) that prevents it being a living classic. But doubts intrude here too. Clarissa is mistreated by her worldly family who want her to marry an uninspiring suitor. She is loved by the rake Lovelace, who abducts her, lodges her in a brothel, and eventually rapes her while she is drugged. Clarissa refuses to marry him, and wastes away, while Lovelace is killed in a duel. The subject is simple yet terrible, but the loving, lingering detail with which it is treated suggests that it appealed to Richardson in ways he can scarcely have acknowledged to himself. There is pity in the treatment, and horror, but is there not also more than a suspicion of a gloat, of lips being licked?

All this is part of the familiar case against Richardson, and modern criticism has not been able entirely to set it aside. Perhaps our feelings towards the books will always be ambiguous, of admiring distaste. But to concentrate on Richardson's morality – admittedly the feature he himself most trumpeted – diverts our attention from his astonishing realism and psychological insight. For example, the rake Lovelace embodies extremely modern insights into the connection between libertinism and sadism: sex, to have meaning for him, must involve humiliation for his partner. He demands constant recognition of his irresistible fascination. As she submits, his victim must grovel. He is Don Juan, with a dash of Milton's Satan, transposed into everyday London life. On a different level Clarissa's family, the Harlowes, are masterpieces of realism: mean, bullying, ambitious. And the obsessive piling up of detail, which sometimes in *Pamela* gave the impression that the author was stocktaking ('My master has . . . given me a suit of my late lady's clothes, and half a dozen of her shifts, and six fine handkerchiefs, and three of her cambric aprons, and four Holland ones') here adds up to a series of superbly concrete social settings, each as totally *there* for us as a domestic interior in a Dutch painting.

The endless detail of Richardson, inherited from Defoe, was one of the things that Henry Fielding (1707–1754) seized on when he came to write *Shamela*, the first of his attacks on Richardson's successful novel: 'two pair of stockings, one odd one, . . . one clog, and almost another' says Shamela, in a parody inventory of her possessions sent to her disgraceful old mother. Fielding took the suspicion of Pamela's motives that many readers felt to its logical conclusion: Shamela is a vulgar whore who pretends virtue to entrap her master, aided by a disreputable parson, one of her old lovers. Within its small compass *Shamela* is a superb literary spoof.

Fielding was as unlike Richardson in character as the Idle Apprentice in Hogarth's contemporary series of etchings was unlike the Industrious Apprentice. And – as with the Hogarth prints – it is very difficult to avoid preferring the Idle Apprentice. Where Richardson married his master's daughter and rose to the top of his profession of printer, Fielding eloped from Eton at seventeen with a nearby gentleman's daughter; where Richardson surrounded himself with admiring women who cosseted him and admired his moral pronouncements, Fielding wenched and rollicked and had to marry his housekeeper hurriedly. 'He has known more happy moments than any prince upon the earth,' opined one contemporary after his death. But such an opposition is as crudely black and white as Hogarth's morality: Fielding was a first-rate magistrate, a sincere Christian, and the moral codes of his novels are as deeply felt as Richardson's, though they are very different.

Fielding's first novel proper, *Joseph Andrews*, begins (and it is to some

extent lamed by this beginning) as another satire on *Pamela*. Fielding
invents a brother for Pamela, Joseph, who in turn has *his* virtue tested by
his insatiable mistress Lady Booby. Fielding found, however, that there
was a limit to the fun that could be got out of this situation: once the
innocent Joseph had been tempted by a rapacious female, there was little
left to do but repeat the process, with diminishing effect. Fielding
salvages the novel by sending Joseph out on the road with his old teacher
Parson Adams, and the novel thus becomes one of the first of the
picaresque novels (the tradition extends as late as early Dickens), which in
English terms means little more than that the novel centres on the
travels of the hero, the characters consisting mainly of the people he
meets on the road. This sort of novel was much more to Fielding's liking
than the hot-house atmosphere of Richardson, with its 'underclothing
excitements' (the phrase is D. H. Lawrence's). There are many opportunities for physical action – fights, chases, contretemps in the hunting
field. Many of these are described in mock-heroic terms, for Fielding was
very concerned to establish his kind of novel in a respectable classical
tradition. The characters Adams and Joseph meet on their travels are a
comic gallery of remarkable vividness and humanity. To call them types
is to miss the essential quality of his characterization: Parson Trulliber
is no doubt in one sense the archetype of the negligent clergyman that
Fielding loved to chastise; on the other hand, the absurdity of his
overmastering preoccupation, his pigs, lifts him into a realm of ludicrous comedy very different from type humour. Nor is there anything in
the least mechanical or constructed about such characters as Mrs Tow-
wowse or Lady Booby. What Fielding was aiming at, as *Joseph Andrews*
developed, was a panoramic picture of eighteenth-century England, set
in the context of a conservative but tolerant and compassionate social
morality. This is what he was actually to achieve in his next and great
novel, *Tom Jones*.

The title hints at his intention: one of the commonest British sur-
names, allied with a sturdy British Christian name in its familiar form.
Not that Tom is quite a British Everyman. He is too handsome, gallant
and generous for that. But he allies what Fielding sees as many of the
best qualities of his countrymen along with more negative traits: his
impetuousness, for example, continuously leads him into scrapes, both
in love and war. Tom is illegitimate, brought up by the virtuous Square
Allworthy. Due in part to his own imprudence, but also the hostility of
his tutors Thwackum and Square and his cousin, the repulsively virtuous

Blifil, he is cast out of the Allworthy household, and the long central section of the novel deals with his adventures on the road, where his path crosses now and again both with soldiers off to fight the Jacobites (for this is 1745) and with the beautiful Sophia Western whom he loves. The last section is in London, where Tom indulges in fashionable intrigue, nearly gets hanged, apparently discovers he has committed incest, yet finally (chastened and mature) gains the hand of Sophia.

The book is shaped with classical finesse. The opening section is a pastoral idyll, but one in which the darker side of rural life is not ignored: the rustics can be brutal and crudely over-sexed, and Allworthy's Eden is full of snakes. The Squire himself may be all-worthy, yet he employs a sadist and an unprincipled atheist to bring up his adoptive son. Squire Western may be hearty and good-humoured, but he is an ignorant boor and a tyrant to his women-folk.

When Tom sets out on the road the social focus is widened. On the road can be found a cross-section of English life, with the accent, perhaps, on the adventurous and the unfortunate. If we get a sense of the brutal changeability of fortunes in eighteenth-century England, we see, too, many examples of compassion and good-fellowship. More, certainly, than we find in upper-class London, for in the final section a brittle, artificial good-breeding hides cupidity, lust, heartlessness. It is through his experience of life at all levels, and in all these different environments, that Tom's natural good-nature can be tempered and matured to true and wise benevolence. And if Fielding believed in a natural goodness, an in-bred beauty of heart, he clearly believed in its opposite too: Blifil is young, prudent, and neglects none of the outward shows of religion. It is not long before we learn that he is also cunning, grasping and treacherous, and it is in the gradual unravelling of his double-dealing that Fielding's meticulous plotting reveals the master-storyteller. It is significant that though Blifil is cast out of the Allworthy household at the end he is not punished beyond that (unless marriage to a Methodist widow be accounted punishment). Fielding displays throughout this (and his last novel, *Amelia*) the strongest sense of how powerful the forces of darkness are, how many of the levers of power they inevitably control. The 'happy constitution' of which his contemporaries spoke made Fielding reluctant to give the victory to those forces, but the final triumph of good is never easy, or achieved without struggle and loss.

After the brilliant energy and originality of these three great founder-fathers, came a new generation of novelists less original (with one exception), and more competent journeymen than trail-blazers. Tobias Smollett (1721–1771), for example, takes the basic picaresque form as Fielding established it and produced two rumbustious novels (*Peregrine Pickle* and *Roderick Random*) in which we follow the rowdy scamps who are his heroes through a variety of adventures on land and at sea. The characteristic marks of Smollett's genius are his violence and his almost hysterical sensitivity to dirt, disease, smells and ugliness of every kind, which he depicts with almost masochistic relish. There is (in contrast to Fielding) no humanity in the grotesques that populate his novels: they are all part of, and contribute to, the hideous and pointless brutality of the world as Smollett sees it. The morbid, almost pathological side to Smollett's vision seems at times to ally him to twentieth-century writers – to those who use pornographic and scatological detail to point up the cruelty and viciousness of our century. It is only in *Humphrey Clinker*, his last novel, that we sense some slight mellowing: here Smollett re-invents the epistolary novels for ends quite different from Richardson's. A journey through England is seen through the eyes of a company of travellers, and their pictures of each other, as well as their inimitable epistolary styles, contribute to creating a feeling of balance and reluctant humanity that is more acceptable to a tender digestion.

The epistolary novel was developed also by Frances Burney (1752–1840), almost always known as Fanny. Her most famous novel, *Evelina*, written while she was in her mid-twenties, depicts – as the subtitle claims – 'A Young Lady's Entrance Into the World,' and thus the woman's viewpoint enters the novel – the viewpoint, that is, of the average woman, rather than the potential victim of rape who dominated in Richardson. Fanny Burney uses Richardson's techniques, but she is temperamentally closer to Fielding, with her delight in human absurdity and pretension, her zest at the mishaps and misunderstandings which dog all social intercourse – particularly that in which the classes mingle. Her vision is, naturally, more restricted: her experience was less, due to her youth and the limitations imposed on her sex. She had, too, a youthful snobbery which is understandable if not actually pleasing. But there is an energy, a sharp charm about this novel that is irresistible, and which is largely lost in her later books, where a dreadful heaviness of style mars the sharp perceptions. Which is not to say she did not develop as an artist: her genius went into her diary, one of the greatest in the language, where all her mastery of character description and sense of conveying a scene or building dramatic tension are on display. The record there of George III's growing mental disorder in 1788 (Fanny was Assistant Keeper of the Robes to his Queen), culminating in her en-counters with the mad king in Kew Gardens, are as involving and as funny/terrible as anything in her fiction.

The joker in the pack, the innovator and original, was Laurence Sterne (1713–1768), whose *Life and Opinions of Tristram Shandy, Gent* is as unlike any other gentleman's life (or opinions) as it is possible to imagine. For example, it begins not with his birth but his conception, which very nearly does not take place at all, since his mother chooses that inconvenient moment to ask his father whether he has remembered to wind the clock (' "Good God!" cried my father . . . "Did ever woman, since the creation of the world, interrupt a man with such a silly question?" '). Sterne has written four books before his hero even gets born at all, and they are books which employ every conceivable device of whimsy, fantasy, free association, typographical oddity, grotesque or obscene incident to create a comic novel that is light years away from any other comic novel. We must come forward to our own century before we can find anything that relates to it – *Ulysses, Finnegans Wake*, expres-sionist drama, absurd humour. The characterization is of its time – humours, done in a humane, gentle spirit – but it is the only recognizable plum in a very queer pudding indeed.

We get a sense, in many of these late eighteenth-century writers, of 'marking time.' The world was changing: physically the industrial revolution was leaving its mark already on the landscape of England and the day-to-day lives of its inhabitants. In thought and feeling the settled, sure classicism of Fielding or Dr Johnson was being undermined by the spreading cult of 'feeling,' of sensibility, by the onset of a change of heart and mind that we call Romanticism. Eventually the novel was going to have to absorb these sweeping changes.

10

The Birth of Romanticism

In the later years of the eighteenth century, there began a shift in the way educated men and women regarded themselves and the world around them. That shift, in the aftermath of which we still live, was later given the name of the Romantic Movement.

One puts such general statements as cautiously as possible. Of course the main elements of Romanticism were not new: no one would pretend that the works of Chaucer, Spenser or Shakespeare were never Romantic in spirit. Nor did the Romantic poets think of themselves in those terms, or regard themselves as a group. Frequently, indeed, they thoroughly disliked each other's poetry: 'A drowsy frowzy poem, call'd the "Excursion",' growled Byron, about one of Wordsworth's later efforts, 'Writ in a manner which is my aversion.' Nor can one deny that in some of the great Romantic poets, the remnants of eighteenth-century attitudes are sometimes unexpectedly strong.

Nevertheless, when all the nervous qualifications have been made, it remains true that the mode of thinking of intelligent people was changed by the poetry, the critical writings, and the social attitudes of the leaders of the Romantic Movement. By 1830, a man who was brought up in the neo-classical tradition, or who clung to it from innate conservatism, was feeling very lonely in and alienated from the literary world – indeed from his social world in general. The colour of people's thoughts had been changed.

It is not difficult for the modern reader to see what the Romantic poets were reacting against: their feeling that the neo-classical tradition had exhausted itself into cliché, repetition, staleness was understandable, even if (in the manner of young revolutionaries) they produced too blanket a condemnation. Their reaction against the dominant modes of thinking of the eighteenth-century writers and philosophers was vigorous and wholesale. Where their predecessors saw man as a social animal, saw him in his daily relations with his fellows, the Romantics saw him essentially in the solitary state, self-communing. Where the Augustans emphasized those features that men have in common, the interests that bring them together, the Romantics emphasized the special qualities of each individual's mind; they exalted the atypical, even the bizarre, they honoured the hermit, the outcast, the rebel. Where, for the Augustans, literature was a communal activity, likely to be carried on in a metropolitan environment, for the Romantics it was essentially solitary, or at most the communing of two sympathetic souls, and it was inevitably attached not to the city, but to the outdoors. Nature, for the most influential eighteenth-century writers, was more something to be *seen* than something to be *known*. The famous exchange between Boswell and Johnson during one of their early meetings is significant in this connection. When Boswell, mindful of Johnson's famous contempt for Scotland and its people, timidly advanced in its defence that it had many 'noble prospects,' he received this magisterial put-down:

> 'Norway too, has noble wild prospects; and Lapland is remarkable for prodigious noble wild prospects. But, Sir, let me tell you, the noblest prospect which a Scotchman ever sees, is the high road that leads him to England!'

The terms of the exchange are significant. Nature, to Boswell, is a matter of 'prospects,' of panoramic views rather than intimate contact; the prospects, one feels, are seen from the safety of a coach. For Johnson the majesty of nature is something tinged with barbarism, and when he refers to the high road to England, one feels morally sure he was thinking of the high road to London. In the years to come, the years of the Romantic revival, Scotland, and even Norway, were to gain a significant revenge for the Great Cham's lofty dismissal.

It is of nature that the ordinary reader will think when the subject of Romantic poetry comes up, and by and large the emphasis is not misplaced. The natural world now comes to the forefront of the poetic imagination – provides the dominant subject matter, is the major source of imagery, even infiltrates into much of the theoretical writing. Naturally it does not mean quite the same to all the poets. Wordsworth is the closest to nature, though he is not primarily an observer (his sister

Dorothy, in her *Journals*, often *observes* the same scene more sharply); the natural world is known, felt, in Wordsworth – it is an emotional necessity for him, the basis of his spiritual life. Shelley and Keats *know* nature much less well; the natural object tends to be a springboard for philosophical, social or personal meditations. For Byron nature is a magnificent backdrop, in front of which he can make splendid gestures.

But it was Wordsworth's view of the natural world that was the dominant influence in changing people's sensibilities: nature to him was a source of mental cleanliness and spiritual understanding, it was a teacher, it was the stepping stone between Man and God. Such a view was easier to propagate in the wild rolling countryside of England than in, say, a land of deserts or jungles: Aldous Huxley, in the twentieth century, commented on the *impossibility* of reading Wordsworth in the tropics. Natural grandeur was not now a question of *prospects*; it was an image of God more glorious than anything Michelangelo could produce. When Shelley, in the sight of Mont Blanc, gave his profession in hotel registers along his route as 'Democrat, Philanthropist and Atheist' he gave unbounded offence to generations of tourists who followed after: to proclaim atheism, *there*!

With the shift in emphasis from man in society to man in solitude, the very words to express that solitude became dominant ones in poetry, and began to carry an emotional charge very different from that they held in the eighteenth century. 'Alone, alone, all, all alone, / Alone on a wide wide sea!' intones Coleridge's Ancient Mariner, with that bleakly expressive repetition that makes the poem so instantly memorable. 'Behold her, single in the field, / Yon solitary Highland lass!' says Wordsworth, and adds, in case we have missed the point, 'Reaping and singing by herself.' Even Byron, a highly sociable man in a misanthropic kind of way, felt the need to go along with this: 'There is a rapture on the lonely shore, / There is society, where none intrudes.' Only in solitude is man truly himself, only in solitude can he come adequately to know himself. Once one sees the larger social organisms as essentially corrupting, one inevitably comes to see as wiser, holier, those who have not had the chance to be thus corrupted – the peasant, the hermit, the mariner, the child. Wordsworth sees the child as 'trailing clouds of glory ... / From God, who is our home,' but also sees society rapidly closing in on him, extinguishing that glory: 'Shades of the prison-house begin to close / Upon the growing boy.'

It is in solitude, in communion with the natural universe, that man can exercise that most valuable of faculties, the Imagination. 'This world of Imagination is the world of Eternity; it is the divine bosom . . .' said Blake. Where intelligence was fallible, limited, the Imagination was our hope of contact with eternal forces, with the whole spiritual world. The Romantics were fascinated by the faculty of imagination, and elevated the concepts of spontaneity, inspiration, and so on. In general they celebrated the limitless possibilities of the human mind, and explored the means of penetrating down to subconscious levels: dreams, drugs, madness, hypnosis, thought transference occupy a place in the romantic view of things that the eighteenth century would have found unhealthy, untenable, simply foolish. These were the Romantics' ways of escaping from, or at any rate articulating an alternative to, a world that had become excessively rational, as well as excessively materialistic and ugly.

It is not surprising that, finding little sustenance in the world of the late eighteenth century, where even nature was threatened by the burgeoning industrialism, and where all the impulses of spontaneity and free expression were stifled under a reactionary political system, the imaginations of the Romantics tuned in, instead, to other times and places, where the qualities they valued could be convincingly depicted. The medieval or renaissance worlds were particularly favoured (it would be hard to think of more than a handful of romantic operas which were not set in one or the other), but they might range further afield – to the central Asian fief of Kubla Khan, or to India for the vaguely Hindu tales (more vague than Hindu) of Robert Southey. In such settings, it seemed, life was more dangerous, man's individuality more sharply defined; existence had a zest, an edge, lacking in conformist nineteenth-century Britain. There too one could allow free play to the supernatural – witches, curses, visions and prophecies – without arousing feelings of incongruity. The fascination with such aspects of the non-rational could be and was capitalized on: at its lowest form, in the Gothic novels of people like 'Monk' Lewis and Mrs Radcliffe, it becomes a matter of ivy-encrusted castles, threatened heroines, murderous monks, sepulchral prophetic voices. Used with proper discretion, for example by Sir Walter Scott, it opened up new avenues in fiction, drama and poetry.

One last characteristic of the romantic poets may seem hardly compatible with this attraction to the medieval world: they were all, at least when young, radicals. The older generation embraced enthusiastically the aspirations of the first years of the French Revolution: 'Bliss was it in that dawn to be alive,' said Wordsworth. The younger generation, particularly Shelley and Byron, had close contacts with the hard-pressed radical groupings in England, and supported nationalist movements against the creaking tyrannies re-erected throughout Europe after the defeat of Napoleon. Their radicalism is often of a vague, utopian kind, more idealistic than practical, and frequently coming into conflict with their actual experiences. The story of Coleridge's marriage and Shelley's second elopement belong in the realms of high human comedy, and the behaviour of Robert Southey in the first matter and William Godwin in the second prove that double standards were not the sole preserve of the conforming and conservative classes. But at its best, for example in Shelley's superb contempt for the British political establishment in *England in 1819*, or in Byron's noble enthusiasm for the *idea* of Greece, radicalism runs through romantic poetry like a fresh breeze entering a museum.

The childhood and adolescence of William Wordsworth (1770–1850) was spent in the Lake District, in the North-Western corner of England, and it is impossible not to see his poetry as influenced by the beauty and grandeur of that region. The country people of Cumberland and West-moreland had not been reduced (as in most other areas of Britain) to the status of tenants or labourers, and their independence and attachment to their own native soil also set their mark of his poetry. The crucial emotional events of his life were first his sojourn in France (1791–1792) during a year of tumultuous political changes, a year that also saw a youthful love affair that produced an illegitimate daughter; and secondly the close intimacy of Wordsworth, his sister Dorothy and the poet Coleridge, first in the West Country, then back in the Lake District, which was to be his home for the rest of his life. This close friendship of the two greatest poets of their time – a friendship of men very different in temperament and aspiration – is unparalleled in the history of poetry; and the sparks ignited by the relationship started the revolution in English poetry which they jointly achieved.

In Coleridge's *Biographia Literaria* he states that Wordsworth's con-tributions to the volume of *Lyrical Ballads* (1798) which they produced jointly were intended to 'give the charm of novelty to things of every day' and to awaken 'the mind's attention from the lethargy of custom and [direct] it to the loveliness and the wonders of the world before us.' Wordsworth himself in the Preface he later wrote to the volume talked about choosing 'incidents and situations from common life,' and added that the aim was 'to relate or describe them, throughout, as far as was possible, in a selection of language really used by men.' Such descriptions do not tell the whole truth about Wordsworth's aims, but they provide a convenient doorway into what was distinctive and new in his poetry.

Wordsworth's concern to draw at least some of his subject matter from the life of the humble peasantry around him drew easy ridicule in his own time, and even today it is possible to feel that he not merely fell into bathos, but jumped in enthusiastically, in such oft-ridiculed lines as

> For still, the more he works, the more
> Do his weak ankles swell

or

> I've measured it from side to side:
> 'Tis three feet long, and two feet wide.

Yet for all that, and for all the intrusive Sunday school moralizing in many of the poems of simple peasant life, his concern with the uneducated rural population both moves the reader and enlarges his sympathies. Certainly it is more appealing than his contemporary Jane Austen's practical yet briskly dismissive concern: 'She understood their ways, could allow for their ignorance and temptations, had no romantic expectations of extraordinary virtue from those for whom education had done so little . . .' (*Emma*, chapter 10).

Many of Wordsworth's best poems concern encounters of his own with people or natural objects, in which he movingly conveys the very experience of the moment, the complex of aesthetic, moral and emotional reactions that are aroused. For example, in *The Solitary Reaper*, from which the first lines have already been quoted, the physical oneness of the girl with nature, the incomprehensible beauty of her Gaelic song, arouse in Wordsworth feelings of physical and emotional pleasure, mysterious apprehensions of her direct link with folk traditions and 'battles long ago,' appreciation of her dignity and wholeness. And these apprehensions are not analysed, but are conveyed in simple and evocative language – the sort of language, close to normal speech, which for Wordsworth was the only way of decisively rejecting the burdensome formality of Augustan poetic diction. In *She Dwelt Among the Untrodden*

Ways, his reactions to the death of Lucy are all the more poignant because of their heartfelt understatement:

> She lived unknown, and few could know
>> When Lucy ceased to be;
> But she is in her grave, and, oh,
>> The difference to me!

During his greatest, most fertile period of creativity, Wordsworth managed to recapture, or even retain, the freshness of the response to nature that he had had as a boy, freely ranging the mountains, dales and lakes. It was this closeness to his pristine responses that Wordsworth most valued and saw the need to maintain:

> My heart leaps up when I behold
>> A rainbow in the sky:
> So was it when my life began;
> So is it now I am a man;
> So be it when I shall grow old,
>> Or let me die!

The simplicity of diction here mirrors the simplicity of childish responses. But Wordsworth emphasizes that this pristine response grew to have a moral and religious dimension that is an essential part of the function of nature in his poetry.

The modern vulgarization of this, that a walk in the mountains is more spiritually uplifting than a church service, shows the long-lasting influence of Wordsworthianism, and essentially Wordsworth would have agreed. The level of sophistication at which the message is conveyed varies greatly. There is a famous passage in *The Prelude* in which Wordsworth describes how one night, when a boy, he borrowed a boat for an unlawful night expedition. He rowed out into the lake, and as he got further and further from the shore he saw 'a huge peak, black and huge,' which, as it got larger, seemed to threaten him more and more with retribution. The apprehension here has the grotesque simplification of the adolescent boy Wordsworth was at the time. In the *Lines Composed a Few Miles Above Tintern Abbey*, on the other hand, he joyously recalls the freshness of his childish response to nature, but convincingly and movingly expands this to a much more complex, mature response, one in which he hears the 'still, sad music of humanity,' and, more, conceives of nature as 'the nurse, / The guide, the guardian of my heart, and soul / Of all my moral being.' The *necessity* of a response to nature in the full man was something Wordsworth never tired of underlining.

Some of the essentials of the Romantic creed are put appealingly, if over-starkly, in the two companion poems *Expostulation and Reply* and *The Tables Turned*. In the first, Wordsworth is attacked by a friend for mooning away over natural objects, and neglecting the wisdom to be got from learning, from the world of books:

> 'Where are your books? – that light bequeathed
> To beings else forlorn and blind!
> Up! up! and drink the spirit breathed
> From dead men to their kind.'

The ambiguity of that last line makes one feel that Wordsworth hardly conducts a fair argument, and certainly he allots himself the lion's share of it, as well as most of the memorable lines. In the second poem he insists on the singing bird as preacher, nature as teacher, and the essential *destructiveness* (in that they destroy natural, spontaneous apprehensions) of Science and Art:

> One impulse from a vernal wood
> May teach you more of man,
> Of moral evil and of good,
> Than all the sages can.
>
> Sweet is the lore which Nature brings;
> Our meddling intellect
> Misshapes the beauteous forms of things –
> We murder to dissect.

Wordsworth here, one must emphasize, is conducting an argument, so that the obvious objections to all this – that Wordsworth gets from vernal woods only what he brings into them, for example, or that he wildly overestimates the 'sweetness' of nature's lore – are beside the point. Nor was Wordsworth as a rule as damagingly anti-intellectual as he appears here. Nevertheless, the conclusion of the poem, in which the friend is urged to 'Come forth, and bring with you a heart / That watches and receives' is a splendid statement in miniature of the Wordsworthian creed. It was the creation of such hearts that was Wordsworth's great legacy to the nineteenth century, that makes his appeal perpetually renewable to our own day.

The high point of Wordsworth's poetic creativity lasted for ten years or so. He finished *The Prelude*, the story of his development as poet, thinker and man, in 1805. By 1807 most of his best work was done, though there were certainly upsurges of poetic power in the forty-three years that remained to him. Coleridge's period of poetic creativity was even shorter. Many critics, both at the time and since, have associated the poetic drying-up (a *comparative* drying up only, in Wordsworth's case) with the political swing to the right which both men underwent during the Napoleonic wars. Both became staunch, if idiosyncratic, pillars of conservatism. Such a view is not much more than ideological wishful thinking. If conservatism disqualified one from writing good poetry, the twentieth century would lose all its major poets and a good many of its minor ones. More likely is the view that the source of Wordsworth's inspiration was his profound gratitude for his boyhood experiences in nature, and his ability to reawaken the freshness of his responses to them. Such a seam could not be endlessly mined, and as he got further from them the effort to recapture them grew greater, their recall more sporadic. It was not, perhaps, that his heart ceased to leap up when he beheld a rainbow in the sky, but that it leapt up as much from habit as from impulsive joy.

The case of Coleridge is more complex. In fact, everything about Samuel Taylor Coleridge (1772–1834) is complex. His period of poetic creativity was shorter than Wordsworth's, and very much a matter of what in another connection he calls 'half-intermitted bursts.' Of his three major, universally admired poems, only one is complete. He wrote a handful of fine, meditative poems, but these are closer in spirit to Wordsworth than to his own great works. His life was a mess. The popular view is that he was a poet destroyed by opium addiction, but this is no more than a half-truth. Even during his period of most abject slavery to the drug he was productive – of some brilliant lectures, of journalism, even of drama. After he (with the help of good friends, who lodged and nursed him) gained some kind of control over his addiction his output was considerable, though certainly uneven, and aided by turgid padding and sometimes outright thievery from the works of others. The *Biographia Literaria*, the *Aids to Reflection* and *On the Constitu-*

tion of Church and State all date from the last years of his life, and indicate the wide-ranging power of his mind. It wasn't so much that his life lacked direction, more that it had too many directions. Many of the misfortunes of his life, including his marriage and perhaps his addiction, could have been avoided by a stronger personality. Certainly he lacked, in each individual enterprise of his life, will power and staying power. Yet all his friends testify to the charm of his personality, the wondrous power of his conversation, the staggering richness of his mind. When all is said and done it is a more than sufficient claim to fame to be known (as he is to the general reader) as the author of the marvellous *Ancient Mariner*, *Kubla Khan* and *Christabel*.

The contrast in style we encounter on turning from Wordsworth to Coleridge comes largely from their differing temperaments, but also from the plan of the *Lyrical Ballads*: where Wordsworth was to choose subjects from 'ordinary life,' Coleridge was to concentrate on 'persons and characters supernatural, or at least romantic.' Where Wordsworth's poetry is meditative, low-keyed, only occasionally concentrating itself for the unforgettable phrase ('The Child is father of the Man'), Coleridge's is passionate, mysterious, thrilling, seemingly written in moods of total commitment, of surrender to an uncontrollable vision. Though these three poems occupy perhaps twenty pages or so, phrases from them are imprinted on our memory, force themselves upon us on every occasion of conceivable appropriateness. The ancient mariner as the type of button-holding, irresistible narrator, his burden of the albatross, the poet who 'on honeydew has fed' – these have entered popular speech, folk myth.

For Coleridge's tone of voice is obsessive, incantatory, like a witch-doctor crying out formulas from tribal memory. The *Ancient Mariner* is in fact a highly sophisticated poem, but Coleridge disguises this by his brilliant use of every conceivable device from the balladist's art – alliteration, onomatopoeia, internal rhyme, above all repetition, so that every phrase seems carved from ice in one single, brilliant stroke:

> The ice was here, the ice was there,
> The ice was all around:
> It cracked and growled, and roared and howled,
> Like noises in a swound!

That this impression of unforced inspiration is misleading can easily be seen by checking the first published version of the poem – infinitely weaker than that we know by reason of its dogged, distracting medieval-isms. But the poem impresses itself on the reader as an irresistible vision of a world beyond our own, in language of a kind uniquely fitted to force us into that 'suspension of disbelief' which Coleridge saw as necessary in such poetry.

Though the poem begins in a real world of weddings and wedding-guests, of blushing brides and groaning tables, it soon takes on a very different aspect as the Mariner fixes his auditor with his 'glittering eye' (hypnotism fascinated the Romantics and the Victorians, like all other non-rational manifestations that seemed to offer access to areas of the mind beyond the conscious ones). In spite of the debt Coleridge owed to Elizabethan books of travel and mariners' tales, both for incident, super-stition and individual phrases, the voyage soon takes on the air of ritual and of myth, with nature powerfully yet mysteriously animated, the sailors some kind of chorus, half in and half out of the action, and the albatross a bird of priestly aspect and function.

It is the shooting of the albatross – an action unmotivated and unex-plained, as so often in myth and ballad – that cuts the Mariner off from the healing, restorative natural world. Coleridge seems to image here the alienation of modern man, to whom society denies all the conditions of mental and spiritual wholeness. The drought conveys unforgettably a physical equivalent of this state:

Water, water, everywhere,
And all the boards did shrink;
Water, water, everywhere,
Nor any drop to drink.

By reason of his flouting the community between man, beast and the whole natural world, the Mariner suffers a period of virtual death, of near self-annihilation, and only when he begins to recognize again his kinship with the world of nature does the long process of spiritual regeneration begin. In Part IV, the centre of the poem, the Mariner lies on deck with the dead bodies of the other sailors, and progresses from the state of being unable to pray, via that of wonder at the beauty of the moon and stars, to admiration of the beauty of the water-snakes, 'Blue, glossy green, and velvet black,' which previously had been 'slimy things . . . / Upon the slimy sea.' It is when, as if involuntarily, the Mariner blesses the snakes that he can begin to regain that wholeness he had lost, that oneness with his fellow men and the natural world.

Kubla Khan is a poem even more strange and wonderful. Coleridge's account of its genesis is famous: it was composed, he said, at a distant farmhouse in the West Country, in an opium dream — two to three hundred lines of it. When he woke he began to transcribe this composition, but he had written only 50 lines or so when he was interrupted by a gentleman from Porlock, and when he had transacted his business with him he returned to find the rest of the poem had fled from his conscious mind. The gentleman from Porlock has been universally execrated for robbing us of Coleridge's greatest poem. The question is, whether there ever was a gentleman from Porlock. Coleridge made a great many claims of a similar kind, claims of being in the grip of some power that results in his falling *involuntarily* into verse, a mere instrument of a higher spirit. Most of these claims modern scholarship has disproved. They seem to be the result of congenital nervousness, a wriggling-out from under responsibility for what he had written. It is best to take the poem as it stands.

And yet it can never be a poem like any other. An opium dream would certainly seem to enter the picture somewhere. The incantatory voice is heard again in parts of the poem, but so is a softer, more beguiling one, that depicts 'gardens bright with sinuous rills.' The idyllic, enchanted nature of Kubla's pleasure palace and its gardens is always married to its opposite — sunless seas, measureless caverns, savage chasms and fountains in which rocks play. The sacred river Alph, perhaps the river of poetic inspiration, connects all the various parts of the landscape. Many of the features have strong sexual overtones, some suggestive of the guilt and panic Coleridge seems to have felt on this subject.

Until line 30 – 'And 'mid this tumult Kubla heard from far / Ancestral voices prophesying war!' – the poem seems set to become a narrative, in which the idyll of the pleasure palace is threatened, perhaps destroyed, by war. Then the poem (and perhaps the dream) begins to fragment. The next lines seem to repeat material, rather than following on, and suddenly we switch to a vision that the poet (entering the poem for the first time) once had of an Abyssinian maid, singing: she seems to have become a symbol to him of the poet's inspiration, of the need to capture, make permanent, evanescent visions. If he could recapture his vision of *her*, he could recreate Kubla's palace in such vividness that people without his miraculous power would regard him not merely as a poet, but as seer, soothsayer, prophet, possessor of mystic secrets.

At this point, and only at this point, the poem seems to take as its subject the poetic vision as such. For the rest it is wild, mysterious, contradictory, bewildering – a marriage of opposites, a narrative fragment without narrative, momentarily suggestive, impenetrable as a totality, yet always strangely haunting.

Coleridge's other notable work in the romantic/supernatural vein is *Christabel*, an unfinished yet superbly accomplished piece in the Gothic vein, with threatened maidens, wicked witches, all the paraphernalia of the romantics' view of the medieval world. *Christabel* had a prodigious progeny in the works of Scott, Keats, Tennyson and others. The tendency is to regard it as inferior to the other two great exercises in the supernatural – 'an exquisite piece of decor' it has been called by Graham Hough. Yet its use of an apparently irregular metre, based on stress rather than syllables, is masterly, and many of the lines cleave their way into the memory, just as in the other poems. The strength and imaginative commitment of the poem, it might be argued, rescued the medieval world from the tushery of the Gothic novelists, and opened up new paths for the serious use of the past by later writers. It was certainly a path they trod with enthusiasm.

11

Romantics and Anti-Romantics

In 1812 Lord Byron (1788–1824) published the first two cantos of *Childe Harold*, and in his own words 'awoke one morning and found myself famous.' Born into the disreputable fringes of the aristocracy, he had previously published feeble lyrics and an unsuccessful satire; suddenly he was the darling of the fashionable and literary worlds, the popularizer and personification of Romantic values. Wordsworth and Coleridge, whose poetry and ideas had been greeted by the public with a scepticism verging on contempt, might justifiably have felt a twinge of jealousy. In fact, one can imagine them contemplating the poem with the fascinated horror of Frankenstein staring aghast at the monster he himself had created.

For *Childe Harold* is a very odd affair indeed. It teems with features recognizably Romantic, yet vulgarized sometimes to the point of comedy. It starts, apparently, as a tale of a medieval knight, and the early stanzas teem with mock-medieval, mock-Spenserian usages ('Whilome in Albion's isle there dwelt a youth, / Who ne in virtue's ways did take delight' and so on) – the sort of thing Coleridge had wisely pruned from *The Ancient Mariner*. Before long, however, the pretence of a medieval setting is abandoned, and soon after the archaic diction too. We get reflections on contemporary politics, the Peninsular war, the character of the Portuguese (disgraceful), the Elgin marbles, the sad state of modern Greece – a sort of travelogue with digressions, in fact, in which Childe Harold gets increasingly forgotten. In the first two books Byron makes nervous bows in his hero's direction ('So deem'd the Childe,' he will say, or – justifiably – 'But where is Harold?'), but by the time of the third and fourth cantos he has more or less disappeared, and the identity between him and the narrator becomes complete. The pilgrimage thus reveals itself as the story of Byron's European travels in 1809–11, and (for the later cantos) those during the first years of his self-imposed exile from England following his disastrous marriage. It is a Gentleman's Travel Notes, with his thoughts on war, politics, and anything that happens to strike him.

But what captured the public, and what made Byron the most famous writer in Europe of his day, and for long after, was the figure, sketched here and elaborated in later narrative poems such as *The Corsair* and *The Giaour*, of what came to be called the Byronic hero. Handsome, licentious, moody, doomed, he carried on his shoulders the burden of unpardonable – nay, unmentionable – sins and he shook his fist at the world order, the world's rules, even the Creator himself. Childe Harold was 'not unskilful in the spoiler's art,' and 'through Sin's long labyrinth had run,' and now 'Apart he stalked in joyless reverie.' The rebel outcast, stained with sin yet irresistibly virile was a figure both new and thrilling, and contemporary readers were not slow in identifying it with the poet himself, who also seemed burdened with a past stained by crime (in fact he felt a Calvinistic sense of guilt for having slept with his sister). Byron himself, no mean publicist, the first of the modern image-projectors, played up to the public's expectations of him.

It is easy enough to find in *Childe Harold* vulgarizations of almost every Romantic preoccupation – the medieval, the outcast figure, love of nature, hatred of tyranny, preoccupation with the remote and savage, and so on. Though even here it must be said that an energy and gusto, a flair for grand gestures and grandiose phrases, keeps one reading. But perhaps the most important point to make about *Childe Harold* is that it shows Byron working towards his own individual mode: in *Harold* we hear the discursive-rhapsodic. He darts from subject to subject, enthusing or execrating, always with the same energy. But the more one reads the poem, the more oddly eighteenth-century it sounds: the diction, the classical references, the recourse to personification ('Vice, that digs her own voluptuous tomb,' for example). It was when Byron rediscovered the eighteenth-century part of himself – urbane, worldly, companionable – that he found his real mode, the discursive-comic. In *Beppo*, a spicy tale of Italian sexual mores (of which Byron knew a great deal), in *The Vision of Judgment* (the hilarious story of George III's arrival at heaven's gate – savage, witty and blasphemous), and above all in *Don Juan*, this voice becomes a marvellous means of conveying the personality and views of the tale-teller. *Don Juan* was decried at the time of publication as shocking, and a degradation of the poet's gifts. Even today the term *comic poetry* carries a taste of music-hall recitations. *Don Juan*, however, is robustly comic and farcical, but also pathetic, thrilling, satirical and passionate – for Byron's sexuality, albeit ambivalent, was no invention of his fans. All these elements are united by the witty gusto of the teller himself, one man of the world talking to another, digressing into personal reminiscence, swerving aside to tell you a story someone told him last night, puncturing pretension and rhapsody, perpetrating dreadful jokes and comic-appalling rhymes:

> But – Oh! ye lords of ladies intellectual,
> Inform us truly, have they not hen-peck'd you all?

Don Juan himself is nothing – a pretty stick, no more – but his sexual exploits, in which he is seldom the initiator, enable Byron to expatiate on his favourite subjects – sexual habits, and the hypocrisy surrounding them:

> A little still she strove, and much repented,
> And whispering 'I will ne'er consent' – consented.

Juan visits Greece, Russia and England, giving Byron ample scope for radical invective and political philosophising: Wellington, for example, in those years of post-Napoleonic reaction, is 'Called "Saviour of the Nations" – not yet saved, / And "Europe's Liberator" – still enslaved.' *Don Juan* is the most glorious rag-bag in all literature: its point is that it *is* a rag-bag, into which Byron can cram a motley collection of reflections, witticisms, political propaganda, and the worldly wisdom culled from a long, raffish career.

If Byron impressed on his contemporaries an image of brooding glamour, tinged with Satanism, Percy Bysshe Shelley (1792–1822) was seen by them either as a literally insane radical, or as a noble if impractical idealist. His character, and most of the central actions of his brief life, are still matters of dispute. Like all the second generation of Romantic poets he was a radical. They grew to maturity and political consciousness not in the years of hope and disillusion of the French revolution, as Wordsworth and Coleridge did, but in the years of black reaction during and after the Napoleonic wars. 'Those who now live,' Shelley wrote in 1817, 'have survived an age of despair.' It is significant

of the uneasy temper of the times that, though his radical and revolutionary plans were of a most impractical kind, his activities were
observed by spies and reported back to the Government. In personal
relationships Shelley was beloved and generous, but, towards women in
particular, he displayed a streak of ruthless egotism, a refusal to let
anything stand in the way of his impulses of the moment. Indeed, one
doubts whether he ever had the imaginative sympathy truly to understand another person's mind: he needed constantly to stamp *his* mind on
the other person's.

Shelley's reading was voracious and voluminous, and many of his
poems have at their core a relationship to ideas, rather than a relationship to actuality. This has led, in our century, to much damaging
criticism — words like 'gaseous' are heard — and he is frequently compared, to his disadvantage, with Keats. It is certainly true that Shelley
was an extremely unequal poet: we must remember not only that he died
young, but that, unlike Byron, he never attained any audience, even of a
section of the England of his time. One senses, in the weaker poetry, that
he is in a sense writing in a void, or for the intelligent but too admiring
circle around him, which did not really provide him with the sort of
rigorous criticism he needed.

It is perhaps a certain want of toughness that keeps readers today away
from most of Shelley's longer poems. They teem with ideas, but the ideas
are not always fully absorbed, they do not become part of Shelley's poetic
character. The reader senses a certain insubstantiality, a lack of humanity, an amount of idealistic flim-flam. The exceptions are the superb
poetic drama *Prometheus Unbound*, on the subject of tyranny and revolution, and *Adonais*, an elegy on the death of John Keats, fruitfully
indebted to Milton's *Lycidas*, and like it concerned as much with the poet
himself as with the dead man.

For most readers today Shelley is the poet of the shorter anthology
piece, and some of these have become so well known as to work in a way
doubly to his disadvantage. On the one hand, some of these pieces do not
stand up well to repeated re-reading: in *To a Skylark*, for example, or *The
Cloud*, there is too much effusion, too much fancifulness, too little firm
grasp of structure. There seems no reason why either should not be half
as long as it is, or double. On the other hand, the very familiarity of
the other pieces obscures qualities which we do not find elsewhere in
Shelley, which might have been nurtured had he lived longer. *Ozymandias*,
for example, a simple yet scorching meditation on earthly power, has a

control, a unity of structure and effect, that is hard to find in the longer pieces. *England in 1819* is a superb piece of scorn for the arthritic body politic of his homeland. The sonnet form adds compression to his contempt as he runs through the power-structure – king, princes, politicians, army, church – with images of a muddy river, of blood-sucking and blood-shedding, of blindness and insensibility. Only the last two lines, in which glorious revolution is predicted as springing from the death-throes of the old system, seem a typically unsubstantiated piece of wishful thinking.

Best of all these well-known pieces is the *Ode to the West Wind*, for here Shelley's rhapsodic and declamatory tendencies, his other-worldliness, find a subject perfectly suited to them. The autumn wind, burying the dead year, preparing for a new Spring, becomes an image of Shelley himself, as he would want to be, in its freedom, its destructive-constructive potential, its universality. 'I fall upon the thorns of life! I bleed!' calls the Shelley that could not bear being fettered to the humdrum realities of everyday. 'Be through my lips to unawakened Earth / The trumpet of a prophecy!' Poet and wind coalesce, decay followed by regeneration in nature are mirrored in the poet's imaginative faculties. The whole poem has a logic of feeling, a not easily analysable progression that leads to a triumphant, hopeful, and here convincing conclusion: 'If Winter comes, can Spring be far behind?'

If Shelley's early death leaves us with some unanswerable questions about his likely development, the even more tragic early death of John Keats (1795–1821) leaves few queries in our mind about his stature. Even as it is, he is one of our greatest poets; had he lived he would have developed, refined, widened his already formidable powers. In his short writing life of six or seven years he produced a variety of *kinds* of work, including verse plays (all the Romantic poets were afflicted with the urge to write Shakespearean dramas), an epic, *Hyperion*, which was never finished, narrative poems, light verse, and so on. But if we only had left to us the poems written in 1819 we would have no doubt that Keats is with Shakespeare, Milton and Wordsworth, one of the indisputably great English poets. It was in the early days of 1820 that Keats coughed up blood, and having nursed his brother through tuberculosis understood its meaning at once: 'that drop of blood is my death warrant.' His poetic career was over, at the age of twenty four. His last months were given over to his disease.

Not surprisingly, the early poems of Keats reveal the influence of other poets – fleetingly that of Leigh Hunt, the radical journalist and (dreadful) poet to whose circle Keats for a time belonged; more lastingly that of Spenser and Milton. He was dissatisfied with the poems written under these giant shadows almost as soon as they were written, and Shakespeare is the most potent influence in the later poems. In the three narrative poems *Isabella*, *Lamia* and *The Eve of St Agnes*, all written in 1819, Keats found his voice and shrugged off the immaturities, excesses and wilful indulgences that marred many of his earlier poems. *The Eve of St Agnes* is in the romantic-medieval mode of Coleridge's *Christabel*, only recently published, but the emphasis on narrative is much less – there is, in fact, hardly any story to speak of. The poem delights in the sensuous, colourful sides of the medieval world, and the poet gives himself up so completely to the sensations of the moment that the poem becomes a succession of these – cold, music, colourful ceremony, the beauty of the body, food, and so on. It is easy to accuse Keats of wallowing in a technicolour dream which has nothing to do with the medieval world, but the sensual richness of the poem is far from uncontrolled: it works by contrasts and comparisons, and no one sensation is without its opposite. The sensual world of the young lovers is enclosed by another world of old age and superstition; the luscious feast Porphyro sets for Madeline is counter-balanced by the extreme cold of the opening sections, which is not romanticized or distanced, but is real cold:

> St Agnes' Eve – Ah, bitter chill it was!
> The owl, for all his feathers, was a-cold;
> The hare limped trembling through the frozen grass . . .

The vividness of the life of the sensations conveyed in *St Agnes Eve* and in the great odes is in part due to the remarkable empathy Keats can feel with all creation: 'if a sparrow comes before my window I take part in its existence and pick about the gravel,' he once wrote. Allied with this ability to feel himself into the being or essence of all created things is Keats's receptiveness to ideas, for he is the reverse of the committed or didactic writer: 'The only means of strengthening one's intellect is to make up one's mind about nothing – to let the mind be a thoroughfare for all thoughts.' He is very quick, too, to imagine pictorially – in the widest sense, of seeing all round. It was a faculty that never deserted him. In the last words he wrote, in a letter of farewell before dying, he said: 'I can scarcely bid you goodbye, even in a letter. I always made an awkward bow.' He sees himself there stumbling clumsily out of life, friendship, society, like a socially inept youth from a gay party. This pictorial faculty informs the great odes: Autumn is *seen* 'sitting careless on a granary floor, / Thy hair soft-lifted by the winnowing wind.' In the *Ode on Melancholy*, in which the union of contrasting feelings is most tellingly presented, melancholy

> dwells with Beauty – Beauty that must die;
> And joy, whose hand is ever at his lips
> Bidding adieu . . .

Pictures of parting, farewell, the evanescence of life and love, not unnaturally haunted Keats. Two of the Odes have this as a central theme. In the *Ode on a Grecian Urn* the permanence of the picture on the Greek frieze, the figures caught in unchangeable attitudes, contrasts with the decay and change of real human activities and natural processes. In the *Ode to a Nightingale* the apparent permanence of the bird's song, unchanging through the centuries, is contrasted with a world where 'Beauty cannot keep her lustrous eyes, / Or new love pine at them beyond tomorrow.' The poem depicts poignantly the poet's desire to immerse himself in the bird's song, be at one with its immortality, and shake off the world where 'men sit and hear each other groan' (what seems like adolescent exaggeration here was Keats's understandable response to the long illness of his brother). Having considered drugs and wine as means of uniting himself with the bird and partaking of its 'immortality,' Keats chooses 'the viewless wings of Poesy' as his means. But even as he imagines himself into the forest glen with the bird, he cannot slough off thoughts of death – the bird can only render the thoughts more acceptable. And as he chronicles the ages past that have heard the self same song, in a passage of unique loveliness (Stanza 7), he climaxes his vision with the song having 'Charmed magic casements, opening on the foam / Of perilous seas, in faery lands forlorn.' And the double meaning of the last word (long ago, as well as lonely and desolate) brings him back to the real world, as the nightingale's song, like everything else, fades.

To Keats thought and feeling had to exist in unison, the body and mind in equilibrium, and the fruitful tension between the disparate elements in his nature informs the great poems of 1819. He was one of the most sympathetic figures in our literature, and one of the most complete poets.

The early years of the nineteenth century were as notable for their novelists as for their poets, and almost all of them, after a rather arid period for fiction, were trying to do something new. Maria Edgeworth (1767–1849) had a brilliant success with *Castle Rackrent*, the story of the decline of a family of Irish gentry, seen through the eyes of their servant Thady Quirk – original both from its opening up of new areas for the novel, social as well as geographical, and for its clever use of point of view. A didactic element became too pronounced for her other novels to be complete artistic successes, but *The Absentee* and *Helen* are still very readable, and both British and Continental writers acknowledged her influence.

Among these were Sir Walter Scott (1771–1832), the most popular novelist of his day, both in Britain and in Europe, and a powerful literary influence, for good and ill, throughout the nineteenth century. After establishing himself as a writer of romantic historical narrative poetry, Scott switched to novel writing when he felt that Byron was stealing his thunder, and his audience. Through Scott's pen, Scotland became *the* romantic country *par excellence* for the whole of Europe: the rugged grandeur of its scenery, its sturdy, independent peasantry, the bloody yet poignant nature of much of its history all added to its appeal. For Scott really established the historical novel as a viable and worthwhile fictional form, by setting the personal dilemmas of his characters against a background of historical events, and rooting both in the on-going, densely realized life of the whole community. He is at his best, for this reason, when dealing with his own country, most notably in the century and a half before he writes: he not only feels most at home in the late seventeenth and early eighteenth centuries, he feels ties with the life of that time through his ancestors, through stories of them handed down in his family. And though he was by temperament conservative, by politics Tory, he was able to feel instinctive, understanding sympathy for all points of view, political and religious, in Scotland's troubled and quarrelsome history.

His narrative style was that of a born story-teller with time on his hands. Thomas Crawford tellingly relates this to his years as an advocate waiting for briefs, when he would hear the experiences of lawyers 'to whom it was natural to begin a story slowly and deliberately; and then, when once it was fairly under way, to digress into the minute description of attendant circumstances.' It is a characteristic that has lost Scott readers in more recent times, as has his use of Scottish dialect speech, but both are essential to his art and aims. In *The Heart of Midlothian* we may get impatient as minor character after minor character is introduced, accounted for, given a history, allowed to parade his peculiarities in marked, sometimes near-impenetrable Scottish dialect. What has all this to do with a girl accused of child-murder, the main story of the novel? But in the end we realize that Scott's stories are nothing without the firm bed-rock of communal activities, group and religious animosities, class differences which Scott has depicted. And the characters exist through their language: ' "I dinna ken muckle about the law," ' says a chorus-character in the novel, ' "but I ken, when we had a king, and a chancellor, and parliament-men o'our ain, we could aye peeble them wi' stanes when they werena gode bairns." ' David Deans, father of the accused girl, opinionated, stubborn, self-righteous, disputes the lawyers proposed as defenders of his daughter on the grounds that he disagrees with them on matters of faith:

> 'When you call in a physician,' [says another character] 'you would not, I suppose, question him on the nature of his religious principles?'
> 'Wad I *no?*' answered David.

The other character, speaking educated English, makes no impression, but one can *hear* David Deans. Even when his story is much more conventional, for example in *Guy Mannering*, with its smugglers and lost heir theme, or *The Bride of Lammermoor*, with its Capulet and Montague situation, the sense of community gives depth and individuality, for one senses Scott's total understanding of the Scots throughout their recent history. He was loved throughout Europe for his romantic and leisurely-told stories, but perhaps readers also responded to the dignity that he gave to his own country and its people. In the age of nationalism, especially for small, oppressed peoples, this was something they could feel on their pulses.

But even as the Romantic movement was at its height, and perhaps because of its decidedly fervid nature, voices were to be heard expressing doubts and reservations. One of these voices was that of Thomas Love Peacock (1785–1866), whose satirical conversation novels made hilarious fun of the beliefs and foibles of intellectuals of his time. Of these *Nightmare Abbey* is perhaps the most notable, with its splendid pictures of Coleridge, Byron and Shelley. It is ironic too that the indisputably great novelist of the Romantic period was also the one who carried most determinedly into the new century the values of the previous one.

Jane Austen (1775–1817) habitually mocked or was suspicious of Romantic excesses: 'Do you remember . . . Scott's beautiful lines on the Sea?' demands one of her more absurd Romantic enthusiasts. 'That man who can read them unmoved must have the nerves of an Assassin!' Jane Austen's clear-eyed, realistic appraisal of life and its possibilities, her understanding that humans must make the best of unsatisfactory fates, that having made foolish decisions they must endure what cannot be cured, gives her novels a very different feel from the prevalent tone of the Romantic poets, with their all-or-nothing, bliss-or-suicide assumptions. Not surprisingly she had in her day only a small, select circle of ad-mirers, which included Scott and the Prince Regent, and throughout the nineteenth century she aroused devotion in a coterie rather than wide-spread enthusiasm. Only in our own time has she become a popular classic, admired for her wit, her common-sense, her insight into charac-ter and social relationships.

Jane Austen's subject was the country gentry of England: she occasion-ally went up into the fringes of the aristocracy, almost never lower than the middle-class tradesman. Even servants are seldom individualized in her work. Her novels centre on girls or young women, and always end with their engagement or marriage. The idea that her subject matter is limited hardly holds water: the gentry were at the time the backbone of England; men are quite as well done in Jane Austen as women are in Scott; the choice of marriage partner is the most important anyone can make in his life. Nevertheless, it is true that Jane Austen took very good care not to move out of areas that she knew not just slightly, but through and through. It was only thus that her irony could attain due weight. If she had applied it to aspects of life she knew less well, it would have seemed flippant and brittle, as it sometimes does in her letters ('Mrs Hall of Sherborne was brought to bed yesterday of a dead child . . . owing to a fright. I suppose she happened unawares to look at her husband.') In the mature novels the continuous ironic surface, which makes them very funny, nevertheless provides a thoughtful fun, because it is so securely based. *Pride and Prejudice*, which the author herself thought 'too light and bright and sparkling,' opens with a typical example of her irony: 'It is a truth universally acknowledged, that a single man in possession of a good fortune, must be in want of a wife.' The irony is double-edged, making fun both of enunciators of universal truths and of husband-hunting mothers. The hilarious fun of the first chapter, in which Mrs Bennet plots to get one of her daughters (it scarcely matters which) married to the newly arrived rich young man, is underpinned by Jane Austen's understanding that Mrs Bennet is *dangerously* silly, that she is playing irresponsibly with the most important decision her daughters will ever have to make.

Elizabeth Bennet is the most loved of Jane Austen's heroines, and the most witty and independent-minded. Being the child of parents both, in their ways, irresponsible, she takes much of the moral burden of the family on her own shoulders. She is fully integrated into the upper-class society of her time, and accepts its values by and large, but she often shocks the more shallow characters by her readiness to utter her own opinions: to the more foolish members of polite society strong opinions were themselves ungenteel. With such a view of polite behaviour Jane Austen will have nothing to do.

The danger for all Austen heroines is that, through immaturity or an undisciplined heart, they will make a wrong decision on the vital matter of a life partner. Elizabeth Bennet is in danger of this when she feels attracted to the handsome and plausible Mr Wickham, with his tale of being romantically wronged, and when she rejects the remote and reserved Mr Darcy. When she comes to accept Darcy's second proposal, the factors that make up her decision are complex: she knows she has totally mistaken his conduct towards Mr Wickham; she has discovered his kindness towards his sister and his dependents; he has aided her family; she is convinced of the soundness of his principles; she has seen his fine estate at Pemberley. Most of these would be considerations of no weight at all to a Romantic, but then, to Jane Austen the Romantic view of love was a dangerous madness. The factors that make for successful marriages are esteem and affection – added to a dash of self-interest. Elizabeth does not accept Darcy because she has seen Pemberley, but Pemberley has its place in the making of her decision: 'at that moment she felt, that to be mistress of Pemberley might be something!'

Emma is suffused by subtler but hardly more gentle irony. Emma Woodhouse is, like Elizabeth Bennet, clever and independent, but she is spoilt, and too used to having her own way. In the first chapter a beautiful balance is maintained: Emma's father is shown to be amiably selfish and demanding, intellectually no more than a cabbage. We admire the good-humour and self-restraint with which Emma ministers to his wants and protects him from anxiety or irritation. On the other hand, we see that her solicitude comes in part from her desire to maintain and increase her own independence, and we see the dangers of one so limited in experience being so powerful within her own small domain. For Emma wants to play God. She does not want things to happen, she wants to make them happen. She enjoys the feeling that, unknown to themselves, people are dancing as she pulls the strings. She contemplates life aesthetically, and tries to bring about things that she would find fitting, nicely patterned, appropriate. Even when she imagines herself in love with Frank Churchill it is the artistic appropriateness of such a relationship that she seems to gain most satisfaction from.

And of course she brings about disaster. Every step she takes into the world of feelings is mistaken, whether she is trying to promote or prevent marriages. As always in Jane Austen moral questions are illuminated by social behaviour. When the self-important Mr Elton, the vicar, refuses to dance with the illegitimate Harriet Smithson at a ball, Mr Knightley, not a dancing man, immediately takes her on to the floor. Similarly, the consequences of Emma's self-will and too-great freedom are finally made clear to the reader when she is rude to poor, silly Miss Bates at the Box Hill picnic. Excessive courtesy is likely to be distrusted in Jane Austen, as denoting insincerity, but a failure of courtesy is almost always a sign of egotism and hardness of heart. It is when the enormity of her breach of decorum is brought home to her that the process of regeneration begins in Emma, climaxed by her realization that she is in love with Mr Knightley, who will give her life the firmness of principle it has so far lacked. This is something the reader has had the chance to realize all along, because though Emma is not aware herself of the real nature of her feeling for Knightley, the reader has been given the clues that should have enabled him to guess it. In fact, the novel is plotted with all the minute, deceptive skill of a detective story: the surface appearance of the action always allows for a variety of interpretations, and the reader alive to subtle hints will understand the truth of what is going on better than the heroine from whose point of view we see the action.

Jane Austen's view of life is a totally realistic one. She has no sentimentality, no time for emotional excess. Though her subject is love and marriage, her books never produce a warm glow, never for a moment aspire to the poetic. She honours the Augustan virtues of moderation, dignity, disciplined emotion and common sense, and she used her ironic wit to deflect heartbreak. She was a lonely voice in the age of Byron and Shelley.

12

The Early Victorian Novelists

The popular image which one period impresses on succeeding ones is always interesting, and popular usage of the word 'Victorian' is particularly instructive: its connotations are respectability, church-going, prudishness, the close-knit, patriarchal family circle, the businessman of unimpeachable probity. This is how the Victorian middle classes imposed themselves on the world and on posterity, and they would be pleased and proud that this image – or this false front, some might say – has endured. To modify this picture one has only to look into Mayhew's *London Labour and the London Poor* to enter a vital, chaotic, amoral world that makes the bourgeois facade look considerably less stable than the Victorians liked to pretend. Or, on the other hand, one has only to consider the round of pleasures of the Marlborough House set, led by the gross and promiscuous Prince of Wales, to see that upper-class life had changed in little but inessentials since Regency days. Victorianism was a creation of the middle-class, an expression of their new self-confidence. Fortunately they found the perfect figure-heads in the worthy, earnest and energetic couple, Victoria and Albert, who were the nominal leaders of society.

The moral and religious roots of Victorianism reach well back into the eighteenth century, to the Wesleys and the revival of evangelicalism. By the beginning of the nineteenth century people were beginning to find writers like Fielding and Swift unacceptably outspoken. In 1818 Dr Bowdler presented to his countrymen his edition of Shakespeare – a well-scrubbed Shakespeare with all the sexual outspokenness silently dropped and all the moral sententiousness emphasized. By the mid-1840s there were severe limits to what a novelist could say without losing his family audience, and to most of them the family audience –

gathered together to read the novel aloud, like a jollier sort of church service – was the basis of their readership and hence their livelihood. It is because these limits were so strictly set that we find many subjects such as sexual immorality, sexual deviance, prostitution etc, either avoided entirely, or treated with a falseness of tone that shows that the author feels he is treading on quicksands. On the other hand, the reading-aloud habit, combined with the monthly or weekly publication method that many writers used, made for an immediacy, a closeness between novelist and reader, that animates and invigorates all aspects of Victorian fiction, especially its social conscience and its humour. The joyful vigour of this relationship makes the inhibitions that it imposed on writers like Dickens seem comparatively unimportant.

Part of the vitality which one feels springing from the pages of Victorian novels arises from the newness of their vision of the world. Britain was being transformed rapidly from a rural to an urban civilization, a process both terrible yet exciting in its consequences and potentialities. What is more, the railways were opening up every corner of it for inspection and admiration. Where once the circuit of people's lives was tens of miles or less, now it was hundreds. Whole sections of the population were on the move, geographically and socially: in the new industrial towns – which were not only new, but new *kinds* of towns – fortunes were made and lost in a matter of months. These commercial miracles involved everyone, not just the new capitalists and the workforce, lurching year by year from comfortable prosperity to starvation: the railway boom and subsequent panic sent reverberations into so remote a stronghold as Haworth Parsonage, where Emily Brontë had invested the family's small capital in railway shares, and characteristically refused to reconsider her decision. The new religion of the new capitalists (who still paid ostentatious lip-service to the old) was 'laissez-faire,' often called Political Economy, or Benthamism: the new economic doctrines of an unrestricted market economy and total freedom for the industrialist (though not for the trade-unionist) seemed to the early Victorians to be dogma as undeniable as any preached from the pulpit, iron laws proven beyond denial. And the new industrialist, preaching these laws and profiting by them, was the national hero, the modern equivalent of the Elizabethan freebooter.

The intellectuals, of course, saw a very different age, and a much less attractive one: the crisis of faith, which became a matter of popular debate with Darwin's *Origin of Species* in 1867, had in fact been fought in the minds of writers like Tennyson and George Eliot decades before; Matthew Arnold looked at Victorian England and saw it as a hideously ugly playground of Philistines and Barbarians; John Stuart Mill saw the degradation of the labouring classes and the subjection of women. But in the early years of the reign the novels reflect the confidence of the man in the street, rather than the doubts and dejection of the man in the study. In fact the transition from exuberant optimism to disgust and despair is nowhere better illustrated than in the works of the Victorians' first and favourite novelist, Charles Dickens.

Dickens (1812–1870), the greatest novelist in an age rich in novelists, had his first success in the year before Victoria's accession, and his career spanned almost exactly the first half of her reign. *Pickwick Papers*, probably the most successful fictional debut ever, looks back in many ways to the past, to a pre-industrial world of stage-coaches, sleepy villages and genteel watering places. Perhaps it was a nostalgia for these aspects of English life, that were even then threatened with extinction, that accounted for some part of *Pickwick's* fantastic success. In these settings Dickens places a series of comic adventures for Pickwick and his fellow travellers – adventures which take up all the popular subjects for humour at that time (sport, politics, sexual misadventures, class, and so on) and beat his competitors at their own game. The picture of Pickwick himself begins in a hard, satirical, eighteenth-century manner, but Dickens soon endows him with a nineteenth-century heart and (in the sequence in which he is imprisoned after a ludicrous breach-of-promise suit) a nineteenth-century social conscience. But at this stage of his career his vision of the world was mostly sun and sparkle, with very little shade.

As if in reaction against Pickwick's high spirits, his next great success, *Oliver Twist* (1837–1838) is a much darker affair, though the energy of his indignation, the luxuriance of his invention, ensures that it is by no means a depressing novel. Dickens's theme is man's inhumanity to child, and his social target is the new workhouses established on Benthamite principles which laid down that relief of the poor and starving should be made so unpleasant, and should be so meagre, that it would upset as little as possible the natural 'balance' of iron economic laws. Oliver is thus not just the representative of childhood, but a symbol of all suffering humanity. When he escapes, it is to the criminal slums of London, into a thieves' and prostitutes' gang run by the Jew Fagin: a terrible world, but one with an energy and warmth about it that makes us wonder if it is not preferable to the workhouse. Periodically Oliver lands up in the bourgeois world of the Brownlows and the Maylies, but these episodes suffer from a loss of vigour and sharp observation, and sometimes lapse into gross sentimentality. Dickens does not seem to realize, in making Oliver's goal that of becoming a clean, pious middle-class boy, that it is the middle-classes who save Oliver who have also dictated the social policies that created the workhouses.

Both *Pickwick* and *Oliver* are full of the exuberant caricatures that made Dickens so popular, and made his works seem like a sort of moving picture gallery of contemporary types. If in his later works his characters became less lively, this is less because they are 'deeper' than because they have to fit into a social vision that is increasingly despairing. In *Hard Times*, for example, the book is so exclusively centred on Dickens's attack on Benthamite principles, as they worked themselves out in an industrial context, that the characters at times seem mechanical reproductions of his earlier creations. We have to realize that *because* Dickens saw the industrial system as turning men into automata, his characters had in consequence to be robbed of vitality, to become something between men and puppets. It is, significantly, mainly in the novels that spring from a view of childhood that the old energy is maintained. *David Copperfield* – a heavily fictionalized but emotionally truthful account of his own childhood – contains some of his most engaging caricatures, most notably the gloriously feckless Mr Micawber (based on Dickens's father) and the repellent Uriah Heep, with his snake-like writhings and his transparently bogus humility. *Great Expectations* is a later and sadder book, in which Pip, in crossing the barriers from lower to middle class, loses the spontaneity and instinctive fellow-feeling of his own class, and can only slough off the corrupting influence of snobbery and class isolation when he discovers that the source of his new wealth, his 'expectations,' is a convict-tramp he befriended in his childhood, before his loss of social innocence.

The pinnacle of Dickens's achievement, and the books that contain the kernel of his social vision, are a series of long, panoramic novels written in the 1850s and 60s, in which he analyses the state of England, outwardly so self-confident and successful, in fact so unjust, inefficient and divided. Perhaps the greatest of these is *Bleak House* (1852–1853) in which the starting point is a critique of the law – its procrastinations, its inhumanity, the graspingness of its practitioners – and which broadens out into social criticism and social prophecy. It is a novel of immense scope, which takes in all classes, from the reactionary yet honourable Sir Leicester Dedlock (whose name is a diagnosis of social relationships in Britain) down to Jo the crossing sweeper, who is himself the sweepings of an ugly and pitiless social structure. The novel opens in fog, and fog becomes a metaphor for the modern state, in which people 'grub on in a muddle,' never coming together in real understanding, never able to show effective compassion. Cut off as they are from each other, all classes in the novel are united by one terrible force: the disease which spreads from the slums inhabited by Jo to the country seats of Sir Leicester and his like. This is Dickens's most despairing novel, and no panaceas are offered: the character who dies of 'spontaneous combustion' seems to image a catastrophic end to a ramshackle and uncaring state.

The basis of Dickens's art, as an observer, as a vivid poet of nineteenth-century urban life, was his eye for the extreme, the grotesque, the abnormal. The modern embarrassment that averts its eyes from physical or mental peculiarities, that tries unconsciously to iron out the differences between men, could not be further from the distinctive Dickens vision. He seized unerringly on the essential spirit of people, places, atmospheres; he heightened them and he forced the reader to acknowledge the infinite variety and richness of what he saw. It is this ability which sometimes attracts to Dickens the sneer that he can only create flat characters, or caricatures; yet there is often more psychological penetration in a wooden leg or a wall eye in Dickens than in five pages of painstaking character-analysis in Trollope. Married to this is an unerring ear for speech, for the sub-text behind what we actually say, that makes conversation in Dickens more devastatingly revealing than anything before the Watergate tapes. He was the complete artist: the poet and craftsman, the miniature painter and the social prophet, the showman and the statesman. He created no school, essentially had no successors: it is no more possible to be Dickensian than it is to be Shakespearian. Perhaps his contemporaries sensed this when they attached to his name the adjective 'inimitable.'

The undisputed pre-eminence of Dickens as entertainer to the Victorian era lasted for ten years. In the late 40s new writers came forward who, if in no way resembling Dickens, could be mentioned in the same breath: Thackeray, the Brontës, Mrs Gaskell. Of these Thackeray (1811–1863) was the novelist whose name was most often coupled with Dickens's, and in the last half of the century he was habitually acclaimed by educated readers as the greater master. This view has not worn well.

Today there are certainly to be found critics who urge the claims of Thackeray's other novels, but for the public at large he is the author of *Vanity Fair*, and probably they are right.

The first impression we get of *Vanity Fair* (1847–1848) is of a wide, vividly alive canvas: the book presents a panoramic view of English society between 1812 and 1830, the central focus of the book being on polite society of one kind or another. We go as high as the sophisticated aristocracy and as low as genteel, bankrupt poverty, but the bulk of the book concerns the landed gentry, the rich city classes, the officer caste in the army, the flashy hangers-on to the world of fashion. Dealing as it does with the years of Waterloo and after, the book captures something of the self-confident, zestful, devil-may-care quality of a nation that has just emerged victorious from years of struggle and privation. Perhaps this is why, though their conduct is frequently odious or disgraceful, the characters have a vitality and an amoral insouciance that prevents the book seeming merely cynical or depressing. The novel centres on the fortunes of its two heroines, Becky Sharp and Amelia Sedley, the first vital, pushing, unscrupulous and entertaining, the second virtuous, loving, clinging and a little dull. The charting of their fortunes has an effortless simplicity of outline: as Becky's fortunes rise, Amelia's fall, and vice versa. Both heroines are viewed with a typically Thackerayan ambiguity, so that the reader gives full approbation or respect to neither. Amelia's is the less entertaining history (she usually gets one chapter to Becky's three in each monthly instalment), but the picture is one of great subtlety. The age demands that women be loving adjuncts to men, uncomplaining slipper-warmers, hero-worshippers, domestic cabbages, with enough brains to appreciate but not enough to see through their husbands and lovers. Amelia conforms effortlessly. Perhaps she is too stupid to do anything else. But she capitalizes on her 'little woman' role, using over and over the advantages (emotional and economic) such a position gave a woman undisposed to take her own initiatives. Her emotional blackmail of her faithful admirer Dobbin is only the most notable example of this.

If the larger outlines of Amelia's life are drawn by men, Becky is one to shape her own fate. That behind the wit, energy and charm she is ruthless, predatory and unscrupulous cannot be denied. The reader can only greet with a cynical smile her claim that 'I could be a good woman if I had five thousand a year.' Even today five thousand would seem a stiff price for any goodness Becky can command. Nor is the reader fooled by

Thackeray's 'Was she guilty?' question when she is caught with Lord Steyne. If she *wasn't* guilty Lord Steyne was even more of a fool than her husband. Nevertheless, we always have a sense that the society that cannot channel the energies and talents of a Becky to better advantage than gaining trivial victories over a small-minded social elite is denying itself something of value, restricting its potential.

Around these two are gathered a superb picture-gallery of saints and sinners, fools and sophisticates, born winners and born losers. The advantage of Thackeray's chosen period is that in his characters of the older generation he can look back to the eighteenth century (the gross, illiterate backwoods M. P. Sir Pitt Crawley, his free-thinking and theoretically democratic sister Miss Crawley), and in his younger generation he can look forward to the Victorian age (the emotionally constipated younger Pitt Crawley, and his evangelical, tract-writing in-laws). If Thackeray's panorama seems to concentrate on the rogues, hypocrites and fools, it is nevertheless worth noting that at moments of crisis many of his characters can behave with a moral or emotional rightness that we might have thought beyond them: Lady Jane Sheepshanks reveals a backbone of moral steel beneath her vapid religiosity; Becky can do her 'friend' Amelia a contemptuous good turn at the climax of her emotional history; the apparently shallow Amelia can respond to *Fidelio*; above all the raffish and stupid Rawdon Crawley can mature into a gentleman with an instinctive grasp of moral principle. The element of Pilgrim's Progress is not entirely absent from this Vanity Fair.

What *Vanity Fair* has above all, and what marks it off from most of Thackeray's other novels, is a superb narrative drive, presenting a whirl of great men and small, making history and being caught up in it. It is this sweep and energy that we miss in such smaller successes as *Pendennis, Henry Esmond* and *The Newcomes*.

The distinctive note sounded by the Brontë sisters was of a very different kind. Perhaps too much has been made of the harshness, solitude and pathos of their lives: true they lost their mother and two elder sisters early, but such early deaths were hardly unusual in Victorian times; true Haworth was remote and rough, yet hardly worse as a childhood environment than the streets of London or Manchester; true they were cut off from other children of their age, yet this was not uncommon for precariously middle-class children in a remote environment. The reverse side of the coin is that within the family circle they enjoyed an intensely vital imaginative life, writing interminable romantic chronicles about their fictional kingdoms of Gondal and Angria; they were treated as equals by their father, who discussed with them current political and social questions (they were infinitely better informed than the child of today); and above all they found in the Yorkshire moors where they spent their lives a source of constant delight and imaginative stimulation.

It was the success of Charlotte Brontë (1816–1855) with *Jane Eyre* in 1847 that established the family with the public, and it remained throughout the century the most popular Brontë novel. All Charlotte's novels are technically unconventional, and are frequently subjected to superficial criticism on this account. The most impressive thing about this novel is the way Charlotte blends the most disparate elements from her reading and from her own limited experience to create a novel with a uniquely personal flavour: one can see the influence of Scott, the Gothic novelists, Byron, the French realists; one can see Charlotte's horrifying childhood experiences at Cowan Bridge school, and her desperate need for sexual love. Yet all these are so blended that no page of *Jane Eyre* could be mistaken for the work of anybody else. To render the central character she uses a variety of devices that in other hands would be melodramatic, crude or merely ridiculous, and by the end we have a picture of Jane – complex, self-lacerating, independent, revolutionary – that is as complete a picture as any in literature. Jane is torn between a side of her which demands passion, excitement and fulfilment, and another side which is attracted by the idea of hardship, self-abnegation, spiritual struggle. The colours red and white, the images of fire and ice, follow her through the novel, right from the miraculous opening, where she sits behind red curtains, reading of the Arctic. The two extremes find human embodiment in the two men in her life, Mr Rochester and St John Rivers. In coming to terms with these two sides of her nature, Jane also comes to understand and rebel against the impossible contradictions in what was expected of a woman at that time, the hypocrisies and concealments underlying the Victorian ideal of 'womanliness.' The same may be said of Lucy Snowe, the heroine of *Villette*, a more repressed and unhappy individual (*snow*, as opposed to *air*), but one who gains our respect by her insistence that it is not the glamorous or fortunate who are generally the most morally or intellectually interesting. The book lacks the romantic sweep of *Jane Eyre*, but it has an awkward, unlovely integrity that makes it infinitely re-readable. It is worth remembering today, since their shock-effect has worn off, that the success of

Charlotte's novels was a *scandalous* success. 'I will not have those women's names mentioned at my table' thundered one clergyman many years after they were all dead; and one conservative woman critic at the time identified the spirit of *Jane Eyre* with the spirit of rebellion spreading through Europe in the year of revolutions, 1848. Though Charlotte herself indignantly resented such suggestions, many feminist critics and others in our own time have rediscovered their truth: *Jane Eyre* was a revolutionary book, and Charlotte Brontë's open declarations about women's sexuality and women's rights make her books milestones, and not merely literary ones.

The one novel of Emily Brontë (1818–1848) has a very different flavour. Like Charlotte she shocked, and this is partly because their upbringing was in so remote and unfashionable a region that they were out of touch with the creeping prudishness and genteel concealments of the Victorian age. But *Wuthering Heights* (1847) shocked by its harshness, its brutality, its unflinching look at subjects that were taboo to writers more in tune with their audience's demands. Even the love in *Wuthering Heights* is more of a wild kinship than a conventional sexual passion, and it is certainly as far as it is possible to get from the verbose sentimentalism of love in, for example, early Dickens. The book is structured simply on the inter-relations of two families, the farming Earnshaws and the country gentry Lintons. Into the settled, socially ordered existence of these two families comes Heathcliff, a gypsy boy picked up on the streets of Liverpool; immediately he and Catherine Earnshaw fall childishly but irrevocably in love. In the course of the novel Catherine marries the heir to the Linton estate, but Heathcliff wrests control of both properties from their rightful owners, pauperizes and degrades the heirs, and becomes tyrant of the little world of the novel. His story is told to us, and to a vapid town dandy Lockwood, by a servant of the two houses, and the comments of the two narrators are like shocked and inadequate human comments on the doings of gods.

Perhaps the most striking thing about the book, especially for its time, is the absence of moral condemnation of the extraordinary beings and doings depicted: here we have incest (or something very like), incessant physical brutality, naked acquisitiveness, and indeed all the less attractive sins in the calender. Towards the end Heathcliff lets his own son die, too mean to get medical attention. Yet the reader is not invited to condemn such actions, nor (a still more remarkable artistic feat) does he do so uninvited. Heathcliff's actions are simply accepted.

This is not, I think, because the depiction of his love for Catherine is so intense that it in a sense 'justifies' his actions after she has married Edgar Linton; nor is it (as some Marxist critics have suggested) that we recognize his savage tyrannies as 'rough moral justice on his oppressors' (justice that rough is mere jungle law). It is that Emily Brontë was singularly free from the moral itch that afflicted most Victorians: she acknowledged the existence of evil in the world without feeling the need to condemn the evil-doer. Heathcliff *is*, and moral judgments miss the point.

This extraordinary tale is played out against a background of the Yorkshire moors, unforgettably depicted, *not* (as sometimes with Hardy) through pages of fine writing laid on to the tale, but by mere throwaway phrases, vivid evocations in the middle of speeches, a sense of their omnipresence, framing the action. In this century *Wuthering Heights* has been the most popular of the Brontë novels, perhaps the most popular of all English novels. It has been adapted for stage, cinema and television times without number, sequels have been written, and recently the love of Heathcliff and Catherine trivialized into a pop song. In view of all these versions, it is necessary to insist that *Wuthering Heights* is not a lovely romantic novel; it is a harsh, intricately wrought tale, of unflinching integrity of thought. It is one of the two or three unquestionable masterpieces of English fiction.

The two novels of Anne Brontë (1820–1849), particularly *Agnes Grey* (1847), are realistic miniatures which expose the brutalities, physical and psychological, behind the middle-class, respectable Victorian facade. If she is the least of the Brontë sisters, it is because she was later developing a style that could encompass the everydayness of her matter. Her importance as a link between Jane Austen and the more realistic novelists of the 1850s and 1860s should not be underestimated.

Charlotte Brontë's friend and biographer Elizabeth Gaskell (1810–1865) led a life as unlike hers as possible: she was wife to a Unitarian minister in Manchester, amid some of the worst squalor and distress of industrial England. Her first novel, *Mary Barton* (1848), is perhaps the most powerful evocation of the industrial scene (and indictment of the industrial system) before the twentieth century. In spite of some melodrama, contrivance and sentimentality, the picture of working-class life in prosperity and depression convinces by its honesty, its meticulous observation of the telling detail, its sympathy which never spills over into special pleading. Mrs Gaskell is not merely concerned with the virtuous poor, the well-conducted chapel-goer who tips his hat to the right people; she takes in the idler, the rebel, the prostitute, the murderer, and she sees them against a meticulously described background of their hovels, their streets running with sewage, the grinding routine of their work, their holidays and small treats, their soul-destroying idleness and hunger during unemployment. It is all, inevitably, seen from the outside, but nobody else brought to the Victorian industrial scene so knowledgeable an eye, or (Disraeli apart) so sharp a brain.

Mrs Gaskell wrote another industrial novel, *North and South*, which many admire, but which seems weakened by her attempt to be fair to both sides of the industrial battle-lines. The rest of her output is very varied, but the best of it springs from her memories of childhood and girlhood in the small town of Knutsford, in the English Midlands. Her best-loved novel, *Cranford*, is a series of vignettes, charming yet clear-eyed, of a town in which the single woman dominates. The best and richest of her novels is *Wives and Daughters* (1865–1866). Here she captures the nuances of class relationships and social differences in a small town, and uses them to enrich her central subject, the study of two girls, step-sisters, growing up within a family circle created by a disastrous second marriage. Elizabeth Gaskell never moralizes, though she is a moralist of the subtlest kind. She deals not with tragedy or undying grief, but with grinding unhappiness and frustration, continued day after day. Her characters make no heroic gestures; they endure, they compromise, they make the best of things. *Wives and Daughters* is one of the landmarks of the new, more realistic novel that was being written in the 1850s and 60s.

The most notable of these novelists who aimed to eschew sensational incident, unreal emotions and conventional melodramatics in order to capture the tones of life as everyday people experience it every day, are George Eliot (1819–1880) and Anthony Trollope (1815–1882). Of these, Trollope can perhaps be treated more briefly (though he seldom treated anything briefly himself). His Barchester novels, centring on a Cathedral city and the surrounding villages, capture beautifully the lives of 'county' people – the rural gentry, the upper clergy, the genteel poor – in mid-Victorian England. The novels are long, leisurely, going into their characters' motives, dilemmas and errors with an elaborate fullness of dissection hardly possible for a novelist today. Even more impressive, and perhaps more real to the modern reader, are his political novels, in particular *The Way We Live Now* (1874–1875), a savage denunciation of the shabby moral standards, the financial double-dealing, the callous money-mania behind the solid-seeming front of Victorian institutions. It has a Dickensian scope as well as a Dickensian disgust, and modifies the somewhat complacent impression made by the Barchester novels.

Unlike Trollope, whose mother and brother were both writers, George Eliot came from a totally non-literary background and seems to have fallen into fiction writing almost by accident. Yet she was undoubtedly the major talent of the mid-Victorian novel. She was an intellectual, at home (as few novelists have been) in discussing philosophy, ethics, and the whole range of contemporary thought. Though she found the Christian religion she had been brought up in impossible to cling to in the face of modern scientific discoveries, the evangelical and moralistic strain in her remained strong: duty, restraint and moral honesty were of paramount importance precisely because there were now no supernatural sanctions to enforce them. She was distressed when people found the Dodson family in *The Mill on the Floss* (1860) 'mean and uninteresting,' because she felt that the code of 'respectability' by which such provincial families lived was the only morality such people – narrowly educated and immersed in commercial drudgery – could grasp, and it was one that kept them from the moral chaos of following their own instincts.

George Eliot's masterpiece is *Middlemarch* (1871–1872), an immense novel which traces a dozen or so interconnected destinies in and around an English provincial town at a turning-point in British history, the years leading up to the Great Reform Bill of 1832. Socially the range of the novel is wide, but not exhaustive: the urban and rural poor play little part except as occasional chorus or fever-sufferers. The novel, like *Vanity Fair*, is built around two characters and their destinies, but it is typical of George Eliot that these are characters of considerably greater stature and potential than Thackeray's: if Thackeray seems sometimes in his comments to approach a sneer at his creations, George Eliot is invariably understanding and compassionate – which might be wearing, were it not for the abundant humour in the depiction of the host of minor characters that surround them. Dorothea and Lydgate, the twin pillars of this novel, are both in their ways characters who express through their lives and fates the changes at work in nineteenth-century society, yet both are defeated by the tenacious conservatism of provincial society as well as by inadequacies and immaturities in themselves. Lydgate is a doctor, aiming to bring the best in modern medical knowledge and ethics to Middlemarch; his efforts are thwarted by unshakeable local habits and superstitions, and by his marriage to the beautiful and cold Rosamund Vincy, whose mind can aspire after nothing but trivial social successes. Dorothea, on the other hand, full of vague yearnings of the soul for a life of spiritual grandeur and social usefulness, commits herself to marriage with a local clergyman, a pathetic yet tyrannical pedant who crushes the youthful enthusiasm out of her. Both are prophetic figures whose time is not yet, most particularly not yet in Middlemarch. Around them are a multitude of characters, some almost Dickensian caricatures such as Mrs Cadwallader, others like the vicar, Mr Farebrother, done with great but economical psychological skill and understanding. The one character who is exempt from George Eliot's compassion is Rosamund Vincy, and this is both odd and limiting: for some reason Eliot cannot see that she is a victim of the same attitude to women, and women's potential, that restricts and frustrates Dorothea.

All the characters, major and minor, are to some degree caught up in the revolutionary changes of the times, yet ultimately what strikes us is the unchanging quality of life in and around Middlemarch. The Reform Bill is a bit of fun and excitement, but for years to come it is going to make very little difference, either in town or country. The near-slum inhabitants of Slaughter Lane are going to live very much as their Elizabethan ancestors did. The gentry divide themselves into Whigs, Radicals and Tories, but their convictions hardly seem to affect the way they lead their lives. George Eliot, whose mental world had been completely re-ordered by scientific discovery, seemed to cling to the stable, unchanging, stubborn character of provincial life as a rock of certainty in a sea of change and disorder. But the characters she most sympathizes with have to compromise totally, or get out.

To write briefly of the Victorian novel – as with Elizabethan and Jacobean drama – is merely to scratch the surface, for it is one of the richest fields in our literature. Writing as well were such figures as Benjamin Disraeli, Frances Trollope, Harrison Ainsworth, Mrs Oliphant, Wilkie Collins and many more. Their works were published and translated throughout Europe and America, and the chorus of sorrow in the European newspapers on the death of Dickens is only one illustration of the very special position the English novelist enjoyed vis à vis his foreign readers, and in the burgeoning fictional traditions of France, Italy, Spain and above all Russia.

13

The Early Victorian Poets

The poets who dominated the first half of Victoria's reign were true children of the Romantic Movement, and all of them looked up to the great poets of that era as models and mentors. Yet the Victorian poets, like the novelists, were facing a very changed state of society from that the Romantics wrote of: the class structure was changing, almost before their eyes, with the middle-class taking over positions of influence from the old aristocracy, and bringing a very different set of values; industrialization, with its concomitants of pollution and squalor, was becoming difficult to ignore; religious faith was being undermined by a spirit of sceptical enquiry directed at the Bible, and by the discoveries of geologists and biologists.

It is all too easy to feel that the early Victorians made rather heavy weather of their loss of faith. A lapse from religious belief is no great matter today (though some who lapse whore after some pretty odd beliefs to fill the gap). But the early Victorians who found their faith slipping away were surrounded by a community which believed and evangelically proclaimed. They were in an intellectual vanguard, and they did not find it comfortable. Where Shelley's atheism is a triumphant fist flourished in the face of conventional Christianity, the typical Victorian doubter is a reluctant backslider, a wrestler with spiritual problems, melancholic or wistful over what he has lost that others retain. It is a loss more than a liberation.

Alfred, Lord Tennyson (1809–1892) demands first consideration, because he was the oldest, but above all because he was seen by the Victorians themselves as embodying poetically the strengths and glories of the age. He still seems to us typical, both in his virtues and his defects. His family background was odd: he was brought up in a

Parsonage, but insanity, drunkenness and melancholy lurked behind the respectable front, and we do well to remember this darker side when we are repelled by some of the blandness and evasions of Tennyson at the height of his fame, for it forms a disturbing undertow to his poetry.

Tennyson's first mature volume of poetry (1832) was much criticized, and ridiculed as of the 'cockney' school, meaning it was influenced by, for example, Leigh Hunt and Keats. Keats was certainly an abiding example – in imagery, diction and metre, rather than thought. Tennyson is an uncommonly musical poet, his natural good ear being refined upon by hard work and constant revision. His best known anthology-piece, *The Lady of Shalott*, imitates the ballad in form, but in a smooth, highly sophisticated way, which has nothing of the rugged urgency of, say, *The Ancient Mariner*. The Lady, immured in her castle, weaving a web of the sights she sees in her mirror, is a haunting figure in her own right. The eruption into the poem of Lancelot, representing activity, the real world, sex, is splendidly managed as a riot of colour, noise and astral imagery, but the desire to see him directly, without the mirror as intermediary, brings on the Lady the mysterious curse, and in the last section she is gradually drained of life as she floats down the river. We may see the lady as representing the artist, removed from life even as she reflects it, who is killed by the touch of reality that she longs for; we may see, in aspects of her fate, a comment on Victorian womanhood, elevated on to a pedestal, yet shut away from the hurly-burly of life which may both invigorate and destroy. It is worth remembering that though in the poem as we have it the end of the Lady is infused with characteristic Tennysonian melancholy, in the original 1832 version there is also something heroic, almost triumphant, in her confrontation of her fate:

> Though the squally eastwind keenly
> Blew, with folded arms serenely
> By the water stood the queenly
> Lady of Shalott.

It is the characteristic melancholy, mentioned above, that constantly undercuts the confident Victorian self that eventually won Tennyson his enormous public. Though some modern critics have seen something almost discreditable in this closeness to a (presumably philistine) public, something ludicrous in his devotion to the Queen herself, the case is not all that simple. For example, in *Ulysses*, the aged warrior finds it impossible to settle down to the humdrum life of everyday after he returns to Thrace, and he and his warriors resolve to return to sea

> strong in will
> To strive, to seek, to find, and not to yield.

The very motto, it would seem, to impress on a Victorian missionary or Empire-builder. And yet – Ulysses's journey is mere random, restless wandering, involving neglect of all the duties Victorians hold dear. It is Ulysses's son, Telemachus, who embodies the Victorian virtues:

> Most blameless is he, centred in the sphere
> Of common duties, decent not to fail
> In offices of tenderness, and pay
> Meet adoration to my household gods . . .

There is, behind these lines, a trace of unfatherly contempt, the contempt of the man of action for the builder and conserver. With all their apparent approval of the civilization they were building, the Victorians were very apt to admire the man who deserted it for a life of action, or of heroic simplicity – as the hero of *Maud* does, or Browning's listener to the slippery Apology of Bishop Blougram. This is the spirit, too, behind Millais's enormously popular picture of 'The Boyhood of Raleigh.' And yet, behind the confident ring of the old warrior at the end of the poem, there is, some critics have felt, the usual undertow, working in the other direction. As Christopher Ricks says: 'rippling underneath that final line, striving to utter itself but battened down by will, is another line, almost identical and yet utterly different: "To strive, to seek, to yield, and not to find." '

Tennyson, as we have said, is beautiful. One has only to read, say, the openings lines of *Tithonus* to see just how beautiful he can be. He is also much more difficult than appears – one has to be alive to suggestions behind the words, to the effects of metre. This is something people who like to characterize him as 'the stupidest of our poets' ignore. But he is also frequently disturbing, even on the surface. *Maud* is a genuinely impressive long poem of murder, obsession, madness, hopeless love, interspersed with more accessible lyrics of great beauty. And if the *Idylls of the King* fail, in spite of wonderful sections, to become the national epic Tennyson would have liked to write, *In Memoriam* does seem to represent the Victorian age, in its spiritual aspect, for the modern reader. It is a series of elegaic poems triggered off by the death of his friend Arthur Hallam, tracing the course of his grief over the succeeding years, and also his consequent crisis of faith. It faces head on the new view of the natural world that scientific discoveries were forcing on educated men: man, Tennyson says, had

> trusted God was love indeed
> And love Creation's final law—
> Tho' Nature, red in tooth and claw
>   With ravine, shrieked against his creed . . .

The poem is haunting in its account of unbearable grief, of the long, melancholy months after bereavement, of doubts and spiritual torments. And if, in the end, Tennyson cannot say much more as a justification for his revived faith than that he believes because he wants to believe, it behoves modern man, easy in his disbelief, to pay tribute to Tennyson's courage in his period of doubt. He was, after all, one of the first generation who faced up to a spiritual challenge in this form, and of this magnitude. Always in Tennyson there is a gulf between his desire to act as spokesman for his age, and his private doubts, reservations and neuroses. He is not a musical genius with little brain or toughness, the poetic equivalent of Grieg or Mendelssohn; he is a lonely, tormented genius, who finally won through to a precarious equilibrium, an uneasy, threatened peace with his own times.

On the surface at least there is less of struggle with the world around him, and less spiritual torment, in the works of Robert Browning (1812–1889). This is not to sanction the way successive hostile critics have wrenched from its context the song from *Pippa Passes* ('God's in his heaven – /All's right with the world!') and pretended this was Browning's own fatuous world view. There is no blinkering of the eyes towards the world's ugliness in Browning, but there is a confidence, an energy, a belief in man's potential ('a man's reach should exceed his grasp, /Or what's a heaven for?') that was for his contemporaries invigorating and uplifting. Browning's poetry was not concerned first and foremost with the social and spiritual problems of his age: to *demand* that a poet occupy himself with these is to confuse his function with that of a Prime Minister, or an Archbishop. It is, perhaps, an implied comment on his age that Browning so frequently took refuge from it in earlier periods –

the Renaissance or medieval worlds, Biblical times – periods with the spice of danger, the flavour of the exceptional or the heroic. Where Tennyson frequently uses myth, Browning uses most often real historical figures which have caught his imagination. Where Tennyson's King Arthur, it is often said, has been transformed into a Victorian gentleman not unlike the Prince Consort, Browning's figures have the feel and smell of the historical times they inhabit and illustrate – and by their very contrast they comment on Browning's own times.

Browning's preferred form was the dramatic monologue, which he brought to perfection and handed on as a vital poetic form to our own times. He speaks, then, from behind the mask of an assumed personality, and we can only guess at the poet's judgment of that personality, for he never appears himself in the poem. Often the characters are at crucial moments in their lives: a young man who has just murdered his lover; a Renaissance prelate on the point of death; a fake medium who has just been caught out in his tricks. This gives edge and zest to their own self-revelations or self-justifications. Sometimes the character is mad, as in *Porphyria's Lover*, where the narrator has murdered his lover to make eternal the perfection of their moment of meeting. Arguably the narrator of *My Last Duchess* is also insane. Here *judgment* hardly enters into the poem. In other poems we accept the speaker's viewpoint for part of the poem, or even all of it, judgment coming later. In *Andrea del Sarto* we hear the apologia of a Renaissance painter who has the most perfect technical grasp of any of his time, yet knows he will never rival the greatness of contemporaries like Leonardo or Michelangelo. He speaks to his wife, whose beauty has enthralled him within the purely worldly, whose extravagance has led to his artistic and moral compromises. The mood is wistful, autumnal, enervated, sad with the sense of opportunities lost. At the end he dismisses her to the lover (her 'cousin') who has been waiting and whistling outside. As we read the poem we accept the artist's explanation for his own second-rateness. Afterwards we wonder whether he has not tried to shovel off on to his beautiful, vapid wife the responsibility for his own essential mediocrity.

The necessary qualities for the reader of a dramatic monologue are emotional sympathy and liveliness of apprehension (for often a great deal is conveyed in an aside). In addition to asking ourselves what sort of man the speaker is, we have to ask: who is he talking to? where are they? what is their business? *why* is he exposing himself like this? is he telling the whole truth? All these questions are relevant to that little masterpiece

My Last Duchess. The Duke (based on a real sixteenth-century figure) is talking in the gallery of his palace to an ambassador, with whom he is arranging the details of his next marriage. He unveils the usually hidden portrait of his previous wife (how many has he had? – we are not told) and tells the ambassador about her girlish frankness, her open pleasure in everyone and everything she saw. Her indiscriminate joy in life did not please her husband, did not minister sufficiently to his *own* over- whelming greatness and importance. He had her murdered. We realize that this is a *warning*, to be handed on indirectly to his next wife. As he goes down the stairs with the ambassador ('Nay, we'll go / Together down, sir' – and we can imagine that the ambassador, as well as giving the Duke his proper precedence, has shrunk ever so politely away) he points to another splendid work of art in his collection – his wife is now no more to him than that.

For some time as we read we are so fascinated by the speaker's suavity, his magnificence, his self-confidence, that we suspend our moral judg- ment of him. At some point (it may be when he confesses to having his wife murdered, it may be when he puts up a paltry pretence of loving the woman he is hoping to marry, it may be when he points to the magnifi- cence of his statue of Neptune) our fascination is overcome by our repugnance, and there floods in the realization that he is either mad, or, if not, a monster of amoral egotism, totally depraved by absolute power, yet essentially petty in his need to surround himself by people and objects that minister to his sense of his own greatness.

Not all of Browning's subjects are so unattractive. The reader is sym- pathetic, for example, to his painter-monk *Fra Lippo Lippi* caught on an illicit night out from the monastery by the night watch, to whom he pours out all his delight in the real world of flesh, pleasure and beauty, repressed by the Prior's concern with the formalized, the spiritual, the ideal. But essentially in Browning the morally ambiguous figure is allowed to make out the best possible case for himself. The dying Bishop in *The Bishop Orders his Tomb* is hardly an attractive person: concerned only with the ostentatious display of his wealth, his old enmities and rivalries, his memories of unlawful pleasures. In the flickering light we imagine the figures of his sons, so-called 'nephews,' watching his agonies, and we feel no outrage that they are going to trick him of his monstrously lavish tomb. And yet, at the end, we feel that twinge of sympathy as the old sinner expresses his delight, long ago, in the fleshly beauty of his mis- tress, his triumph at winning her, over the jealousy of his rival:

I may watch at leisure if he leers—
Old Gandolf, at me, from his onion stone,
As still he envied me, so fair she was!

It is significant that two of his few disagreements with his wife, the poet Elizabeth Barrett Browning, were over the fake medium Daniel Home and the Emperor Napoleon III. Yet, however he disliked them, when he writes poems about them (*Mr Sludge, 'The Medium'* and *Prince Hohenstiel-Schwangau*) he gives these morally suspect characters their due, and more than their due. In Browning moral judgments are tentative and relative, almost anyone may reveal aspects of the divine.

Even the murderer in *The Ring and the Book*, one of the great long poems in our literature, is capable of salvation when he calls on his saintly wife, whom he has murdered, as they lead him off to execution. In this brilliant recreation, in which the sordid murder case is seen from ten different points of view, we catch Browning's energy, his zestful love of the grotesque, his enormous, enthusiastic learning and sense of period. On the other hand, it *is* long; modern life seems too short for a poem of 500 pages. And certain bad habits seem to have grown on him with the years: rambling, wilful obscurity, a fondness for ridiculous rhymes, a tendency to assault the reader's ear with crabbed, tongue-twisting phrases. But at his best he is stimulating in his investigation of historical and psychological by-ways, invigorating in his thrust and confidence. And if his main appeal is on the level of drama and character, the lyric impulse was certainly not lacking in him:

O lyric Love, half angel and half bird
And all a wonder and a wild desire . . .

Most critics would agree that Tennyson and Browning, particularly the latter, wrote too much poetry for their own good. This certainly cannot be said of Matthew Arnold (1822–1888), who wrote almost no poetry after the age of forty, turning to the great prose works such as *Culture and Anarchy* which make him, with Carlyle, Ruskin and J. S. Mill, one of the great commentators on Victorian industrial/commercial civilization.

Most of Arnold's poetic production is beautiful, often formally impressive, yet he found it difficult to forge an individual voice, perhaps because he found it difficult to come to terms with the Victorian world.

Often one feels that he works out his relationship with the cool, ugly, post-Christian world *via* the works of other great writers. When one comes back to re-reading him, one finds many memorable passages that one feels one has always known, but it is astonishing how often these refer to other authors. We feel the rightness of his reflections on Emily Brontë, Shakespeare ('Others abide our question. Thou art free'), Byron ('He taught us little; but our soul / Had *felt* him like the thunder's roll'), 'Wordsworth's healing power,' and so on. We hear, too, strongly, the voice of other poets, notably Keats. Yet it happens seldom that a quote from Arnold comes to our mind and impresses itself as distinctively Arnoldian. When dealing with the modern world his tone of voice is educated, wistful, regretful – not unlike Tennyson's, but much less personally involved. Even in his greatest poem, *Dover Beach*, dealing with the slow ebb of religious faith, we have no sense of anguished personal involvement. The poem is not about how he lost his faith, but about what it is like to live in an age in which faith is decaying:

> But now I only hear
> Its melancholy, long, withdrawing roar,
> Retreating, to the breath
> Of the night wind, down the vast edges drear
> And naked shingles of the world.

Arnold feels himself, as he says in *Stanzas from the Grande Chartreuse* 'wandering between two worlds, one dead, / The other powerless to be born.' It may be that the new world will be better than this empty, faithless shell of a world, that it 'without hardness will be sage, / And gay without frivolity.' But the interim is hard, joyless (as it is for the narrator of Eliot's *Journey of the Magi*). Arnold is the poet not of the struggle to retain faith, but of the uneasy acceptance of its loss.

Arthur Hugh Clough (1819–1861) was a friend of Arnold, his contemporary at Rugby, where he too came under the influence of Arnold's father, Dr Thomas Arnold, who had reformed the English public school system, turning it from a jungle into a high-minded greenhouse. Clough's public career was very much less brilliant than was expected of one of Arnold's star pupils, partly due to the loss of faith that led him to resign his Oxford fellowship. Nevertheless, there is in his poems, at least intermittently, a toughness, a pugnacity, an effervescence, that modern readers find more to their taste than the prevailing melancholy. Faith he lost, but concern with religion never left him. In *The Latest Decalogue*, a version of the Ten Commandments for a profit-grubbing age, he cuts through the hypocrisies of Victorian piety:

> Thou shalt not kill; but need'st not strive
> Officiously to keep alive.
> Do not adultery commit;
> Advantage rarely comes of it.
> Thou shalt not steal; an empty feat,
> When it's so lucrative to cheat.

He was less confident than George Eliot that moral standards might be maintained without the 'opium' of religious promises. Yet there was at times a vitality, a sense of release, even victory – however temporary – in his confrontation with a godless world:

> Ting, ting, there is no God; ting ting;
> Come dance and play, and merrily sing—
> Ting, ting a ding; ting, ting a ding!
> O pretty girl who trippest along,
> Come to my bed—it isn't wrong.
> Uncork the bottle, sing the song!
> Ting, ting a ding: dong dong.
> Wine has dregs; the song an end;
> A silly girl is a poor friend
> And age and weakness who shall mend?
> Dong, there is no God: Dong!

The man who could write that, even satirically, and certainly conscious of the potential emptiness of a religion of pleasure, was nevertheless a bridge between the early Victorian age and some, at least, of the later Victorian poets, with their cynicism, their exuberance, their acceptance of a cooling earth and an empty sky.

14

The Late Victorians

In the second half of Queen Victoria's reign, the most public and protracted widowhood in history, the ethos, tastes and practices of high Victorianism came under increasingly sharp attack. This is perhaps easier for us to see today than it was for those living at the time. The dominance of those guardians of public morals who decided (in Dickens's phrase) whether anything might 'bring a blush into the cheek of the young person' still forced many writers into deviousness, particularly on sexual matters. Then again, Britain certainly put up a tremendous *appearance* of being the confident world leader she had been at mid-century: she ran, without serious threat, the most extensive Empire the world had ever known, and she was central to decision-making in Europe.

Yet both the power and the ideals of Victorianism were on the wane. Agricultural depression (due in part to competition from North and South America) was undermining the financial basis of the landed gentry and aristocracy. Depression in industry was leading to widespread hardship in industrial towns, and the first murmurings of mass socialism. With the publication of Darwin's *Origin of Species* the debate on the literal truth of the Bible came out of the study and on to the streets: it was a strident, acrimonious, and frequently ridiculous debate, but at least the defenders of the literal truth of Genesis showed that they knew what was at stake: the sober, earnest, somewhat repressive temper of the times that the Evangelicals had built up in the first half of the century. With the weakening of the religious sanction, all sorts of liberations, great and small, began and quickly burgeoned. Earnestness itself began to be ridiculed (both Wilde and Butler make fun of it, through its use as a Christian name); Victorian Christianity was by scoffers discovered to be a sham, its morality mere hypocrisy, its taste in the arts debased, materialistic and mechanical.

One can see the change in mood reveal itself in all sorts of aspects of the civilization – in the new popular press, in the theatre, in the hankering of so many after some new religion (socialism, aestheticism, spiritualism, whatever) to replace the faith they had lost. The changes in the sexual arena are particularly interesting. The assumption in the early Victorian novel, at least on the books' accessible surface of meaning, is that sex is straight, monogamous and a side-product of love. Beneath that surface one can catch suggestions of other forms of sexual activity (for example the suggestion of lesbianism in Miss Wade in *Little Dorrit*) but alternatives to the accepted patterns were almost always treated highly obliquely, or melodramatically. Now sexual variations began to be paraded, in life if not in print: the shocking became piquant, the risqué part of the intellectual's life-style. Novelty in sexual behaviour became a form of protest against the tyranny of the Victorian family unit.

No one did more to shock and titillate bourgeois morality than Algernon Swinburne (1837–1909). Impeccably upper-class in background and education, he acted the role of a hairy and tipsy elf who strayed into genteel drawing-rooms with the express purpose of shrieking out the unmentionable. His sexual tastes (he was addicted to flagellation) were indescribable, his opinions (republican, pagan) outrageous, and the constant, trumpeted eroticism of his early verse, their calls to pleasure rather than duty, experimental sensuality rather than self-denial, their exhortations to throw off 'creeds that refuse and restrain,' made them shocking to the older generation, fascinating and liberating to the young.

Swinburne was a highly intelligent man, well-read in the classics, history and mythology, an all-rounder whose work includes the inevitable verse dramas, attempts at novels, some first-rate critical essays, as well as erotica about birching (of interest mainly to the specialist). His poetic technique was dazzling – a seemingly effortless flow of beauty, of rhythmic virtuosity. How is it, then, that his verse seems to say so little to our own age, with its passion for sexual experimentation? The main reason, perhaps, is that almost everything in Swinburne, including his pagan sensuality, seems shallow and somehow insecure. In his celebration of pleasure in pain, there is no Keatsian reconciliation of opposites, and too much of a schoolboyish, hysterical determination to shock at all costs. Again, it happens so often that individual lines are memorable, but are lost in a poem which (as in Shelley's weaker ones) falls victim to a formless, self-propelling lyricism. We remember the lament of the Roman pagan at the victory of Christianity: 'Thou hast conquered, O pale Galilean; the world has grown grey from Thy breath.' Yet the *Hymn to Proserpine* from which it comes, one of his better poems, leaves as a whole only a diffuse, undisciplined impression.

It might have been better for Swinburne's reputation if he had died young in one of his excesses of alcoholic and sexual dissipation. In the late 1870s he showed every sign of intending to do just that. However he was taken under the wing of Theodore Watts-Dunton and lived the last decades of his life in a comparatively sober atmosphere of suburban respectability, under which his poetry cooled, but hardly deepened. His life thus offers a convenient symbol of the way Victorianism could fight back against the disintegrating forces that threatened it, could counter-attack and crush the rebels in its ranks. We may see the pattern repeated with variations over and over again: in Oscar Wilde's imprisonment, in the outcry that led Hardy to give up novel writing, in the smothering of A.E. Housman's lyrical gift because the sexual inspiration behind it was taboo, in the way Samuel Butler wrote a time-bomb of a novel, then sat on it like a broody hen until he died.

Swinburne was in his earlier days associated with the Pre-Raphaelite Brotherhood, a movement in poetry and art which protested against the mechanical literalness of Victorianism, and aimed to recapture some of the spirituality and simplicity of the medieval world. As it developed, it led directly, via Swinburne, to the Aesthetic Movement of the last decades of the century, with its cultivation of 'Art for Art's sake,' and its dangerous separation of artistic activity from the life of its time. The name most closely associated with Aestheticism is that of Oscar Wilde (1854–1900), though one feels that most of his early work belongs more to the history of publicity, of image-building, than to literary history. However, behind the deliberately outrageous behaviour, dress and opinions there was a remarkable brain which produced stimulating essays, fairy-stories, a strange short novel (*The Picture of Dorian Gray*), a great comedy (which will be treated elsewhere), and one long poem of considerable power. *The Ballad of Reading Gaol* was written after Wilde had served a savage sentence of two years' hard labour for homosexual offences (which had recently been made illegal for males). In this poem he has shrugged off the sillier falsities of aestheticism, and writes powerfully of the prison community, as it awaits the hanging of one of its number. The poem is not lacking in adornment, there is some sentimentalism, for example of the man under sentence, but the total effect is savage. We get a sense of terrible waste, of frustration, of the hopelessness of men for whom 'each day is like a year, / A year whose days are long.' And the famous Wilde wit is operative even in these surroundings, with searing effect:

> The Governor was strong upon
>   The Regulations Act:
> The Doctor said that Death was but
>   A scientific fact:
> And twice a day the Chaplain called,
>   And left a little tract.

Wilde's fate was watched with gloomy interest by A. E. Housman (1859–1936), also a homosexual, but one repressed, melancholic, compulsively hiding whatever meagre personal life he managed under an impenetrably English reserve. His poems are deceptively simple, ballad-like in form, continuing the tradition of the pastoral, but in a spirit so wistful and gloomy as to make something genuinely new of it. Against a generalized English landscape his *Shropshire Lad* (1896) deals with unhappy lovers, brief hectic celebrations, the swift-passing beauties of nature, and early death. So obsessed is he with the more doleful sides of youthful experience that Housman inevitably attracts the adjective 'adolescent' (always used derogatorily, though surely adolescence is one of the more interesting and sharply experienced phases of life). But his pithy poems are frequently moving, almost always memorable, and informed by the stoic determination to face the brief, cruel spectacle of life with courage and dignity. The poem that begins rebelliously with 'The laws of God, the laws of man / He may keep that will and can; / Not I . . .' will work itself round to a final, joyless acceptance: 'Keep we must, if keep we can, / These foreign laws of God and man.' One has no doubt that one of the things he is thinking of here are the homosexuality laws that entrapped Wilde, as he is in the savage poem beginning 'Oh who is that young sinner with the handcuffs on his wrist?,' in which the sexual abnormality is transformed into a purely physical one, with devastating ironic effect: 'hanging isn't bad enough and flaying would be fair / For the nameless and abominable colour of his hair.' At his best

Housman sums up unforgettably a small range of moods – our blacker fits, our feelings of unfulfilment, our occasional sense of life as a trick, a firework that fails to ignite:

> Here dead lie we because we did not choose
>   To live and shame the land from which we sprung.
> Life, to be sure, is nothing much to lose;
>   But young men think it is, and we were young.

It will probably be clear by now that there were interesting poets in the late nineteenth century but no giants dominating the scene. Or if there was one, he was a voice silenced, a power virtually unknown. Gerard Manley Hopkins (1844–1889) became a Catholic soon after leaving Oxford, and was a Jesuit priest. He had grave doubts about his ability to combine the practice of poetry with his vocation, and he showed his poetry only to a few friends, whose understanding and appreciation was at best partial. Not surprisingly, for Hopkins was technically the most original poet of the century. His rhythms were unusual and varied, being based mainly on stress; this might have been acceptable if Hopkins had not, in the interests of concentration, wrenched his syntax into novel shape, missed out less vital words to let weight fall on the important ones, played fast and loose with parts of speech ('the achieve of, the mastery of the thing!'), coined new words, adopted dialect words, forced new word combinations into adjectival mouthfuls ('Of the rolling level underneath him steady air'), and so on. The result is a poetry of peculiar intensity, which frequently seizes on and brilliantly clarifies the essence of his subject, as in the opening of his poem on the windhover, a kestrel, where the bird's flight is dizzyingly conveyed, and the wonder of the bird in his pride:

> I caught this morning morning's minion, king-
> dom of daylight's dauphin, dapple-dawn-drawn Falcon, in his riding
> Of the rolling level underneath him steady air . . .

The riot of chivalric, courtly imagery culminates when the poem shifts from the bird, an image of Christ's glory, to Christ himself:

>   the fire that breaks from thee then, a billion
> Times told lovelier, more dangerous, O my chevalier!

No one conveys more intensely the apprehension of God through nature, the ecstasy of that communion, the consequent horror at the destruction of a natural thing:

> O if we but knew what we do
>> When we delve or hew—
> Hack and rack the growing green!

Hopkins is Wordsworthian, too, in his appreciation of the dignity and simple strength of country people, as in his elegy for the blacksmith Felix Randal. But Hopkins's poems are touched with an intenser mysticism, a fiery love of his creator that reminds one more of the metaphysical poets. This odd, self-doubting, powerfully original poet had to wait until thirty years after his death, till 1918, before he was to be published, and his great influence was to be, oddly, on the generation of poets who grew to maturity in the thirties, adherents of a very different theology.

If poetry in late Victorian times seemed to be going through a period of diminished confidence, the burst of fictional energy of the early years of the reign had by no means exhausted itself. Looking back, the last decades of the century seem dominated by two figures, Thomas Hardy and Henry James, with a host of lesser but interesting figures behind them. Thomas Hardy (1840–1928) is a puzzling figure to place, partly because he by no means follows the line towards greater realism pointed out by George Eliot and Trollope (lines of development, in artistic matters, are comforting things for students, but frequently mislead). In some ways he looks back to Scott, with his feeling for natural setting which plays a still larger part in his novels. On the other hand, he has little of Scott's sense of a developing community. In other respects he looks back to the eighteenth century, with his free use of chance and coincidence, his sprawling plots. But he has none of the eighteenth-century novelist's optimism or breezy sense of life's possibilities. Hardy is very much his own man.

He was born in Dorset, of parents on the upper fringes of the working class, and all his best novels are set in the area he calls 'Wessex' – that is, the South West of England. The setting may vary – cultivated farmland may predominate, or country towns, or endless, inhospitable heath – but always in Hardy *place* is of the essence, and many of the books seem to divide themselves up not merely by stages in the characters' lives, but by the places they find themselves in. Perhaps some of Hardy's popularity today (he is probably the most read novelist among young people) is due to his matchless evocation of a rural England gone beyond recall but not beyond yearning for. Yet his renderings of nature are never sentimental, or merely lush: he closes his eyes to none of the cruelties of the natural world. In one novel, *The Return of the Native*, Egdon Heath, the setting, is by any estimate the main force in the novel, and its presence is not benign but brooding, unlovely, potent:

> It was at present a place perfectly accordant with man's nature – neither ghastly, hateful, nor ugly: neither commonplace, unmeaning, nor tame; but, like man, slighted and enduring; and withal singularly colossal and mysterious in its swarthy monotony.

Against the still, lowering immensity of the heath, the actual characters seem very small indeed: every journey they take is a slow, difficult one across unwelcoming landscape; every aspiration they have is dwarfed by their surroundings. Hardy's perspective is literally a bird's eye view – from above, at a distance – and it may be said that he is the only novelist who can see the human being in his true, universal perspective: very small. But for the novelist this is a dangerous position to adopt. *The Return of the Native* succeeds triumphantly, but by its nature it is a once-off success. Fiction demands an assumption that man, his affairs, his relationships, are of central interest, and in later Hardy novels nature is not allowed so totally to usurp the front seat.

In fact, many recent critics have felt that readers have tended to ignore the extent to which Hardy is a social novelist, concerned with vital issues of the day, such as working-class education, agricultural conditions, the marriage laws, and so on. It is true that Hardy touches on these things, and many more. The trouble is, that one never gets the sense that he believes that reform in these areas will improve the human condition more than fractionally.

For, however much he hated the label, Hardy's pessimism broods over his novels as embracingly as Housman's does over his poems. And it is deeper-seated than Housman's. Hardy would agree that the world has 'much good, but much less good than ill,' but he sometimes goes much further, apparently believing that the finer the spirit, the greater the potential, the more total the ruin that will be contrived for it. When his finest spirit, Tess in *Tess of the d'Urbervilles*, is hanged, Hardy chimes in with his terrible, ironic ' "Justice" was done, and the President of the Immortals, in Aeschylean phrase, had ended his sport with Tess.' Of course, this view of the Almighty and his relation to the human predicament was not a final, settled philosophical viewpoint; Hardy rather nervously talks in his preface about it being no new thing to 'exclaim illogically against the gods,' and emphasizes that a novel is 'an impression, not an argument' – all true enough. Yet the placing of the phrase, at the climax of the novel and the beginning of its last paragraph, ensures that the reader does not take it as merely a passing impression of the author's. And the God who makes several appearances in Hardy's poetry is either malignant, or too incompetent to rule human affairs better. The idea that Tess, *because* she is so splendid a person, has been the sport of whatever powers there be in the universe chimes in very precisely with the reader's apprehension of the book as a whole. The coincidences and misadventures with which the book is riddled always work in the long run towards disaster for Tess. And her moments of happiness, for example at Talbothays Dairy Farm, are undercut by a menacing drum-beat that tells the reader that even such happiness, close to nature, is likely to be a snare and a delusion.

The only, remote possibility for happiness in Hardy is nevertheless in living close to nature and in 'keeping your head down' – maintaining the very lowest level of hopes and aspirations. Disaster in Hardy almost always comes from the town (as Alec d'Urberville does), or by involvement with the currents of contemporary intellectual life (as Angel Clare, the other disastrous influence in Tess's life, is involved). When the boy Jude, in *Jude the Obscure* (1895) looks towards Christminster (Oxford), and breathes 'The heavenly Jerusalem' we know already he is doomed to a life of frustration and vexation. One reason we cannot take *Jude* seriously as a social novel, a plea for working-class higher education, is that it is made quite clear that no education Jude could have got at Christminster would be worth half the education he has laboured to acquire for himself, spelling through the classics on the back of his bread-cart. Jude is a superb picture of a man both sensual and spiritual, living in an age when the two can scarcely be reconciled. After a disastrous early marriage to the earthy Arabella, he becomes involved with Sue Bridehead, a superbly rounded picture of one whom contemporary sexual hypocrisy has pushed into a state of neurosis – on the surface a liberated woman, underneath a sexual sadist, one who can be excited only by the outré, a tease who sexually torments her men, just as she finally ends up a self-lacerating Christian convert, forcing herself to live with a man who physically revolts her. She is a perverted, neurotic, utterly fascinating creature, the first creation from the abnormal fringes of the New Woman movement, and she brings Jude, never marked for happiness or prosperity, to total disaster. It is only the earthy Arabella, living for the moment, satisfied if her bodily wants are catered for, who will live a life of moderate satisfaction: as she leaves the body of the dead Jude to go off to join in the Christminster boating festivities, she already has another husband in view. Life will always go on through such as her, and in the process the finer spirits will be destroyed.

Hardy's novels are full of moments which cause the reader to rise in revolt – improbabilities, coincidences, changes of mind or attitude that are merely told us, not dramatized. One such moment in *Jude* is the action of his oldest child, who hangs his little brothers and sisters, and then himself, 'because we are too menny.' In *Tess* we have the ludicrous conversion of Alec d'Urberville to evangelical Christianity, and his subsequent de-conversion due to some chance words of Tess. This sort of thing it was, no doubt, that led Henry James to his disgustingly condescending judgment that 'the good little Thomas Hardy' had had a great success with *Tess*, which was 'chock-full of faults and falsity,' but yet had 'a singular charm.' This sort of thing significantly mars the tragic grandeur of *The Mayor of Casterbridge*. But in the end, the rough edges in Hardy's workmanship matter little: the reader is overwhelmed by the poetry, by the integrity, and by the gloomy coherence of Hardy's vision.

If James was condescending about the crudity of Hardy's technique, Hardy was in turn equally scathing about the *matter* of Henry James's novels: he said they were about the sort of thing that one thought about when one hadn't got anything better to think about – which perhaps tells us more about Hardy than about James. Certainly few novelists could be further apart in spirit: Hardy was never one for a minute dissection of delicate moral consciences, and he was never easy when dealing with the class that James is most at home with – the comfortably off class. The fact is that James is a novelist in the realistic tradition, the heir of Jane Austen (whom he oddly failed to appreciate), George Eliot, and (the model he was most anxious to acknowledge) the Russian Turgenev. He eschews the melodramatic, the grotesque, the ramshackle structures of what he called 'loose, baggy monsters,' that is, the typical early-Victorian novel. His characters face problems of love and marriage, of self-interest or renunciation, they confront opposing codes of behaviour – all in a milieu meticulously delineated as part of an action gently inched forward, the moral issues surfacing through acutely detailed analyses of states of mind, or through witty, allusive dialogue.

Henry James (1843–1916) was an American who settled in England, and lived there for his last forty years. Much is made of what is called the 'international situation' in his novels, the interplay between Americans and Europeans, but this is part of his larger theme of the juxtaposition of innocence and experience, purity and corruption, their influence on each other. In bodying forth this theme, his own twin heritage of his New England birth and his European residence naturally loom large, though the issues are seldom as simple as a clash between American innocence and European corruption, as is sometimes imagined.

In his little gem of an early novel *The Europeans*, for example, the two worlds clashing are those of the New England Wentworths and their Europeanized American cousins. The Wentworth civilization is pious, inward-looking, straight, the fine fruit of Puritan civilization. The cousins, the Baroness Eugenia and her brother Felix, are sophisticated, amusing, and (in the case of the Baroness) devious and scheming. The Baroness, with her little house adorned with curtains, blinds and draperies, contrasts with the Wentworths in their white, clean straight-lined residence, and she represents a threat to them. But she also represents a call to them to question their own values. 'There must be a thousand different ways of being dreary,' says one of the Wentworth daughters, 'and sometimes I think we make use of them all.' If Eugenia could do with some of their openness and honesty, they could do with some of the Europeans' gaiety and responsiveness to the arts and the subtler pleasures of life. And if the Baroness is defeated in the encounter because of her addiction to multiple intrigue, Felix her brother, Europeanized but by no means corrupt, carries off the prettiest of the Wentworth daughters, and at the end of the book we find her unimaginative father listening for the sound of their laughter. The process is by no means a simple one of innocence corrupted, or resisting corruption.

The greatest novel of the first phase of James's career is by general consent *The Portrait of a Lady*. The novel came to James, he said, in the form of a young girl 'affronting her destiny.' The girl was Isabel Archer, a young American girl in Europe, and he determined to 'place the centre of the subject in the young woman's own consciousness' so as to get 'as interesting and as beautiful a difficulty as you could wish.' The necessary addition to the character of Isabel – fresh, frank, enquiring – was the endowing her with a fortune, transforming her from a poor relation (though by no means a downtrodden one) to an independent woman and an excellent 'catch.' Her cousin Ralph, in persuading his dying father to do this, says 'I call people rich when they're able to meet the requirements of their imagination. Isabel has a great deal of imagination.' But in spite of all the selfless good intentions of her relatives, in spite of her own eager idealism, the result is disaster. She falls victim to two subtle, devious, empty expatriate Americans, and finds herself trapped in a loveless marriage to Gilbert Osmond, a shell of a man with nevertheless a strong egotistical will. At the end of the novel we see her, in spite of the temptation to escape, going back to her dead marriage, her apparently wasted life.

The remarkable feat of the novel is the vivid creation of the central character, the use James makes of her 'point of view' both to express the growth of her moral being through her European experiences, and to show the gradual self-understanding of the girl, the realization of the full implications of her terrible predicament. It was James's concern to refine the technique of the novel, to make it into a more consistent and sensitive artistic tool, to use it to investigate deeper levels of character, subtler shades of moral awareness. This he achieves in *Portrait*, and to read it is to understand why James has generally been thought of as the father of the modern novel. It is true that the subtlety of his moral sense has its drawbacks: it can only express itself in a style individual, highly parodiable, that is allusive, convoluted, full of double negatives, half-hints, vulgarisms delicately qualified, opaque comparisons. As T. S. Eliot said, he had 'an integrity so great, a vision so exacting, that it was forced to the extreme of care and punctiliousness for exact expression.' Occasionally in the later books the style seems to create the need for a subtle moral awareness in the characters it presents, so that people will be endowed with complex sensibilities which the reader is not satisfied they would have in real life. Yet, when all is said, James is one of the greatest analysers of the highly developed modern conscience. Nor was he as little of a social novelist as is sometimes thought: the anarchist movement, the revival of feminism, the horrors of nineteenth-century capitalism, the aesthetic movement are all subtly analysed in various of his novels – indirectly, often, it is true, but there is little in James that is direct.

James was often disappointed by the lack of critical acclaim his novels enjoyed, but he can hardly have been surprised by their lack of popular success. Yet an audience for fiction was there, larger than ever before. The Education Act of 1870 had provided universal education from the age of five to eleven, and a large, hard-working, half-educated working class audience was now eager for literary entertainment to beguile their leisure hours. The age did not produce a Dickens, a literary giant who could bestride class barriers, but it did produce Robert Louis Stevenson (1850–1894), a sensitive stylist and born story-teller. If one of the nightmares of English childhood is the opening churchyard scene of *Great Expectations*, another is the tapping stick of blind Pew in the early chapters of *Treasure Island*. Stevenson's short, sickly life produced a great deal of uneven fiction, but there are some superb stories among his production, notably 'Markheim' (a miniature *Crime and Punishment* with some very Scottish overtones), 'The House of Eld' and 'The Beach at Falesá.' At his early death he was engaged on *Weir of Hermiston*, which promised to be his masterpiece: here Stevenson's familiarity with national types is deepened by an effortless grasp of the economic class structures of both urban and rural Scotland, so that the romance elements in the fragment take on a new substance and seriousness. The conflict between Archie Weir and his father, the hanging judge, is at the centre of the story, but when the action moves to rural Scotland Stevenson is equally successful with 'the Black Elliots,' a family who seem to exist on the borders between civilization and savagery, and who are equally rooted in the national life.

Another writer adept at appealing to a wide readership in his stories, poems and novels was Rudyard Kipling (1865–1936). Kipling came to be seen as the literary personification of the ideals of Empire, but his case is much more complex than that. Even in the well-known Jubilee poem *Recessional* we feel contrary pulls: on the surface it is a call to the nation to remember its duty to God, its need to rule justly under God, and the fate of past, crumbled Empires is put sternly before it – 'Lest we forget – lest we forget!' Yet the measured, stately, processional quality of the verse suits it for a celebration of Imperial might, and it is not surprising if, in retrospect, we cannot quite remember what it was we were supposed not to forget. Kipling is, at times, a mass of contradictions; sensitive portraits of individual Indians clash with a 'white-man's-burden' contempt of them in the mass; a taste for brutality and lynch justice jostles with subtle psychological understandings. His code spoke of fair play, obedience to the powers that be, a good day's work. None of these have great appeal in Britain today, and it is significant that the great revival of interest in their Imperial past that is a notable feature of English fiction in the 1960s and 70s did not bring in its wake a revival of Kipling as a living classic.

Stevenson and Kipling to some extent bestraddle class and intelligence divides. But in the last years of the century there was developing a dangerous split between what the intelligensia read and what the ordinary Englishman read. With storytelling as such in low critical esteem, as though there was something easy or even unworthy about it, the need for an engrossing read was supplied by a new breed of popular writers, among them Rider Haggard, Ouida, E. W. Hornung (creator of the Raffles stories), and, greatest of all, Conan Doyle, the master of every popular form he turned his hand to. Such writers kept alive the art of tale telling in a dark age, but it was an unhealthy state for literature that 'serious' fiction was not popular, and popular literature was not held to be 'serious' enough for critical consideration. The bridges thus broken down in the late nineteenth century have only begun to be mended in our own times.

15

The Birth of Modern Poetry

The typical twentieth-century educated Englishman is not rural, but urban; not leisured, but working; not Christian, but buffeted by the thousand ideologies, political creeds and pseudo-sciences that claim to give meaning and wholeness to his life. We like to think of the Edwardian age as gracious, plush, civilized, an endless round of croquet and crumpets on sun-lit lawns. But the First World War did not blow to bits a stable, prosperous social fabric. On the political front it was already riven by the bitterest political struggle for a century, the Suffragette campaign; and in 1914 the long fuse that had been spluttering under the Irish question was about to lead to an explosion. The average British worker was less acquainted with sun-dappled lawns than with the sinister urban streetscapes in Conrad's *Secret Agent* or in Eliot's early poetry — those

> Streets that follow like a tedious argument
> Of insidious intent . . .

The anarchists who populate Conrad's novel had for decades been undermining Western society with assassinations, casual destruction. The Socialist party was already a force to be reckoned with in English life, and the gradual ebb of religious belief (which the ear of Matthew Arnold had detected half a century before) had left the average Britisher open to what Orwell was to call 'the smelly little orthodoxies which are now contending for our souls.' The prophet, in the Edwardian era, was as likely to be Madame Blavatsky as Marx or Freud, but the twentieth century, right up to our own day, is littered with short-lived faiths and shoddy prophets, and little bands of pilgrims have laid trails to spiritual

Nirvanahs, workers' paradises or prosperous market economies in search of the spiritual-cum-social crock of gold at the end of their particular rainbow.

In this waste ground of disputing ideologies, the poetry of T. S. Eliot fits snugly, answering the needs of that generation of intellectuals who saw the ugliness and the emptiness of modern life, the spiritual thirst of a people cut off from its traditions. Indeed, the orthodox account of modern poetry used to be that Eliot and Pound came to rescue poetry from an effete and nerveless late-Romantic tradition, out of touch with the physical and intellectual realities of the age. As usual, there is some truth in this account; but the whole picture is considerably less neat.

There was, no doubt, among the Edwardian and so-called 'Georgian' poets, a great deal of genteel poetic dabbling, any amount of enervated nature-versifying, mere weekend-cottage-in-the-country stuff.

> Stands the Church clock at ten to three?
> And is there honey still for tea?

asks Rupert Brooke. Much more dreadful, there was the public-school pieties of Sir Henry Newbolt, with his cricket-match moralities:

> The voice of the schoolboy rallies the ranks:
> 'Play up! play up! and play the game.'

Nevertheless, what this account ignores is the continuing strength, the late renewal, of traditional English poetic themes and modes. We have recently come to appreciate Thomas Hardy's poetry as among the most notable achievements of the century. Much of it was written after he forsook novel-writing, and it has some of the strength and individuality of his best fiction. His language is spare, sometimes crabbed, with coinings and dialect usages. The themes and their treatments are drawn from a wide spectrum: laments for a godless universe jostle with poignant episodes in near-ballad form; current events such as the sinking of the 'Titanic' are as impressively recorded as the wistful personal poems he wrote after the death of his estranged wife:

> Yes: I have re-entered your olden haunts at last;
>> Through the years, through the dead scenes I have
>>> tracked you;

> What have you now found to say of our past—
> Scanned across the dark space wherein I have
> lacked you?

Another poet working with strong individuality within traditional themes and modes was Edward Thomas (1878–1917), whose quiet, unexcited tones mask an exceedingly subtle and suggestive poetic technique. Through poets like Hardy and Thomas, poetry was still speaking directly, singing traditional music.

The date of Thomas's death was, give or take a year or two, the date of the deaths of many other poets: Rupert Brooke, Julian Grenfell, Isaac Rosenberg, Charles Sorley, Wilfred Owen – the generation of poets killed, along with three quarters of a million other young British soldiers, in the First World War. It was this war, the most horrific the world had known, that proved the turning point for many British poets who hitherto had been writing contentedly in the old manner. This was the moment when there was emphatically no longer honey for tea. In the early stages, of course, the traditional heroic note of war poetry could be sounded, the usual organ-swell maintained:

> If I should die, think only this of me,
> That there's some corner of a foreign field
> That is forever England

wrote Brooke in *The Soldier*, and throughout the poem he relies on the reader's response to the words England and English to do the poet's work for him. People at home, people such as Laurence Binyon or Vera Brittain, could write in that vein even late in the war. The poets at the front learned earlier. In the mud and slaughter of the trenches the heroic, patriotic note was what Charles Sorley called it: 'it is a living lie.'

The poet who for posterity has most terribly summed up the tragedy of his generation, sent to the front to be slaughtered in droves by generals who knew that, man for man, they outnumbered the other side, was Wilfred Owen (1893–1918). It is Owen who, slowly and painfully, evolved a poetry that could convey the horror of the Somme or Paschaendale. Sometimes a Keatsian, contrived note intrudes, relic of his pre-war poetic ideals:

> Red lips are not so red
> As the stained stones kissed by the English dead.

But the note is soon overwhelmed by the anger on behalf of 'these who die as cattle,' by the need to impress on the outsider the specific hideousnesses of this war:

> If in some smothering dreams, you too could pace
> Behind the wagon that we flung him in,
> And watch the white eyes writhing in his face,
> His hanging face, like a devil's sick of sin;
> If you could hear, at every jolt, the blood
> Come gargling from the froth-corrupted lungs . . .

And that long sentence ends with the most direct statement of Owen's purpose in his war poetry – to disabuse men of their heroic notions of war, of the sweetness of courage and death:

> My friend, you would not tell with such high zest
> To children ardent for some desperate glory,
> The old lie: Dulce et decorum est
> Pro patria mori.
> > [it is sweet and proper to die for one's country]

In his best known poem, two men meet in some profound, long tunnel, away from the noise of battle, and Owen, dead, hears from the other that he is the man he killed only yesterday. In a prophetic message he looks ahead to the world after war:

> Now men will go content with what we spoiled,
> Or, discontent, boil bloody, and be spilled.

The poem ends on a note of resigned weariness: 'Let us sleep now.' Owen died a week before Armistice day.

Technically Owen was an innovator, for instance in his use of half-rhymes, but he was always innovating within a poetic tradition which he firmly adhered to. But innovation much more radical than this had in fact come to English poetry some years before. The American Thomas Stearns Eliot (1888–1965) had written *The Love Song of J. Alfred Prufrock* around 1910–1911, in America and Europe, and the manuscript had preceded him to England, where he settled in 1915. So like London does the urban landscape of *Prufrock* appear, at least to English critics, that one has even suggested that Eliot projected himself forward to London in writing it, via the novels of Dickens and others. But the truth is probably that *Prufrock* is set in London, or Boston, or Paris. It is a poem about urban man throughout the Western world, rootless, dissatisfied, sapped of vitality and decision, infirm of belief. Already in the opening of the poem the evening is spread out 'like a patient etherised upon a table': the image proclaims the need for poetry to haul itself out of dreamy Romanticism, concern itself with twentieth-century realities, to be hard, precise, even unpleasant. The feeling of being under an anaesthetic, of a sleep both unnatural and disturbed, follows us through the poem, particularly in the opening section, where the unstimulating, half-alive suburban streets seem designed to smother life, not nourish it:

> . . . certain half-deserted streets,
> The muttering retreats
> Of restless nights in one-night cheap hotels
> And sawdust restaurants with oyster shells . . .

Prufrock is modern man, split, bewildered, tentative, half-seeing the spiritual desert in which he lives, half-conforming to its values. His name divides two ways: Proof and Rock suggest certainty, faith, stability; Pru and frock suggest prudence, prudery, femininity, conformism. As he walks the streets, as he attends his tea-party, where the women trivialize greatness in their chatter about Michelangelo, as he talks with the woman who distracts him with faint suggestions of sexuality, he is tormented by modern, genteel man's self-consciousness, his inability to act spontaneously: he imagines the Eternal Footman, still grander version of his lofty equivalent on earth, holding his coat and snickering; if he says what is on his mind, the woman will say 'That is not what I meant at all. / That is not it, at all' – for indeed, he and she do not converse, but talk in parallel lines of self-obsession. And even as he endures the shabby triviality of his life, he cries out in desperation: 'I have measured out my life with coffee spoons,' and struggles to articulate his frustration, his need for something to give meaning to the emptiness. He aches to 'disturb the universe,' to ask some 'overwhelming question' – what it is he has not quite formulated, but it is something to do with the 'lonely men in shirt-sleeves,' smoking pipes in the windows of the streets he has gone through, each in his own compartment, shut-off, sterile.

And in the end, he will never ask it – afraid of the crushing, uncomprehending scorn of the lady, of the eyes that 'fix you in a formulated phrase,' so that he sees himself, like a living butterfly in a collection, 'pinned and wriggling on the wall' – another of the cruel-scientific images that run through the poem. Prufrock, like so many twentieth-century people, tries to define himself through literature, and though he would like to be Lazarus, risen from the dead, returned with eternal truths, he knows he is more likely to be a balding, ridiculous version of John the Baptist, his head served up at a middle-class feast. Though he would like to be Hamlet, he cannot even aspire to be Polonius, merely an attendant lord. And though he would like to be a modern beau, in white flannel trousers with turn-ups, parading the beach, listening to the mermaids, he knows such contacts with mythic sensuality are not for him. In the evocative conclusion Eliot produces a picture of extraordinary romantic beauty and suggestiveness, only to deny its relevance, insist on its escapist nature:

> I have seen them riding seaward on the waves
> Combing the white hair of the waves blown back
> When the wind blows the water white and black.
>
> We have lingered in the chambers of the sea
> By sea-girls wreathed with seaweed red and brown
> Till human voices wake us, and we drown.

It is not the sea that drowns us, it is the life we live, the daily round of streets and tea-parties and coffee-spoons. Prufrock, in that sense, is already a drowned man.

The originality of *Prufrock*, with its disjointed starting after subjects that are immediately forgotten, its juxtaposition of speech rhythms with traditional verse patterns, its scattered learning and its harsh modern images, is carried several stages further in *The Waste Land*. Evelyn Waugh, in a significant scene in *Brideshead Revisited*, has one of his undergraduate characters intone the poem through a megaphone to the startled citizens of Oxford, a scene which captures the excitement the poem aroused among the elite, the sense of discovery, allied with a recognition of its power to shock and annoy. Yet Eliot's poem is a deeply conservative piece in spirit. It analyses the modern world in terms of its cut-offness from tradition, from faith, from fruitful contact with nature.

Now all that once gave meaning and wholeness to life stirs only wistful half-memories, tormenting regrets:

> April is the cruellest month, breeding
> Lilacs out of the dead land, mixing
> Memory and desire, stirring
> Dull roots with spring rain.

The difficulty of the poem is quite deliberate — connecting links are dispensed with, to produce an effect of jaggedness, discord, fragmentation. Memories of Shakespeare's Cleopatra in her barge merge unexpectedly into a neurotic modern woman and her lover ('My nerves are bad tonight. Yes, bad. Stay with me'), which in its turn merges into a hideous comic parody of love and marriage in an overheard conversation in a pub:

> Now Albert's coming back, make yourself a bit smart.
> He'll want to know what you done with that money he gave you
> To get yourself some teeth. He did, I was there.
> You have them all out, Lil, and get a nice set.
> He said, I swear, I can't bear to look at you . . .

It is not just the disjointedness, mirror of our inability to connect, that bewilders: the poem builds up a formidable range of literary and mythological references — Wagner jostling with the Tarot pack, Egyptian religions with Webster and Baudelaire. All of this serves its purpose of contrasting the modern, parched spirit with civilizations more in touch with the unknown, with faith, with their own traditions, but it undoubtedly presents problems: the modern reader equips himself to understand the poem, reads critical elucidations so that he recognizes the allusions; but the reader who actually *responds* fully to the wealth of reading and learning is even less plentiful today than he was in the twenties.

Eliot's own spiritual and political progress in his later years is perhaps implied in *The Waste Land*. One of his most moving poems in the twenties describes *The Journey of the Magi*, or the wise men, who visit the Bethlehem stable and attest the birth of Christ. The magus who narrates the poem ends up caught in a sort of spiritual interregnum, the old religion dead for him, the new religion waiting to be revealed. If this represents a personal dilemma, Eliot solved it by joining the Church of England (he was a High-Churchman, or Anglo-Catholic) in 1927. Much of his later poetry, notably the *Four Quartets*, is concerned with religious themes, and is quieter, more personal in tone than his early poems. Like his friend and contemporary Pound he went to the right politically, though he never gave himself over to dotty obsessions in the whole-hearted manner of Pound. A commission in the thirties to write a play for Canterbury Cathedral provided a new direction for Eliot, and much of his later production belongs to the history of English drama.

The pattern of English poetry in the early thirties was odd indeed: all the young, left-wing, anti-Fascist poets of the Auden generation looked for their models to the great trio of older poets, Eliot, Pound and Yeats, all of them profoundly (or, in the case of Pound, hysterically) conservative, all of them ambiguous or positively welcoming towards Fascist movements in Europe and their own countries. But we are talking here about the very old Yeats. For Yeats's writing career spanned nearly sixty years, and many, many changes of poetic and intellectual fashion.

W. B. Yeats (1865–1939) was born in Dublin, son and brother of painters, and art in his early years looked like being his profession too. His formative adolescent years were spent in London, and later, in the nineties, he was one of the founder members of a group of English poets called the Rhymers' Club (a horribly mock-modest title, but many of the group had a lot to be modest about). England, however, was never more than marginal in Yeats's imaginative world. Even in his earliest, aesthetic phase, when the shadows of Pater and Wilde loom large, the best poems are those stimulated by Irish peasant life, by Celtic folklore:

> *Come away, O human child!*
> *To the waters and the wild*
> *With a faery, hand in hand,*
> *For the world's more full of weeping than you can understand.*

The drug-like influence of the cult of beauty, of art that is self-sustaining and removed from the dross of everyday realities, is difficult to get rid of. In the early years of the twentieth century Yeats became more involved with life and public matters, due to his long, hopeless love for the beautiful Maud Gonne, and his involvement with the

Irish theatre movement (which, inevitably, was closely associated with the various phases and factions of Irish nationalism). His attitude to the Irish struggle for independence was usually ambiguous: he disliked the grubbing, bigoted spirit of many of the Irish middle-class people he saw engaged in the struggle, the sort who

> . . . fumble in a greasy till
> And add the halfpence to the pence
> And prayer to shivering prayer . . .

In his finest poem to Maud Gonne, who left him for a (in Yeats's opinion) ranting Nationalist rabble-rouser, his fear for the democratic spirit of some members of the Irish movement comes out at once:

> Why should I blame her that she filled my days
> With misery, or that she would of late
> Have taught to ignorant men most violent ways,
> Or hurled the little streets upon the great,
> Had they but courage equal to desire?

His bitterness here must be seen in connection with his devotion to the cultured, leisured life of the Irish country gentry, a life 'where all's accustomed, ceremonious' – a life which was, indeed, destroyed during his lifetime, partly by the nationalist struggle.

Yet for all his doubts and prejudices, this was a struggle in which he could only engage himself, one which, leaving aside the personalities involved, aroused his most deep-seated romantic loyalties. And when the serio-comic Easter rising of 1916 in Dublin was turned into tragedy by the British response, execution of the Nationalists involved, Yeats saw that his old contempt for the ranting rebels would no longer do:

> This other man I had dreamed
> A drunken, vainglorious lout . . .
> Yet I number him in the song;
> He, too, has resigned his part
> In the casual comedy;
> He, too, has been changed in his turn,
> Transformed utterly;
> A terrible beauty is born.

Easter 1916, written in the months after the executions, is the finest
political poem of our century. It is also, incidentally to the celebration of
national heroes, a meditation on the psychological consequences of
political dedication, of the fanaticism that can 'make a stone of the
heart.' By now, without question, Yeats could claim to have realized a
hope he expressed many years earlier, to leave poetry of 'longing and
complaint,' the poetry of his misty Gaelic world, and to write poetry of
'insight and knowledge.' Yet more, and stranger, developments in his
vision were still to come.

In 1917 Yeats at last married (having been refused again by Maud
Gonne and by her daughter), and from this time his interest in spiritual-
ist phenomena, always strong, came to the fore. Mrs Yeats practised
'spirit writing' – possibly faking writing that she knew would be of
the kind her husband's faith-craving mind needed. From these writings,
and from his immense learning in religions and cults, myths and
folklore, Yeats constructed *A Vision* (as he called the book in which he
gave his system explicit shape). The vision is in part an eccentric scheme
of historical cycles, with regular high-spots (Byzantine greatness, ca 500
AD, the Renaissance, ca 1500 AD), and periods of catastrophe and
change, such as Yeats saw before us in his terrifying poem *The Second
Coming*:

> Things fall apart; the centre cannot hold;
> Mere anarchy is loosed upon the world,
> The blood-dimmed tide is loosed, and everywhere
> The ceremony of innocence is drowned . . .

The theory is much wider than this, embracing individual personality,
development and fate, but the important thing is that it gave Yeats a
basis, a framework of belief, within which to operate, and to make
further advances. His poetry becomes both richer and more concentrated, as is attested by two of his greatest poems of the twenties, *Sailing
to Byzantium* and *Byzantium*. In the first, the more approachable of the
two, he rejects the sensual world of the young, casts off his ageing,
ridiculous body ('An aged man is but a paltry thing, / A tattered coat
upon a stick') and craves to be taken 'into the artifice of eternity.' The
impersonality of great art is now his ideal – one sees the continuity with
his aestheticism of so many years before, but the poem is infinitely more
profound than anything a nineties poet could have conceived. When he

is rid of his natural bonds, he will take the form of something totally artificial, something pure of form:

> . . . such a form as Grecian goldsmiths make
> Of hammered gold and gold enamelling
> To keep a drowsy Emperor awake;
> Or set upon a golden bough to sing
> To lords and ladies of Byzantium
> Of what is past, or passing, or to come.

In the Byzantium poems, it would seem that Yeats has cast off the itching, troublesome flesh, but the last poems reveal a man still (in Dylan Thomas's phrase) refusing to 'go gentle into that good night,' still rejecting the role of the serene sage that the public tries to impose on its senior literary men, still praying:

> That I may seem, though I die old,
> A foolish, passionate man.

Read in selection, the poems of Yeats lose some of their effectiveness – sometimes, even, seem too much inclined to posturing. It is a good idea to read one or two *volumes* of Yeats, for there the balance is more clear, the poems comment on each other, enrich each other. Yeats was the last great poet of the Romantic movement, and the first of our modern age.

16

The Birth of the Modern Novel

The history of the English novel in the first three decades of the twentieth century is essentially the story of a few writers who felt the need to do new things, and invented ways of doing them. The balance in fiction shifted from man in his social relations to man as an isolated entity; the focus is on his thought processes, his unconscious impulses, the essential well-springs of his being. The bland face we present to the world, the hardly less bland face we present to ourselves in our self-musings, no longer suffices: 'I don't care so much what the woman feels . . . I only care for what the woman *is*,' said D. H. Lawrence, epitomizing the central concern of the new kind of novel.

These, of course, were the aims of the revolutionaries, and they were by no means the most popular of the serious novelists of the time. There were many solid, readable novelists writing in the realistic tradition. Their books took up matters of social concern, or rendered meticulously the habits and attitudes of one or other of Britain's social groupings. Virginia Woolf called them the 'materialists.' Galsworthy is a good example, with his endless analysis of his rich business family the Forsytes — satirical in the early volumes, almost admiring by the end. It adapted splendidly for television, and in fact the materialism of the materialists is ideally suited for the medium, and the viewer might be forgiven for feeling that television gave him the essence of the books, and that he might be excused from reading them. Arnold Bennett is a more sensitive, more consistent materialist, and some of his novels of Midlands life are readable today, with an interest over and above that of the social document. This does not seem to me true of H. G. Wells, whose bouncy, punchy fiction in the realistic tradition has aged badly. With his incurable curiosity about life and his active social conscience he ought to be enjoyable still. But when, in a novel like *The History of Mr Polly*, he invites comparison with Dickens, one can only feel that these are comparisons that a wiser man would have ducked.

Of the great names who came to maturity or began writing in the Edwardian period, the least innovative was undoubtedly E. M. Forster (1879–1970). He writes, indeed, as if Henry James had never existed, interrupting his narrative, speaking directly – even preaching – to the reader, and so on. But we cannot see him as an odd throwback to mid-Victorian practices, for allied with his old-fashioned narrative techniques was a very un-Victorian impatience with plot. Vital events in the novel will be brought about by a wholly arbitrary twist, or be treated in a throwaway manner, as if he can be bothered neither to motivate nor even describe them. The most notorious of these is the casual 'Gerald died that afternoon. He was broken up in the football match' – shoved baldly at the reader, as if Forster is daring him to protest that healthy young men do not get killed playing soccer as an everyday event. In context the effect is as disconcerting as if one of Jane Austen's young ladies had died of excitement at the card-table.

What Forster is really interested in is the values we live by, and the books provide a constant evaluation and criticism of bourgeois values, as well as suggesting the compassionate, civilized, joy-loving life-style he would set against them. Forster's own personal preoccupation, homosexual love and values, was impossible to treat directly, yet it does glimmer beneath the surface of the novels. In the early *Where Angels Fear to Tread*, for example, we see the usual opposition of life-styles: the constricting, imaginatively poverty-stricken middle-class life of Sawston, symbolized by Mrs Herriton's scratching out straight lines of peas in the gritty earth, is contrasted with the liberating, natural life of Monteriano, in Italy, where body and spirit can be perfectly in equilibrium – the towers of the city are plastered at the base with notices of everyday concern, but the summit is 'radiant in the sun.' The opposition is not a simple one of right and wrong ways of living. Lilia, who escapes Sawston to marry her earthy Italian lover finds that a woman's life in Italy is lonelier, more constricting than it ever was at home. Her husband, Gino, who seems so gorgeously natural when placed over a bowl of spaghetti, reveals brutish primal instincts when his son is killed. And the whole pattern is complicated by the reader's understanding that Philip Herriton, the rather pathetic English middle-class boy at the centre, is in love with Gino, but that convention did not permit this vital plot element to emerge openly.

Undoubtedly Forster's greatest novel is *A Passage to India*, in which his concern for the 'holiness of the heart's affection,' the need for more spontaneous fellowship between people, is played out against a background of racial differences, in a world where the white man rules, and the Indian resentfully, grudgingly or satirically accepts his rule. On the realistic level the novel is a superb picture of the human consequences of Empire, of the domination of one race by another: we see the early good intentions that wither under the prevailing master-race contempt for the subject peoples; we see the tentative hands held out in friendship, frustrated by the appalling complexities of differing races and customs. The emotional constipation of English middle-class life, Forster's prime topic in his novels, is reproduced by the British in India; oblivious to the fascinations of the sub-continent, they produce a version of 'home' that is as tasteless and stale as the tinned soup and bottled peas they eat at dinner. For all Forster's belief in friendship, spontaneity, loving communion, the novel has to end in frustration and separation, with the horses of the two main male characters, Aziz and Fielding, swerving apart, and the earth and rocks saying 'not yet' and 'not there.' On the symbolic level the novel is extraordinarily rich, especially in the figure of Mrs Moore, the old woman who is destroyed, physically and spiritually, by India, yet who, by an irony of fate, becomes a sort of goddess figure for Indians after her death. The central incident of the novel, the delusion of Miss Quested that she has been sexually attacked in the Marabar caves, works on both levels: it images the fear the rulers have of the greater vitality of the ruled, here as so often assuming sexual form; and on the deeper level the caves seem to give back to the Europeans entering them a hideous parody of their deepest fears of the moment – in Mrs Moore's case a fear of the emptiness and valuelessness of life, in Miss Quested's a fear of sex associated with her forthcoming marriage. As a whole they seem to image the blankness at the heart of Britain's imperial splendour.

When E. M. Forster was publishing his youthful novels, Joseph Conrad (1857–1924) had already begun that lifelong exploration of the English language, of the possibilities of the novel form, of the frontiers and wastelands of human behaviour, that was to make him, a Pole, the first great twentieth-century novelist in the English language. The Poland of Josef Korzeniowski was then, as for long after the Second World War, part of the Russian Empire, and the Korzeniowski family was exiled for a time in Russia – the beginning, no doubt, of the lifelong suspicion of Russia and Russians in the young Conrad. His chosen career, an odd one for a boy of good family, was the sea, and in the years between 1874 and 1896 he served on or commanded French, Belgian and British ships, on voyages all over the world which sowed the seeds of numerous novels and stories. His choice of Britain rather than France as his second motherland was the result of a complex set of calculations and chances. He always spoke English imperfectly, but he wrote it – not like a native, but like a native who was enabled miraculously to rediscover his own language as a mature man. It was lucky he did not get into the hands of a present-day language teacher, or he would have spoken it well, written it indifferently, and would never have been heard of again.

In his early years as a writer Conrad made his name as the teller of tales of the sea, and the remoter parts of Empire. They were never 'good yarns' in the popular sense, but stories in which the codes men live by are tested, in which man is forced to look into himself and see the realities beneath the civilised veneer. For such testings and self-explorations Conrad's life at sea had equipped him. He was conservative in his attitudes, without illusions about men and motives, yet still in touch with the youthful romanticism that had sent him to sea, still able to recapture the thrilling novelty of travel, adventure, the exotic, the unknown:

> I see it now – the wide sweep of the bay, the glittering sands, the wealth of green infinite and varied, the sea blue like the sea of a dream, the crowd of attentive faces, the blaze of vivid colour – the water reflecting it all, the curve of the shore, the jetty, the high-sterned outlandish craft floating still . . .

The great work of the first part of Conrad's career, the turning-point, was *Heart of Darkness*, and it concerned a turning-point in his own life, his brief command of a river steamer in the Belgian Congo in 1890. 'Before the Congo I was a mere animal,' he said later. In the years that followed, the British were to learn more of the reasons why it was so crucial an experience for Conrad, for it was in the early years of the century that the full, disgraceful story of King Leopold of the Belgians' colonization of the Congo was to emerge – a story of greed, trickery, brutality and enslavement. It was this, the shabbiest colonial enterprise in the whole history of nineteenth-century colonialism, that Conrad saw at first-hand and made the starting point of his great short novel.

The story begins on the Thames, where Marlow (narrator of many

Conrad stories, and a sort of English alter-ego) tells the story of his Congo expedition to a party of men waiting for the tide. One of the other men narrates directly to us – a complex method worthy of Emily Brontë. The listening men, in effect, vouch for Marlow: he is a solid man, no neurotic; but the principal value of the narrative scheme is that it relates Congo to the Thames: 'And this too,' meditates Marlow, looking around him in the dusk, 'has been one of the dark places of the earth.' To the young Roman legionary, Britain was as mysterious, as 'other,' as the heart of Africa was to the young Victorian colonist. And this was only 'nineteen hundred years ago – the other day.' We are not allowed to take this as a tale of exotic, escapist fantasy: the heart of darkness is here on the Thames, as well as up the Congo.

After a brief stay in Brussels, an episode full of eerie presentiments of unnamed horror concealed beneath fine-sounding pretences, Marlow reaches the Congo, and immediately the realities of colonization are set before us: the enslavement of the natives, the degeneration of the colonists, caught by the 'flabby, pretending, weak-eyed devil of a rapacious and pitiless folly.' Conrad underlines not only the inhumanity of the enterprise, but the futility. The colonists import European notions to a setting where they are absurd: a boat, shelling aimlessly into the jungle, symbolizes the futility. The Africans are labelled 'enemies' or 'criminals,' and the slaves are hired 'in all the legality of time contracts,' some of them paid with little bits of gold wire which is useless to them. Most horrible of all is the pretence of a civilizing, Christianizing mission to the peoples who are in fact being brutalized, robbed, worked to death. Marlow's contempt for the shabby greed of the colonists he meets makes him fix on the one man they all fear and hate, Kurtz, an up-river agent, as the only man in the whole enterprise he can feel kin to. As the steamboat proceeds up river to fetch Kurtz (as Conrad was himself sent to fetch an agent called Klein, the name, in fact, that was used for Kurtz in the manuscript), Marlow feels himself more and more attuned to the jungle, and to the dark shapes on the river bank. And, noticing that even Marlow feels the 'faintest trace of a response' to the darkness around him, we begin to understand what has happened to Kurtz; we hear of a memorandum of his that Marlow has read, full of fine-sounding clap-trap designed for the Christian-philanthropic Society to which it is addressed, but containing the ominous phrase that to the savage the white man must necessarily appear 'with the might as of a deity.' The address ends with the scrawled phrase 'Exterminate all the brutes!'

For Kurtz has become some sort of god and leader, in his remote station – bloody, revengeful, greedy, but yet something supernatural to his tribe, a totem. The details are left vague. The notion Conrad got from the greediest of the Congo ivory collectors, and, surely, from the appalling doings at the base camp of one of Stanley's expeditions in the area (an episode dramatized by Simon Gray in the 1970s). Kurtz, when he finally appears, is a horrific figure – sick, mad, half 'civilized' man, half 'savage.' He babbles in the same breath of his fiancée and the source of his hoped-for wealth: 'My Intended, My Ivory.' For Kurtz is the image of colonialism, he is colonial greed, seen naked. But he is also all of us, the savage core beneath the sophisticated veneer. 'All Europe contributed to the making of Kurtz,' and Conrad subtly underlines Kurtz's kinship with all that is most delicate and refined in our civilization when, at the end, Marlow visits the fiancée. In her conversation we hear all the time the drum beat of 'I, I, me, me,' and when Marlow lies to her, telling her Kurtz's last words were her name, we hear her 'exulting and terrible cry,' a cry which establishes her kinship with Kurtz's African woman that Marlow has seen on the Congo banks. Kurtz's last words were, in fact, 'The horror! The horror!,' and the ending leaves us in no doubt that the horror is not some localized thing, something special to the Congo. It is in all of us.

In *Heart of Darkness* Conrad looked at the dark underside of the human personality that the Victorians preferred to look away from. In his greatest novel, *Nostromo*, he examines critically some Victorian assumptions about society, progress and enlightenment, and finds them empty. In this novel Conrad creates an imaginary state in South America, Costaguana. Though Conrad's actual experience of the area amounted to only a matter of days, it is a totally convincing, solid, haunting creation. We see the progress of Costaguana from a Spanish colony, represented by the statue of the Spanish king in the main square, through the corrupt, inefficient or simply barbaric dictatorships that succeeded 'liberation,' to the establishment of a stable modern state, or one with the appearance of stability. We do not see this in any chronological order: the book darts about in time, bewilderingly, and Conrad exemplifies the modern novelist's need to treat time fluidly: a chronological progression for the book would imply progress, but past, present and future are locked together, instinct in each other, and one thing the novel certainly is not is a celebration of progress.

For the stability of Costaguana is brought about by the silver of the

San Tomé mine, by the idealism-cum-self-interest of Charles Gould the owner, allied with the strong backing of American capital. 'I pin my faith to material interests,' he says, and the phrase echoes through the novel. For the great capitalist enterprise *does* bring a sort of stability, because that is the only social climate in which it can flourish. But it is an inhuman, remote stability, foreign to the soil, overseen by the multi-national company in California. And by the end of the novel the mine represents in the popular mind a tyranny greater than the random bloodthirstiness of the old dictators. And in the process, the mine has destroyed the fine relationship between Charles Gould and his wife – the personal imaging the larger social destruction.

Embedded in the novel there is a superb adventure story, but it is very much embedded: it is as if Conrad had invented the exciting story, then asked himself how he could tell it so as completely to avoid the vulgarity of 'yarn-spinning.' But *Nostromo* offers high rewards for the reader who perseveres through its difficulties: it is austere, remote, pessimistic, one of the towering masterpieces of European fiction.

The distinguishing marks of the novels of D. H. Lawrence (1885–1930) are very different. It is often said that *Sons and Lovers* shows the working-class finding their voice in fiction: for the first time they are depicted from the inside, by one of themselves. In a limited sense this is true: D. H. Lawrence was the son of a miner, and he grew up in the typical environment of the industrial working class. On the other hand, when, late in his short life, he was visited in Italy by his sisters, he got very annoyed by their working-class habit of referring to him as 'Our Bert': 'I am not "our Bert." Come to that, I never was.' This is profound-ly true: D. H. Lawrence had very little in common with working-class people, and was always the sensitive, talented child who would inevit-ably fly the nest. He was somehow inside working-class life, but not of it. Nothing could be less convincing than the protestation of Paul Morel (the Lawrence-figure in this novel) that 'I like my common people best,' on the grounds that what they have is not ideas, as middle-class people do, but 'life itself.' His mother sees through it – but then, it is his mother who has marked him with her artistic and middle-class ambi-tions.

Sons and Lovers is the story of the struggle of Mrs Morel, a woman who has married 'beneath her,' first against her life-loving, vital, drunken husband, then to gain and hold the love of her sons. Paul struggles against the Oedipal situation he is involved in, first with the sensitive, repressed Miriam, later with the more sensual Clara. At the end of the novel, after the death of his mother, he seems totally broken, only waiting to go into the darkness to follow her. Then, in a final paragraph which suggests possibilities but solves nothing, he turns back to the lights of Nottingham, and walks towards life and the future.

It is impossible to ignore the pressures of autobiography in the book. It was begun while his mother was still alive, finished when he had run off with his future wife Frieda, and established a tumultuous but happy relationship with her. Though in the last stages of writing he was introduced to the ideas of Freud, the dominant impression of the novel – it is what makes it so moving and rich – is of Lawrence struggling to give shape and meaning to a situation he was still involved in, and was still far from understanding. *Look! We Have Come Through!* was the title he later gave to a book of his poems; what makes *Sons and Lovers* so immediate is that he has not yet come through. Thus, for long stretches of the book he seems, through Paul, to be trying to shift the blame for the failure of his great adolescent love from himself on to the girl, Miriam. In real life, Lawrence told the original of Miriam at his mother's funeral that he loved his mother 'like a lover,' and that was why he could not love her, Miriam, fully. This truth is only intermittently acknowledged in the novel.

It is not just in the fraught, Oedipal relationship that we are placed in the centre of the situation, with all its conflicting impulses pulling us different ways. Anyone who has discussed the book with students will know what varied reactions there are to the conflict between Mr and Mrs Morel: perhaps in the radical sixties the sympathy tipped towards the former, and in the feminist seventies towards the latter, but there is never in fact a unified response. And this family situation is one that Lawrence remained possessed by all his life. Later he was to feel he had done his father an injustice in the book, was to come almost to hate his mother, and certainly to hate most of what she stood for. But he lived only to be 44: who can say what would have been his final reaction? *Sons and Lovers* is moving and fascinating precisely because of the closeness of the conflicts, the fluidity of the situations, the uncertainties they generate, which are the uncertainties of real life.

Lawrence never returned to live in Nottingham once he had cut off the family bond. Many of his later novels are the result of his travels in Mexico, Australia and elsewhere, and all of them show him working towards a mature social and sexual ethic, often battering through to a conviction across the barriers of his own divided personality. By general consent his greatest achievements are the two novels centred around Ursula Brangwen and her family: *The Rainbow* and *Women in Love*. The first takes us through three generations of the family, exploring the delicate balances of their love and marital relationships, the kinship of man and nature which withers under the blight of urban living, and the tense bond between the generations. In *Women in Love* Lawrence concentrates on right and wrong ways of loving, on the potential and limitations of the marriage relationship. The novel is far from the erotic picnic it was at the time taken to be: in fact, one of the difficulties about the book is Lawrence's difficulty in finding language to convey sexual experience, though most of the other bodily sensations are described with the tang of reality. An awful lot of electricity passes between people in *Women in Love*, but it does not always result in illumination.

The germ of the novel was the pair of contrasting sisters, Ursula and Gudrun Brangwen, who bear the weight of the action. Gudrun is lively, original and attractive, but flawed by a need to possess and dominate, by a desire to use others. Her love affair with the virile and wealthy Gerald Crich ends with his self-destruction, while Gudrun progresses to an affair with the degenerate Loerke, a sculptor who, like Gudrun, reduces and degrades life. Ursula, on the other hand, establishes a difficult but fruitful relationship with Birkin, the Lawrence-figure in the novel, and much of the book is devoted to establishing the type of fruitful marriage relationship that can flourish in our society — a relationship of independent beings, not stuffy and exclusive (Lawrence believed passionately in non-sexual relationships between men, and the need to relate to natural things by touch, by *tactile* understanding), but full, supple, tender and capable of growth.

The novel is difficult, because Lawrence as a teacher is often weak and hectoring when speaking directly, subtle and unanswerable when using action, symbol, gesture. There *is* a problem, even for us today, with Lawrence the teacher. He has been the writer who has led the revolution in our attitude to the body and its relation to the mind. Yet when he talks about 'blood-consciousness,' and when he proclaims that what the blood tells us is always right, he is pointing the way to a valuable readjustment of values, but he is also pointing the way to Fascism. When, in *Sea and Sardinia*, he looks into the face of an old Italian convict, sees evil there, and decides that in a sane society such a man would be destroyed, we can only reply that since Lawrence's time we have seen such societies, and they have not been sane. We must always, reading Lawrence, remember he was by temperament a man for extreme solutions, a millenarianist, a man for whom around the next corner was a great crash, or paradise, and very probably both. The evangelical preachers his mother patronized spoke on through Lawrence, though sometimes they spoke a language his mother would hardly have understood. Preaching was far from fashionable in fiction when Lawrence was writing, and it has never been popular. In the years since his death his reputation has suffered extreme swings, and his apocalyptic tendencies seem to suggest it is likely to do so in years to come.

The greatest, most difficult, most stimulating, most infuriating of the innovatory generation of novelists was the Irishman James Joyce (1882–1941). Joyce was the great experimentalist in the modern novel, though (like all good Irishmen, and bad) he grounded his thought and practice in the past. Like Dickens he spent his childhood moving house, from good to less good to not at all good addresses, and as in the case of Dickens this contributed to his rich consciousness of his own city: Dublin has the same status in *Ulysses* that London has in *Bleak House* or *Our Mutual Friend*. Joyce's father was a grubby, grandiloquent man (not unlike Dickens Senior) whose downward path presented a tragi-comic performance which the young Joyce closely and dispassionately observed, for reproduction later. Joyce had the rigorous education of the brilliant young Catholic in Ireland, but he early showed signs of unease with his religion. During his university career he became aware of the various traps presented by the Irish situation to a man who wished only to fulfil himself as an artist. Not long after taking his degree he left the country, not for England, which he clearly felt could teach him nothing, but for the Continent, where he lived almost entirely for the rest of his life – in Trieste, Zurich and Paris. The great paradox about Joyce is that he was *par excellence* the modern, international writer, yet all his work is grounded in the day to day life of Dublin. And, paradoxical again, his *Ulysses* was first published in Paris, was not available freely in Britain or the States until the thirties, and not available in his homeland until the sixties.

Part of the surface difficulty of Joyce's work is due to the fact that he was a man of immense learning, and immense ingenuity. He was a joker, a prankster, a linguistic reveller, a constructor of puzzles and a parodist of genius; but the bedrock for all these skills is his enormous store of sheer knowledge – hoarded, loved, gloated over like miser's gold. This magpie instinct for facts, ideas, means that, however revolutionary the works are, tentacles reach out from them to the whole cultural heritage of Europe. Equally important were Joyce's theories about the artist, which are rooted in the aesthetic movement, but go well beyond it. The artist is the man apart, a man who is bound to reject the values and tastes of the man in the street, and who must, if necessary, alienate himself from the life around him. Similarly, he must refine himself out of his own work, must be, like God, 'within, or behind or beyond or above his handiwork.' Yet with all this rigorous withdrawal and self-exclusion, Joyce's work concerns itself, as no other great novel does, with the man in the street, and the streets themselves; and one gets the vividest sense from the totality of his writings not, admittedly, of Joyce's personality, but of the unique cast of his mind.

When Joyce, for his first novel, uses the cliché painter's title *A Portrait of the Artist as a Young Man* we are meant to note that it is *A* portrait – not *The*: it selects aspects to illuminate a theme; it does not present the whole personality, but takes a slanted look at aspects of it. *The Artist* both acknowledges the book's personal application (it keeps even closer to autobiography than *Sons and Lovers*), but insists on the larger application as well: it is about what it is to be an artist. And the last part of the title insists that (unlike Lawrence's book) this is about a phase of life that is over and done with, that can be looked back on with a fair degree of objectivity.

The first pages recreate with immediacy the sensations and thought processes of infancy, with Stephen Dedalus becoming aware of his five senses, his gradual apprehension of his immediate environment. This environment is established concretely in the early sections, and gradually enlarges itself, but it is impressed on us from the beginning that it has dual aspect: it is both the setting that contributes to making Stephen what he is, and the force that imprisons him and that eventually, as an artist, he will be impelled to flee from. From the beginning the voices around him urge him to apologize, to conform, confess, fit in; they put before him images to aspire to – to be a gentleman, a good Catholic, a good Irishman. Only half of him listens to those 'hollow-sounding voices;' his deeper urge is escape into his imaginative world, to commune with 'the insubstantial image which his soul so constantly beheld.' In the course of the book Stephen casts off his religion, which presents itself as both fascinating and terrible to his imaginative boy's mind. But he comes to see that in general life in Ireland presents perils for the creative spirit – not just the danger of *suppression*, which the Catholic-puritan temper of the Irish church has presented for all the country's imaginative artists this century, but the danger of irrelevant diversion of energies and sympathy. Riven by faction – religious, nationalistic and political – drawn hither and yon by groups crying up their own panaceas for national ills, life in Ireland, as Stephen comes to see it, is a series of *nets*, set to trap him, to prevent his flying (like his namesake Dædalus) free above earthly impediments.

For in the process of registering and avoiding these 'nets,' he is both developing as artist and coming to terms with the artist's function. We register this through his 'epiphanies,' or moments of spiritual revelation, where the common material of life suddenly takes on an intense spiritual significance, and marks one more stage in his mental growth. For Stephen, in the true Romantic tradition, the essential condition of being an artist is 'freedom' – 'the mode of life or of art whereby your spirit could express itself in unfettered freedom.' It is to find, or rather achieve, that freedom that Stephen leaves Ireland at the end of the book.

But he goes, too, to 'forge in the smithy of my soul the uncreated conscience of my race,' and it is to the Dublin of his early manhood that he returns in *Ulysses*, the vast, varied, tragi-comic picture of one day in the life of Dublin: 16 June, 1904. Meticulously detailed, constructed on a framework incredibly complex yet kept out of sight – each section parallels or parodies a section of the *Odyssey*, each has its own part of the body, its own musical motif, and so on – the book traces the courses through Dublin of Stephen Dedalus (returned to his home city for the death of his mother) and Leopold Bloom, an unheroic, cuckolded solicitor for advertisements, an Irish Jew, and thus one both inside and outside Dublin life. As their paths cross and get diverted in the course of the day we enter their minds in a seemingly unprecedented intimacy through the 'stream of consciousness' technique. The technique (of which pre-echoes can be found in a variety of novelists) was pioneered a few years earlier by Dorothy Richardson, but it is used with unexampled richness in *Ulysses*: we seem to enter directly, without authorial intervention, into the flux and muddle of the characters' actual thoughts, and the novel moves insinuatingly from descriptions of characters, into their minds, and out again. After an inconclusive meeting at the end of the day between the two male principals, the novel ends not with them, but with Molly Bloom, Leopold's unfaithful Penelope, as she drowses through the events of her day and her life in a virtuosic, unpunctuated drift towards sleep:

he was awfully fond of me when he held down the wire with his
foot for me to step over at the bullfight at La Linea when that
matador Gomez was given the bulls ear clothes we have to wear
whoever invented them expecting you to walk up Killiney hill
then for example at that picnic all staysed up you cant do a blessed
thing in them in a crowd run or jump out of the way thats why I was
afraid when that other ferocious old Bull began to charge the band-
erillos with the sashes and the 2 things in their hats and the brutes
of men shouting bravo toro sure the women were as bad in their nice
white mantillas ripping all the whole insides out of those poor
horses . . .

The novel is a parade of learning and virtuosity – as in the episode in the
maternity hospital, where the development of the foetus is imaged by a
series of parodies of English prose style over the centuries. It is also
funny, bawdy, continuously fascinating, and sad. For all their moments
of tentative contact, people in *Ulysses* are as solitary and lost as those in
Eliot's *Prufrock*. Many of the difficulties of the book disappear in later
readings, though it remains a work that will be immeasurably enriched
by critical exegesis. It is often said that Joyce led the novel up a blind
alley. Certainly it is true that few have followed him, and those that have
almost all have disappeared from sight. Yet no one writing novels since
has been unaffected by Joyce's experiments, which have fructified every
area of fiction, and indeed of drama. In search of his blind alley, Joyce
explored many incomparably fascinating paths.

The novels of Virginia Woolf (1882–1941) are often set against
Ulysses, which is used as a touchstone to reveal their supposed limitations and comparative conventionality. This is unfair: there are few
novelists who could survive such a juxtapositioning unscathed. Nor is
Virginia Woolf's range of characters as limited as is sometimes suggested: it is not true that she can deal only with upper-middle-class
women of quivering sensibilities, women like herself. In *Mrs Dalloway*,
for example, the story of – again – one day in the life of Clarissa
Dalloway and of others closely or tangentially related to her, we slide
into the consciousnesses of Clarissa, her husband, her rejected suitor of
many years before, a mentally unstable victim of the war and his Italian
wife, a working-class woman, and others. The novel organizes itself
around the events of Clarissa's day in Westminster and the West End,
punctuated by Big Ben, and around the meetings and passings of the

various characters, most of them eventually to land up at Clarissa's evening party, if only as the subject of conversation.

The writing is poetic and evocative, and the management of the significant incident is superb: for instance, the early sections of the novel organize themselves around a magnificent car proceeding through the West End bearing Greatness – of what precise kind no one can say, but it seems like a reassertion of stability, order and traditional values after the chaos and slaughter of war. A superb comment on the fragility of this reassertion of middle-class values comes in the scene where the crowd, waiting outside Buckingham Palace for a glimpse of the Royal car, has its attention diverted by a stunt plane in the sky, doing advertizing sign-writing, so that they miss the arrival of the car. A similar moment occurs at the end, where the Prime Minister, arriving at Clarissa's party and causing a frisson of something between patriotism and snobbery, is perceived by Clarissa's old suitor to be no more impressive than a grocer: 'You might have stood him behind a counter and bought biscuits.' One's criticism of the book is that such perceptions are too few (and that the latter is merely a substitution of one snobbery for another). Too often we see Clarissa's complacent, conventional world without adequate correct-ive. Indeed, one feels that the author is too affected by her membership of this world, that she fails to capitalize on her perception that it is a brittle, limited, doomed survival from another age. And as a result, this haute-bourgeois intelligentsia seems more dated today not only than the earthier worlds of Lawrence or Joyce, but even than the aristocratic world of Evelyn Waugh. But the book survives – and, still more, her masterpiece *To the Lighthouse* survives – for its poetic evocation of a small area of life, its immediate rendering of civilized consciousnesses, its embodiment of a certain type of liberal conscience.

We have concerned ourselves in this chapter with the novel, where the revolutionary changes are seen most clearly. Nevertheless, this was, too, the first great age of the English short story, both Lawrence and Joyce (in *Dubliners*) being masters of the form. But perhaps the greatest of them was Katherine Mansfield (1888–1923), the New Zealand writer who spent most of her brief maturity in England and Europe. She learned her techniques from Chekhov, and remained the quintessential short-story writer, whom one would not wish to see attempt the longer form. She had the ability to load the brief scene, the passing incident, with such meaning that it carried with it the seeds of the past and future – as in the meeting of two old lovers in 'A Dill Pickle.' In her masterpiece, 'The

Daughters of the Late Colonel,' we follow two sisters in the week after they have been liberated by the death of their absurd, monstrous old tyrant of a father. We see their faint struggles to assert long-suppressed personalities, to recapture old hopes and desires, we see the humour that has kept these underlings sane. And we know at the end that the brief flickerings of life will soon again gutter and die out. These stories are replete with great psychological insight, including an understanding sympathy for perversity, neuroticism and madness. A handful of stories – the New Zealand childhood memories, 'Bliss,' 'Je ne Parle Pas Français' and others – are among the great stories of our language, and though it is now the fashion to denigrate her influence, there is no modern short story writer who has not learned from her.

17

Depression and War

The generation of writers who made their mark in the thirties were, almost without exception, the generation that had grown up during the Great War (as it was then called), but had been too young to fight in it. Implicit in many of their attitudes is a mixture of relief and guilt— natural enough in a generation whose early memories included school assemblies where roll-calls of the dead, their immediate seniors, would be called out. They were conscious of being, in a sense, replacements for a lost generation. They almost all were middle-class, products of the public school system, and thus economically placed to enjoy that brief fling of joy in survival which was the 'gay twenties.' But they grew to political awareness in the period of disillusion after the war, when the crass indifference (as it seemed) to the slaughter displayed by generals and politicians was just coming home to the public. The events which made them all, willy-nilly, politically aware were the General Strike of 1926 and the Wall Street Crash of 1929, with the resulting depression in America and Europe. Evelyn Waugh had written about his own generation in his farewell as editor of his school magazine in 1921. He said: 'It is a queer world which the old men have left them and they will have few ideals and illusions to console them.' This was true enough. But he went on to say: 'they will not be revolutionaries, and they will not be poets.' And there he could hardly have been more wrong.

It was in fact the poets who led the way in the thirties, they who impressed their image on the educated reader's mind, they who insisted that the new poetry had to be modern, socially aware, left-wing. The foremost names of this little group – very involved with each other – were W. H. Auden (1907–1973), Stephen Spender (1909–   ). C. Day Lewis (1904–1972) and Louis MacNeice (1907–1963) – and, associated with them, the novelist and dramatist Christopher Isherwood (1904–1986). The group were lively, pugnacious, tireless publicizers of themselves and each other, energetically parading their modernity and their social consciences, yet never losing the Cain-marks of their public-school education. Thirties poetry, one feels, ought to be totally antipathetic to us today: all that ominous talk about 'Leaders,' which suggests that their anti-Fascism was merely a desire to substitute a left-wing Tweedledum for a right-wing Tweedledee; all that hearty exhortation, like scout-masters addressing a troup of backward boys; all that cliquishness, that schoolboy matiness – suggestive of nothing so much as an afternoon's rugger, secret feasts in the dorm after lights out, and a bit of friendly buggery on the side.

And yet, thirties poetry is still enormously readable, enlivening, amusing: it comes off the page with a zing and a zest that few poets of our own time can match. To be sure there are figures that arouse stirrings of unease: the total theoretic devotion of John Cornford (1915–1936) to Communism makes him unlovely and slightly sinister in the way ideologues have a habit of being. Still, such was the political commitment of the time that even his devotion proved not quite sufficient: when in one of the poems written in Spain (where he was killed in the Civil War) he said 'Now, with my party, I stand quite alone,' this had to be changed in print to 'Now, with my Party . . .' The Party, like God, demanded the dignity of a capital letter.

But Cornford is very much an exception. For the rest, the *social* vision is fresh, immediate, quivering with genuine observation; but as soon as they try to place it in a political context they suffer from a failure of nerve, or else the superficiality of their left-wing commitment becomes embarrassingly evident. The result, most often, is blurring and muddle, though admittedly it is often a very endearing muddle. The way almost all these poets tinkered with their poems after publication, trying to give them some sort of ideological consistency, is a sure pointer to their bewilderment. A poem like Spender's *Elementary School Class Room in a Slum* illustrates this. The first three verses are a damning, angry, painful picture of a slum school, with the physical and mental abnormalities to be seen there, and the evidences of hunger and deprivation. The poem implies a swingeing indictment of the society that could produce such an environment for its young, and demands that they be offered, not escapes, but teaching about slums to nourish their anger. Then suddenly, in the last verse, Spender draws back from his anger, unable to face its

full implications, and produces to finish with a bit of wet-liberalism,
misty hope for the future, pure mush. And however much he fiddled
with it, and he fiddled incessantly, it remains mushy and muddled.
Similar things happen when Spender writes in praise of the new techno-
logy which brings hopes of a new and better life. In *The Pylons* he hymns
these new phenomena, striding across the countryside and the crum-
bling villages of England, emblems of the future. Yet one cannot help
feeling his heart is in the villages and fields, for the splendid pylons seem
less to thrill him than to frighten him:

> Bare like nude, giant girls that have no secret . . .
> But far above and far as sight endures
> Like whips of anger
> With lightning's danger
> There runs the quick perspective of the future.

The poets, in other words, almost all try to face both ways. Pacifist
through the early years of the thirties, they became exuberantly belligerent on the outbreak of the Spanish Civil War; sentimentally pro-
Stalin, they accepted the great purges, but even they found the
Hitler-Stalin pact too tough a morsel to swallow; having spent the last
years of the thirties drumming up support for a fight against Fascism,
they found two of their leaders ducking off to America before the fight
started. They were Socialists who were always destined to enter the
Establishment, atheists with their noses turned towards the Anglican
Church. Though they looked forward to 'the hour of the knife,/ The
break with the past, the major operation,' as Day Lewis put it, they had,
in reality, very little stomach for blood.

All this is said with the hindsight of their later careers, and is perhaps
a little cheap too: they were not the only young revolutionaries who
turned into pillars of the orders they had mocked. If they were confused
and less than honest with themselves, their disgust at slums, at the waste
and misery of the dole, was real enough, and gave poetry a topicality and
relevance it had seldom had. What makes these poets so alive still today
is their technical accomplishment, and the immediacy of the speaking
voice we hear. Auden in particular had a dazzling facility, a command of
every conceivable form and manner, from the ballad style of *Miss Gee* to
the intimate, reflective tone of *Lullaby*, from the hortatory voice of *A
Communist to Others* to the superbly controlled movement of *Seascape* – a

poem which places itself firmly in the long tradition of English nature-cum-nationalism poems:

> Look, stranger, on this island now
> The leaping light for your delight discovers,
> Stand stable here
> And silent be,
> That through the channels of the ear
> May wander like a river
> The swaying sound of the sea.

And Auden's virtuosity did not only dazzle, it stimulated. For all one's irritation with the 'in-group' quality of thirties poetry, we have only to read the poet's more personal writings to feel the invigorating effects of his personality and ideas. One can see everywhere in the poetry the traces of his directness of approach, his assured handling of ideas, his metrical vitality. One can hear him, in his populist mood, poking his nose into the normally rather staid Louis MacNeice's *Bagpipe Music*:

> It's no go the Yogi-Man, it's no go Blavatsky,
> All we want is a bank balance and a bit of skirt in a taxi.

I have given the impression that all the thirties poets were left-wing, at least as long as the thirties lasted. There was, in fact, the odd exception such as Roy Campbell who (claimed to have) fought for Franco in the Spanish Civil War, and wrote some quite embarrassingly bad poems on the subject. But broadly speaking poetry in the thirties was in the hands of men of the left. The situation was rather different as far as the fiction writers were concerned. When the poet, translator and upper-class eccentric Nancy Cunard organized an appeal to the writers of England to take sides in the Civil War, few failed to reply in the terms which the appeal obviously intended they should. Few, that is, except the predictable Eliot and Pound among the older generation, and Evelyn Waugh from the younger: 'If I were a Spaniard I should be fighting for General Franco. As an Englishman I am not in the predicament of choosing between two evils.' But then, Waugh was a very odd fish, politically and in every other way, and nothing would have displeased him more than to find himself among a majority.

The image which Evelyn Waugh (1903–1966) successfully imposed on the public mind in his later years was that of an irascible country squire of appalling manners and opinions which would have been bigoted in the eighteenth century and in the twentieth bordered on the ridiculous. It was very much a performance, and one in which Waugh found himself trapped. At best it represented, or parodied, one side of his nature – that side which pulled him emotionally towards institutions, social systems, that were authoritarian and instinct with tradition. The other side was rebellious, anarchic, revelling in chaos, disaster and absurdity, and this led him into a stance of perpetually ridiculing and undermining those men and institutions that he ought to have held most dear – the aristocracy, the leaders of the Catholic Church, the army which he had worked tirelessly to join in the war, and could only kick against when he got in: when reprimanded by a General for being drunk in the Officers' Mess he told him that he 'could not change the habits of a life time for a whim of his.'

As a technician of the novel, Waugh was, on the surface, equally conservative. He himself talks of his generation as one of 'artists and craftsmen,' coming after a race of 'originators, the exuberant men,' which is a fair enough summary. As one who from the start aimed to make a living from writing, in the family tradition, he can hardly have been unaware that people in the twenties were not reading Lawrence or Virginia Woolf, but Agatha Christie, Dorothy Sayers and John Buchan. His first novels, therefore, were riotous comedies which looked backwards in many ways – their Dickensian grotesques, their faux-naif heroes, their outrageous names (Margot Metroland, Miles Malpractice), their fantastic plots. On the other hand, they are lean, economical books that gain much of their effect from cinematic techniques of quick fades and sharp cross-cutting from scene to scene, making for significant juxtapositions: thus the long, loving description of Simon Balcairn's suicide by gas-oven, caused by his conviction that his journalistic career is over, cuts immediately to his boss, the megalomaniac Lord Monomark, praising his initiative and determining to give him a rise.

These techniques make *Vile Bodies* (1930) an appropriately fast, variegated celebration of the Bright Young Things – the twenties generation, Gadarene swine giggling, dancing and drinking their way to the cliff edge. The tone is satirical, but hardly unsympathetic: the war has destroyed their immediate elders, and the politicians have muddled on in the years since, able neither to re-establish the old world, nor to create anything better. The Bright Young Things career through a round of activities increasingly hectic, apparently bent on self-destruction, and their doings are watched by hordes of gossip-writers and sensation-seekers, and by the appalled and fascinated older generation. These last are not sentimentalized: Edwardian stability was always a fake, and the upper-classes are less decayed remnants of former greatness than part of a continuing process of congenital decay. Attending the upper-crust Bollinger dinner at Scone College, in the superb opening chapter of *Decline and Fall*, are

> epileptic royalty from their villas of exile; uncouth peers from crumbling country seats . . . illiterate lairds from wet granite hovels in the Highlands; ambitious young barristers and Conservative candidates torn from the London season and the indelicate advances of debutantes . . .

And watching this college bun-fight, hoping against hope that the chaos will increase, so that the fines will be enormous, are the College authorities, guardians of order who no longer guard: 'please God, make them attack the Chapel.'

In later novels the drive towards anarchy is kept in check, the nostalgia for an (imagined) era of stability in the past becomes strong. *Brideshead Revisited* was potentially Waugh's masterpiece, but the circumstances of composition (it had to be written in six months' leave from the army during the Second World War) led to the second half, which carried the Catholic burden of the novel, being skimped. The first half is a rich, evocative symphony of remembrance of a past world, subtle in its relationships, superb in its orchestration of the comedy of the generations. Charles Ryder, the narrator, is caught up into the world of one of the great English Catholic families — apparently rich, stable, confident, in fact divided, unhappy, part of a race doomed to extinction. Already here the figure of Lady Marchmain arouses some misgivings: a disastrous mother, combining good intentions with catastrophic effects, she is also given symbolic overtones which at times seem to identify her with the Catholic Church itself, and notably fail to convince. The doubts increase as the story comes to concern itself with 'the operation of grace.' Waugh is a novelist who is also a Catholic, but whether it was in him to write the great Catholic novel is less clear: it may be that his religion was too quirky and idiosyncratic for that, though he does come close to it in the war trilogy, *Sword of Honour*, with which he ended his career. What is certain is that he is one of the great comic novelists of the century, his novels teeming with brilliant invention, marvellous comic *figures* (one uses the word in preference to *characters*) who play their part in the rich social pattern, and a style that is one of the civilized pleasures of life.

Waugh, for all the increasing oddity of his social attitudes, went on developing throughout his career as a novelist. The same cannot be said of Christopher Isherwood, but his early novels place him securely among the 'craftsmen' of whom Waugh spoke. Particularly brilliant are the two novels of Berlin life: *Mr Norris Changes Trains* and *Goodbye to Berlin* (the latter really a collection of linked stories). Isherwood was in Berlin in the last years of the Weimar Republic, and witnessed the rise of Fascism. Berlin, to Isherwood, meant boys, as he was to say much later, when it was safe to, but the omission of his central concern, or rather the veiling of it, adds to the strength of these novels. He creates a central figure – himself, but only part of himself – who observes people and events from a cool distance. 'I am a camera,' he proclaims at the beginning of *Goodbye to Berlin*, implying that he is aiming at an objective, scientific record. But we soon see he is a camera with a splendid eye for the significant, weighted image. In these opening pages we see his landlady's house, furnished with hideous, heavy objects which bespeak the German past, objects in which nationalism and religion are jumbled together: 'Bismarck faces the King of Prussia in stained glass;' the hatstand is three medieval halberds, and the ornaments seem fit only to be 'melted down for munitions in a war.' Berlin is a gay, amoral, zestful city, memorably evoked in the 'Sally Bowles' episode, but we are kept in touch with the brutal nationalism of its recent past, and with the confusion of patriotism and militaristic expansionism which will open the door to Fascism. As the novel proceeds the menacing drumbeats increase. In 'On Reugen Island' a struggle for dominance takes place in a homosexual relationship, and in the background lurks a sinister proto-Nazi doctor, talking of 'degenerate types.' In 'The Nowaks' we have an unforgettable picture of the stench and squalor of a working-class slum, and the final scene, in a T. B. sanatorium where Frau Nowak is being treated, brings into focus the images of fever and disease which have permeated the book. To the end the central character is a cipher – absorbing experience, but not trying to order it; participating, yet skirting both political and emotional involvement. Even in the final diary section he proclaims that the 'real masters of Berlin are not the Police, or the Army, and certainly not the Nazis,' but are 'the workers,' and we realize that he has not assimilated the point of what he has seen, but has nevertheless communicated it to us. It is a subtle, sad, and infinitely memorable evocation of one of the tragic turning-points in our century.

Many novelists in the thirties made intelligent attempts to come closer to their audience, sometimes by a recreation in modern terms of the Victorian 'baggy monster' novel – jam-packed with characters and disparate threads of plot. J. B. Priestley's *Angel Pavement* and Winifred Holtby's *South Riding* are first-rate examples of the genre. But the writer who made the boldest bid to bridge the gap between 'popular' and 'serious' fiction was Graham Greene (1904–1991), who, throughout the thirties and forties, used techniques from the thriller and crime story within novels that were serious social, moral and religious explorations. It was Greene who saw how ripe the times were for such a marriage of forms. With the world split up into warring or hostile camps – Communist, Fascist, democratic, colonial etc – the possibilities of using for serious ends the spy or chase story were infinite. Borders figure prominently in Greene: borders between countries, borderlines between safety and danger, borderline areas in human conduct, where the moral guidelines have become smudged. His typical characters are rather shoddy, unheroic personages, lost and bewildered in hostile landscapes, looking for direction-posts, both geographical and spiritual. And the land they find themselves in has acquired the name 'Greeneland.'

The typical setting for a Greene novel is a sleazy, sweaty, unlovely country: vultures lurk on the rooftops, and dead pi-dogs litter the streets. It is also a country ripe for political upheaval. It is legendary that, whether the country be Vietnam, Cuba or the Congo, just before the trouble starts, Greene will have been there, nosing out material for a novel. And he can create a Greeneland from apparently unpromising materials. In *England Made Me* (1935), inspired by the fall of the Swedish industrialist Kruger, he turns Sweden into something infinitely sinister, ambiguous and drear. In *Brighton Rock* (1938) the English South coast holiday resort – a jolly enough place – becomes a hell of shrill vulgarity, shoddy luxury and Chicago-style gang-warfare. Morally *Brighton Rock* also inhabits typical Greene territory. Ida Arnold, a cheery barmaid, is out to pin the murder of her friend Hale on Pinky, a small-time gang leader, a teenage sadist around whom hell has certainly lain in his infancy. In the course of the novel Ida becomes a monster of narrow-minded self-righteousness, imprisoned by her inadequate Protestant notions of Right and Wrong; while Pinky, the Catholic bound for Hell, gains accretions of ambiguity which leave the reader in a puzzled state of modified repulsion.

But Greene's finest exploration of the 'ravaged and disputed territory between the two eternities' is *The Power and the Glory* (1940), the fruit of Greene's visit to one of the Mexican states where the Catholic Church was outlawed. In this setting Greene places a classic chase story – the sole remaining priest, on the run, pursued by a single-minded lieutenant, devoted to destroying the old order and building a new socialist, godless paradise on earth. As always with Greene, the pattern is by no means the black-and-white of the old-fashioned thriller, but a complex mass of greys. The priest is drunken, has an illegitimate daughter, deep self-doubts, a terrible fear of death; the lieutenant lives like a monk, seems incapable of human relationships, is a sort of mystic and theologian, envisioning 'a dying, cooling world, of human beings who had evolved from animals for no purpose at all.' Amid the usual Greene imagery of cancer, fever, repulsive animals and insects, the duel between the two develops, structured around the three meetings the two men have, notably one in the prison where the priest firmly enunciates his kinship with the poor, the sinful, the dispossessed. If Waugh is especially concerned to show God's grace to the great Catholic families of England, Greene seems to find it most manifest among petty criminals and the committers of the more depressing sexual sins. Heaven knows what God makes of it all. But Greene is a superb story-teller, an artificer of fables that convey his slightly warped spiritual vision, and he compels our assent, at least for the period of reading him.

Where the reputations of Waugh and Greene are safe and growing, that of Joyce Cary (1888–1957), dead for considerably more than a quarter of a century, is still uncertain. He is the object of intense enthusiasms rather than of universal respect. Certainly if one judged him by his early African novels (products of a period in the Colonial Service) one might feel that he had a sharp, humane intelligence, a quirky humour, real human feeling, yet lacked the essential story-teller's gift, the thing that gives impetus and zest to the mundane process of reading. In fact, he remained, throughout his career, a rather hit-and-miss writer, with several novels that fail to get off the ground imaginatively. His masterpiece, by common consent, is the trilogy of novels *Herself Surprised, To Be A Pilgrim* and *The Horse's Mouth*, all published in the early forties. The first is told by Sara Monday, earthy, cunning and exuberant, and involved both with Tom Wilcher, who tells his life-story in the second book, and with Gulley Jimson, an artist, who displays himself in all his unscrupulousness and genius in the third. *The Horse's Mouth* is generally recognized as a glorious comic tour-de-force, but the more sober *To Be A Pilgrim* has equal claim to be recognized as Cary's greatest work. The ageing Wilcher, under the care of relatives after some embarrassing sexual episodes, remembers his own life while observing the developing relationship between the two young people who are taking care of him. Always the dull, plodding member of the family, repressed and burdened by his sense of responsibility he has nevertheless grown mentally over the years to have a deep respect for the essentially questing nature of the English spirit. Now old, garrulous, opinionated, conservative, he tries to crystallize his sense of life as a spiritual forward progress, of people being 'pilgrims who must sleep every night beneath a new sky.' Switching fluidly backwards and forwards in time, developing the family home, Tolbrook, as a central symbol of a changing yet enduring England, *To Be A Pilgrim* becomes a deeply impressive 'condition of England' novel – a genre that embraces Dickens, Forster (*Howards End*) and stretches to Margaret Drabble (*The Ice Age*) in our own times. Such a novel tries to distil the essence of Englishness, and to diagnose the state of the commonweal at the time of writing. There are few more moving, more individual, more cunningly structured than Cary's. For this reader it is one of the handful of great novels of this century.

Behind the intense re-appraisal of Englishness in *To Be A Pilgrim* there is war. So there is too behind *Loving* (1945), the masterpiece of Henry Green (1905–1973). Born into the plushy industrial class, and spending much of his life as managing director of the family firm, Green is nevertheless highly ambiguous about his own class, and in *Living* (1929) wrote one of the most remarkable working-class novels. Here the poetry and directness of the speech rhythms create a feeling of life that is earthy, yet vivid and full of dignity. And it is experienced, it seems, directly, rather than mediated through a middle-class consciousness. Always a stylist, he aimed at concentration through such devices as the omission of articles and words of lesser weight – devices which, in *Living*, bring the passages of narration close to the working-class speech of the protagonists. He was, in fact, an aesthete, but one of a very special kind, one for whom all human experience had value and beauty, all equally demanding to be captured and relished. Thus, his characters are seldom morally judged, however tawdry their behaviour, but are given their full individuality within a morally neutral standpoint. There are exceptions to this in *Loving*, however, which is set in an Irish castle owned by Anglo-Irish gentry, and it is they who certainly do not escape censure. Living out the war in the safe fastness of neutral Ireland, they dignify their snobbishness, selfishness and triviality by somehow imagining they are part of the war effort, part of a keeping up of 'standards.' By focusing on their niggling concern with trifles – their inability to get blotting paper of the right shade of pink, for example – Green exposes a whole class: he said himself his aim was to 'torpedo' the employers in this novel. The body of the book is a poetic, intense, yet unromantic recreation of the experience of loving and sex, mostly enacted below stairs among the English servants at the castle. The total effect is strange and beautiful – very actual apprehensions of real-life emotions combining with moments that have the oddness of a Gothic novel.

One other notable novel of the war years, written in its last months, was *Animal Farm*, a stinging satire on Soviet Russia intended as a corrective to the delusions of left-wing intellectuals of the thirties, and romanticizations of Stalin since his belated entry into the war on the anti-Fascist side. It was also a warning about the likely pattern of post-war politics. George Orwell (1903–1950) had written novels in the thirties, but he had not been too happy in the naturalistic vein. His richest work had been *Homage to Catalonia*, the best book to come out of the Spanish Civil War, and *The Road to Wigan Pier*, which combines reporting from the Northern centres of unemployment with polemic which seemed to preach the need for socialism while regretting the need for socialists. Both had aroused the ire of the left-wing Establishment and its publishers, and it was not surprising:

> One sometimes gets the impression that the mere words 'Socialism' and 'Communism' draw towards them with magnetic force every fruit-juice drinker, nudist, sandal-wearer, sex-maniac, Quaker, 'Nature-Cure' quack, pacifist and feminist in England

he wrote, in a sentence which even today a publisher might have second thoughts about giving his imprint to. So popular was Soviet Russia in 1945 that it was touch and go whether *Animal Farm* would find a publisher at all.

In this fable, Orwell relates with a cunning humour that initially cloaks his anger the rebellion that ousts humans from Manor Farm, and puts it in the collective control of the animals. They work with a will for the common good, but the control – inevitably it seems – is gradually seized by the pigs, who set up all the apparatus of a police state, and (like Stalin) stage show trials of supposed traitors. By the end the main slogan of animalism, 'All animals are equal' has received the addendum 'but some animals are more equal than others.' The odd thing is that some episodes – the carting-off of Boxer to the slaughter-yard, for example – affect us emotionally as strongly as a novel about humans, have almost, in fact, the pity and terror of tragedy. It is Orwell's deep feeling for animals, combined with his rage at the betrayal which he saw as the essential fact about Soviet Russia, that create this paradoxical reaction.

The Second World War produced no 'war poets' of consequence – no servicemen, that is, writing about their service. But the war involved as never before the civilian population: Waugh, reading while in the army letters from home full of air-raids and fire-fighting, caught the paradox well: 'The armed-forces cut a small figure. We were like wives reading letters from the trenches.' The poet who articulated for many the horror of the time for the civilian population was, oddly enough, Edith Sitwell (1887–1964). She was born into a rich, titled family, but in every other respect she was underprivileged – starved of love, ridiculed, 'guilty of being female' as she put it. She grew up into a weird figure: paranoid, self-consciously odd, theatrical, enacting the most outré idea of 'the poetess,' and presenting with her brothers Osbert and Sacheverell the queerest example of the family that brought together birth and artistic talent. Her early poems were surrealist in style, experiments in sounds and rhythms in strange juxtapositions. But through the *Facade* poems (which, with William Walton's accompanying music, proved one of the most notable pieces of the twenties, and caused the sort of scandalous success that Edith loved) there emerge, obsessively, such recurrent pre-occupations as the mad, authoritarian old man (based on her father, no doubt), negresses, parrots, the languor of tropical climes, and so on. All this is interesting and engaging, but hardly prepares us for the changed tone of her poetic production in later years. Throughout the thirties she was a butt for younger poets, though her poetry was in fact becoming philosophical and religious in theme. Then, when war came, Edith came into her own. By now a vatic figure, both preposterous and impressive, she caught the anguish of the bombed civilian, the horrors of the destroyed cities, the terrors of the nuclear age, the guilt of a generation that at the end of the war woke up to the culminating horror of the concentration camps. In *Still Falls the Rain*, the rain (of bombs) draws together all mankind in a religious agony:

> Still falls the Rain
> At the feet of the Starved Man hung upon the Cross.
> Christ that each day, each night, nails there, have mercy on us—
> On Dives and on Lazarus:
> Under the Rain the sore and the gold are as one.

Dame Edith presents a problem: around 1950 she seemed to some to be the hope for English poetry; a few years ago shares in her were lower than if she had been some South American mine whose rumours of silver deposits were long since exploded. Recent rumblings suggest that critics are no longer resting comfortably in such total denigration, and nor should they.

Something of the same wild fluctuation attends the reputation of Dylan Thomas (1914–1953), her protégé. In the thirties he was, without conscious intention, one of the leaders of a reaction against the style and political commitment of the Auden generation. Thomas's themes were Wordsworthian, mediated through Freud: the womb, the innocence of childhood, the corruption of the world and sex, the majesty of death. His manner, like Dame Edith's, was startling: prophetic, declamatory – in his case derived from the chapels of his native Wales. No one, however hostile, can quite resist the sound of Thomas reading his own poetry: oracular, fervent, totally self-convinced. In the last years of his life he carried his fervour and his alcoholism round the colleges and women's clubs of America, and he died of a brain haemorrhage ('I've had eighteen straight whiskies, I think that's the record' being among his last recorded words), complicated by appalling medical treatment in his New York hospital.

The common charge against Thomas is that he is adolescent, that his treatment of sex is mere grubby sensationalism, and that poetically he has only two or three themes which he works the changes on monotonously. The old charge of stupidity, overworked for Tennyson, is resurrected for Thomas – another lyricist, in love with the sound of what he wrote. To these charges, which are certainly not going to die away in the face of his popularity, it may be said that if Thomas's themes are few, they are great and basic ones, and the variations he works on them are full of superb effects. He risks everything, and is never afraid of the grand gesture, as in the majestic opening, sermon-like, of *A Refusal to Mourn the Death, by Fire, of a Child in London*:

> Never until the mankind making
> Bird beast and flower
> Fathering and all humbling darkness
> Tells with silence the last light breaking
> And the still hour
> Is come of the sea tumbling in harness

and so on for another twelve lines before he condescends to punctuation. Thomas's obscurity is sometimes wilful, yet the poems were obsessively crafted, worked over incessantly. In *Fern Hill* the seeming randomness gives way on closer examination to a regular scheme of half-rhyme and rhythm which keeps the verbosity in check. The theme is simple, certainly – the brief innocence of the childish vision – but it is conveyed with such brightness as to be totally winning, and the ominous fore-shadowings of his journey out of endless sunshine culminate in a final verse which produces the genuine *frisson*, rare in recent poetry:

> Oh as I was young and easy in the mercy of his means
>   Time held me green and dying
> Though I sang in my chains like the sea.

The freshness of Thomas's vision, the rhetorical splendour of some of his poems on death, should not be too easily despised. He is one of the few modern poets to have created for himself a public, and the public has gone on renewing itself, to judge by the pilgrimages to his home in Wales. He and Edith Sitwell were, it seems, the last poets to act, consciously, as poets, yet he speaks to people, through his obscurity, directly and movingly. Since his death the Muse has fled to reside among academics and university librarians, and we are not in all ways the richer.

18

Twentieth-century Drama

In the last decade or so of the nineteenth century there began a revival of British drama in the wake of which we are still living. It is as well, though, to define what we mean by a revival, for in the earlier years of the century theatre was by no means dead: indeed, the nineteenth century was a period of great acting, with names such as Kean, Macready, Henry Irving and Ellen Terry. But they performed, for the most part, classics of former ages (especially Shakespeare, trimmed and tailored to suit the requirements and egos of the principal players), or trivial modern comedies and sensational melodramas. The revival was of drama as a vital, living force via new plays written for, and usually reflecting the lives and concerns of, an intelligent audience of the time. The absentee father of the revival was Henrik Ibsen.

True, attempts had been made, before the name of Ibsen had been heard of in Britain, to import into the theatre the lively social concerns of the Victorian novelists. T. W. Robertson (1829–1871) had made brave but rather ham-fisted attempts in that direction in such plays as *Society* and *Caste* (1867). But the battle against the triviality of the English theatre was not one that could be won by a second-rate talent. It was when Ibsen began to be performed – usually in small or private theatres, by groups of enthusiasts – that audiences and actors began to perceive what had been lacking in the drama, what was necessary for its revivification. The Ibsen they elevated to the status of leader and prophet was the Ibsen who explored social problems and drew the veils from public hypocrisies. This view ignored or misrepresented whole areas of Ibsen's genius and achievement, but each age takes from a supreme talent what it most needs itself. An accompanying impulse, more native born, was the impulse to retrieve the energy and style of English comedy, totally lost since the days of Sheridan. Both impulses, the Ibsenite and the comedic, have been important in the century since British drama began to emerge from its long slumber.

Not surprisingly, some of the first attempts to transplant Ibsenism as they understood it were tentative. The social plays of Arthur Wing Pinero (1855–1934) are effective in a limited way, but their social concerns do not go deep. Shaw's hilarious review of *The Notorious Mrs Ebbsmith* is still a classic analysis of the sorts of compromise with conventional melodrama and conventional morality that social dramatists in the nineties felt they had to make. Pinero's talents are more surely revealed in farcical comedies such as *The Magistrate*, and bitter-sweet comedies such as *Trelawny of the Wells*: here he shows a brio and theatrical command that is only fitfully evident in the more serious plays.

Something of the same may be said about Oscar Wilde (1854–1900). His early plays dally with social topics, no more. They mostly concern themselves (as indeed do Pinero's, all too frequently) with the question of whether a 'woman with a past' can become acceptable to 'polite society' – not a topic of vital interest if you don't think that society worth getting into anyway. What remains with us from such plays as *An Ideal Husband* and *Lady Windermere's Fan* are the grotesque eccentrics, and particularly the witty figures who were the means by which Wilde preserved his best epigrams. Wit, style and fantasy were Wilde's forte: social subversion by laughter, not social analysis. He triumphantly forged a form that could achieve this in his last play, *The Importance of Being Earnest* (1895).

Earnest is a play that one's first instinct is to treat as a piece of exquisite and witty fantasy, remote from human concerns, a bubble that will burst at the touch of analysis. Yet the paradoxical thing is that at all sorts of highpoints and crises of life, and confronted with all sorts of personalities, the lines that occur to one are from *Earnest*: lines like 'The General was essentially a man of peace, except in his domestic life,' or 'Divorces are made in Heaven.'

On the surface the play is drawing-room comedy raised to the point of fantasy: Wilde takes certain literary conventions (babies mixed up at birth, girls with impossibly romantic dreams about the man they will marry, people with double identities and so on) and he pushes them into the realm of absurdity. But always, even at its most preposterous, there is an undertow of reality, a tang of wildly unorthodox social comment, and above all a desire to shoot down Victorian morality. Wilde places matters where moral judgments are usual next to matters where moral judgments are absurd, and in the inextricable jumble of the moral and the non-moral, morality emerges looking very groggy indeed: 'Charity, dear Miss Prism, charity!' intones the local clergyman, 'None of us are perfect. I myself am peculiarly susceptible to draughts.' As in Butler's *Erewhon* illness seems to be a crime, and the imperatives of life are to be healthy, to enjoy yourself, and to live with style. Every possible sentimental cliché of Romanticism is paraded and overturned with paradox: 'You have a town house, I hope? A girl with a simple, unspoiled nature, like Gwendolen, could hardly be expected to reside in the country.' Indeed, like the newly-widowed lady whose hair has 'turned quite gold from grief,' the characters cheerfully defy all natural laws. When it is finally revealed who it was who, twenty years before, had inadvertently 'lost' the infant Ernest Moncrieff, Lady Bracknell turns on her with an awesome: 'Prism! Where is that baby?' Wilde asserts the primacy of style, of artifice, of polish; he is the father of the twentieth century 'dandies' of literature – Waugh, Coward, Orton and many others – who refuse to be intimidated into solemnity, commitment or orthodoxy, who dance or prance with grace on the edge of the abyss.

Within weeks of the first night of *Earnest* Wilde was arrested. From now on it was the committed Ibsenites who made the running in the London theatre. For the next thirty years the towering name was that of George Bernard Shaw (1856–1950), who proclaimed his adherence to the precepts of Ibsen (as he chose to understand them) but brought to his own plays a wit, an exhibitionism, an argumentativeness and a tendency to farce that gave them a very different flavour from the Norwegian master's.

Shaw's early plays were very much concerned with contemporary social problems: slum landlordism, armaments manufacture, or – above all – the woman question, which was often in the forefront of his plays, and never less than in the background. In *Mrs Warren's Profession* (1898) he found the ideal subject which enabled him to treat both the woman question and the capitalist system as a whole: that subject was prostitution. The play was banned for many years, not because of the way Shaw treated his subject (which was really quite oblique) but because he treated it at all. It was easy for those in Shaw's socialist/radical circle to read the play as a scathing condemnation of the limited opportunities for talented and energetic women; and to see prostitution as an image of the capitalist system as a whole. In both cases they were right, but Shaw's play is in many ways surprisingly ambiguous and even-handed. Mrs Warren – a rather endearing old blackguard – has taken to prostitution because it is an infinitely more attractive prospect than factory slave-labour. But she stays in the profession because she has an instinct for power, and the use of it. Vivie Warren, her daughter, is a 'new woman,' blazing trails; but she is hard, emotionally undeveloped, and in the end we find that the trails she blazes lead her to a position unequivocally inside the capitalist system. She, too, has an instinct for where the power is, now. The play organizes itself around two superb dialogues – duets might be a better word, for Shaw learnt as much from opera as he did from Ibsen – between mother and daughter, which, properly done, have the fizz and tingle of high theatre, as well as providing a real insight into the problems and causes of prostitution.

The use of the play form as a means of *debate*, pure and simple, was something that Shaw's contemporaries often deplored in him. We now see that it is one of his great strengths. A play like *Getting Married*, which contains next to no plot or action but is simply a debate on sexual and marital issues seen in a social context, proves to be quite as absorbing and theatrical as a piece whose surprises are based purely on the mechanical manipulation of turns in the plot. In fact, Shaw is at his weakest when he relies on surprising turns in the action: a figure such as the burglar who breaks into *Heartbreak House* and turns out to be one who specializes in getting caught, appealing to his victim's sympathy and milching them of charitable hand-outs, strains the audience's credulity beyond breaking-point, as well as being theatrically ineffective. In his best plays, such as *Pygmalion*, Shaw marries concerns central to him (in this case language and phonetics, and how a woman can maintain her individuality in a world where men call the tune) with characterization which, although much thinner than Ibsen's, is theatrically effective, bringing them together in action which is often simple, traditional and involving.

Shaw's versatility can be seen in a late play, *St Joan*, which at first sight seems way outside his traditional concerns. Simple piety and nationalist fervour seem uncongenial subjects for him. But though St Joan interests him as a proto-feminist, the weight of the play rests not on her but on the issues raised by her career and death. As he said, many members of the audience didn't care a fig *why* she was burned, so long as they saw it happening. He, on the contrary, did not show the burning, refused to arouse the religio-erotic feelings that a pageant treatment of her story would have appealed to, but concentrated instead on the issues of the Protestant conscience and the rise of nationalism, seeing these as the central issues which the career of Joan brought into focus. To what extent Shaw's view of the fifteenth century was a valid one need not be argued here. What is important is that the duel between Warwick and Cauchon in the fourth act is one of the highspots of theatre seen as a place of intellectual debate. And it is surely true that by the end of the play Shaw has indeed shown, as he claimed, how such an act as Joan's burning can be brought about by men who are not villains, but men of fine conscience and dedicated religion: 'It is what men do at their best, with good intentions, and what normal men and women find that they must and will do in spite of their intentions, that really concern us' said Shaw in the Preface (his prefaces, at their best, are masterpieces of argument, and enticing conveyers of out-of-the-way information).

When, shortly after his death, Shaw had his centenary, the occasion went by with a minimum of celebration: he was an exploded bomb, an extinct volcano. Within a few years he had had a magnificent revenge: practically all his major plays and most of the plays that had hitherto been considered minor had been performed in London, many in the commercial theatre, enjoying long runs. If doubts about Shaw remain – and they *do* remain, particularly when one reads rather than sees him – they might be summed up by something Lord Melbourne said about Macaulay: 'I wish I was as cocksure of anything as Tom Macaulay is of everything.' The reader often feels that about Shaw. He pronounces, confidently, on everything under the sun; he castigates hypocrisy, obscurantism and the entrenched interests that prevent the betterment of society; he offers common-sense advice on everything from drains to breast-feeding. The reader sometimes feels impelled to enter a squeak of protest: there is a dark, irrational side to humanity that hardly gets a look-in in Shaw's world picture. Man is not so commonsensical, even *in posse*, as Shaw tries to bully him into being, and the reader wonders whether, if Shaw's ideal state of society were ever by a miracle to be attained, it would not prove to be intolerable to live in.

Shaw's devotion to Ibsen was always part sincere, part a ploy in his fight against the philistine public and theatrical 'establishment.' His plays are much more polemical than the Norwegian master's, and cheerfulness keeps breaking in more often. A more sober kind of realism was provided by John Galsworthy, in such plays as *Strife* and *Justice*, and by Harley Granville-Barker, in for example, *The Madras House* and *Waste*.

The realism of these authors, though, is the realism of *An Enemy of the People*, with no trace of the seeds that could lead to a *Master Builder*. A much more creative use of the Ibsen inheritance was made, in the 1920s, by Sean O'Casey (1884–1964).

The revival of a native and distinct Irish theatre (as emphasized earlier, many of the distinguished names in the metropolitan 'English' theatre were in fact Irish) goes back to the late nineteenth century, and its shape and nature are inextricably bound up with the Nationalist movement. In the hands of the poet Yeats the new, distinctively Irish drama was primarily poetic, even ritualistic, and – in his earlier plays – was allied with folk traditions. The brief career of John Millington Synge (1871–1909) pointed the way ahead for Irish dramatists, for both in his tragedies (notably *Riders to the Sea*) and his comedies he was exploring the potential of Irish peasant speech. More ominously, the riots at the 1907 premiere of *The Playboy of the Western World*, which reads today like a charming, idiosyncratic folk comedy, showed that it was not going to be easy for Irish dramatists to tell the truth as they saw it about their country and its people.

This was part of the tragedy of Sean O'Casey's career. In his early plays of Dublin life, particularly *Juno and the Paycock* and *The Plough and the Stars*, he profited by the use earlier Abbey Theatre dramatists had made of working-class language; but the framework of his plays was realistic, topical, and informed by burning indignation and socialist conviction. The background of *Juno* is the civil war in Ireland in the early twenties; elements of the play that once seemed tinged with exaggeration and melodrama seem less so now, when the conditions of civil war have recurred. In O'Casey the men are irredeemably tainted with futile visions, empty boasting and posturing, while the women are the workers and realists. It is a somewhat sexist posture, but dramatically effective. In the figure of Juno Boyle – loving, nagging and fighting for her family – he created one of the few roles of tragic stature in twentieth-century literature.

If O'Casey had been content to create more *Junos*, all might have been well – though the furore at the premiere of *The Plough and the Stars* (which actually dared to suggest an Irish woman might be a prostitute) pinpointed the dangers of plain speaking. But O'Casey was a questor, an experimenter, as well as a political ideologue. When *The Silver Tassie* was rejected by the Abbey he cut himself off from his own country, and became increasingly reviled by its politicians and its all-powerful

Catholic hierarchy (who, to be fair, served almost all major Irish literary figures in the same way). Of O'Casey's later plays it is almost impossible to speak, because they are increasingly bound up with the stage, stage conditions and theatrical possibilities – they are 'total theatre,' involving song, dance, mime, spectacle, stage magic, and so on – and yet they are almost never performed. O'Casey became a man without a theatre, and the Irish stage withered into nostalgia and provincialism. A sad tale of unrealized possibilities and wasted opportunities.

The dominant mood of the 1920s, the desire to forget war and the generation blighted by war and have a good time, was accurately mirrored in the plays of Noel Coward (1899–1973), who triumphantly revived the comedy of manners and extended its range. He was, *par excellence*, a man of the theatre: he had been that most loathsome of beings, a child star, and in the course of his life he acted, directed, sang and danced. This was one reason why he was admired by the very different generation of playwrights in the fifties and sixties – men of the theatre themselves. On the printed page his plays make little effect: almost everything depends on timing, delivery, a theatrical fusion between great comedy performers. A line like 'Oh, he's not dead; he's upstairs' says nothing in the play text; in context, in the theatre, it sounds like great wit. Coward's scripts are raw materials – time bombs that need great actors to light the fuse. Like Restoration comedy dramatists he was writing for a class that had had their confidence shaken by war; but where they, mostly, strove to reassert upper-class values, Coward, by his brittle surfaces and action that tends to the anarchic, delicately exposed the cracks and seams that had appeared and marred the bland facade. He is not at his best when he attempts overt social comment (though *The Vortex*, a play about drugs, with Oedipal overtones, is a disgracefully effective wallow), but in their own, oblique way his plays make a comment on the society they entertained.

One third strand in inter-war and immediate post-war drama that was perhaps surprising was the revival of poetic drama. In fact, verse plays, like old soldiers, never die, though they do frequently fade away. The nineteenth century is littered with verse dramas: all the major poets attempted them, undeterred by their inaptitude for the theatre. There were rather more distinguished attempts to revive the form in the early twentieth century, but the play that really showed that verse still had a valid place in the theatre was T. S. Eliot's *Murder in the Cathedral*. Avoiding all the platitudes and ghastly good taste usually associated with religious drama, Eliot created a powerful play-cum-ritual which focused on the spiritual crisis of Thomas à Becket and the balance between the demands of the secular and the spiritual. Using devices from Greek drama, from expressionist drama, a degree of Brechtian 'alienation' and a title suggested by detective fiction, Eliot welded these disparate elements into a distinctive whole by the force of his spiritual conviction and his distinctive poetic vision. He was less successful, later, with his plays of contemporary life, such as *The Cocktail Party*, where the poetic impulse is weaker and the spiritual impulse fails to gell in the upper-crust settings. These plays tend to be elitist in a limiting, debilitating sense.

Nevertheless the success of *Murder in the Cathedral* encouraged various writers to experiment with the possibilities of a verse drama that was not burdened with the Shakespearean inheritance. Auden and Isherwood collaborated on a series of plays that were lively, untraditional, and combined social comment and propaganda with private themes. After the war Christopher Fry (1907–   ) enlivened the stage with plays like *The Lady's Not For Burning* which, if thin in intellectual content, had a dazzling verbal surface which delighted audiences for the duration of the performance. The verse drama was destroyed by the theatrical revolution of the 1950s, but there are signs at the time of writing that critics and theatre men are preparing to revalue this period of our drama.

It must be said, though, that the theatre on which *Look Back in Anger* burst in 1956 was a pretty moribund affair. Christopher Fry spinning words, Terence Rattigan providing well-crafted plays for middle-class audiences, *The Mousetrap* already in its fifth year. To make the situation more galling, this was, in America, the period of Tennessee Williams and Arthur Miller. Terence Rattigan christened the typical theatre-goer 'Aunt Edna' – a lady of impeccable middle-class respectability, who 'took in a play' on her trips to London, and did know what she liked – which was plays that were 'nice.' Aunt Edna was in for a shock in the late fifties, and though she has fought some rearguard offensive actions, she has never really recovered lost ground.

Look Back in Anger by John Osborne (1929–   ) was a portent and a symbol, and it was the signal for a sudden uprush of theatrical life and vigour which took many different forms. The term 'kitchen sink' was used at the time, and like most journalistic formulations it was inapt, though hardly more so than the term 'Angry Young Man' pinned to the dramatists. Regarded as a piece of realism, *Look Back* is a very odd play indeed. Though it has a realistic surface, it is in essence polemical rather than realistic. Critics might pretend that the country was littered with discontented graduates running market stalls, but such — at the time — was not the case. Indeed, the tone and atmosphere of the play, it has been remarked, is less that of intellectuals slumming it than of touring actors in provincial digs (Osborne's own background). The brilliance of the play lies in the bitter rhetoric, touched alternately with hilarity and hysteria, which is Jimmy Porter's primary response to life. In his way Osborne was as much a phrase-maker as Christopher Fry, but his phrases pummelled at the gut of contemporary neuroses and dissatisfactions. His verbal flailing spoke directly to the provincial graduates doing dead-end, ill-paid jobs in teaching, local government, or libraries; he voiced their discontent at their tentative or constipated emotional lives, their rage at a society that pretended to aim at equality but really contrived to leave 'the old gang' in charge. Paradoxically, he also voiced their nostalgia for the safe, sheltered, socially stratified world of the Edwardians — a world in which, be it understood, they were in the higher social stratum. It is, in short, a brilliant improvization, a muddle that somehow meshed with the muddled thoughts of young men and women in the fifties about themselves and their world. It still leaps off the page with something of the fire of early Shaw.

The success of Osborne's play seemed to release talents and energies damped down by years of tame realism or equally tame poetic drama. The next fifteen years or so were a golden age of our theatre, both from the point of view of the vast number of talented writers that emerged, but also from the point of view of performance and production. The access of energy was not confined to the West End, or the big subsidized theatre companies such as the National Theatre (which got started, at long last, in the early sixties). Much vital and inventive work was to be seen in the theatre companies outside London, which transformed themselves from producers of second-rate reproductions of West End fare, and became innovators with a real relevance to their regions. The theatrical scene of these years is crowded with names and trends; individual authors had brilliant successes with plays that were never followed up. Many, perhaps most, of the new dramatists came from the lower-middle or working classes, areas that had hardly made their marks in the theatre before, except when filtered through genteel consciousnesses and made acceptable. The writers were the scholarship boys whom Somerset Maugham had graciously described as 'scum;' some had worked in kitchens and fairgrounds, been in jail. Above all, many of them, like Osborne, had worked in the theatre. The new drama got rid of the deadly taint of 'literariness,' and made a theatre that was totally theatrical, marked through and through by a knowledge of the potentials of stage performance.

Arnold Wesker (1932–   ) was, of all the new dramatists, the one who at first seemed most at home within the framework of 'social realism.' His political commitment was total and consistent, where Osborne's was merely idiosyncratic, and his *Trilogy* is a movingly worked out study of socialist idealism at grass-roots level. This does not mean that the plays are overt propaganda (as some of the plays of the younger dramatists of the seventies were), for his characters are seen broadly and humanely and are, as often as not, seen through as well as seen. The men, in particular, use political commitment as a refuge from failure, as a means to boost their egos. Beatie Bryant, in *Roots*, is the most sympathetic of the major characters, but even here the audience's sympathies are delicately balanced: her attempts to rouse her emotionally and intellectually torpid family have our support, yet the family make some cogent points when they fight back, and we are by no means sure she really understands what has made them as they are. Nor are we anything but apprehensive about what she will make of her life in the future.

Wesker was the most notable of those dramatists whose work was broadly within the naturalistic tradition. Shelagh Delaney (1939–   ) made a notable debut with *A Taste of Honey*, which took a fairly standard subject for the time – a pregnant, unmarried girl with a horrendous home background – but made it something touching and memorable. Delaney's career petered out, as did that of the very different Ann Jellicoe, disappointing those who hoped that at last women would make an impact on the serious theatre, and open up new perspectives and subject matters.

A very different direction was opened up for British drama by the work of Samuel Beckett (1906–1991) and Harold Pinter (1930–   ). It is as well to try to avoid such labels as Theatre of the Absurd, for labels usually diminish and invariably distort. Applied to Harold Pinter, as it frequently was in his early career, the tag seriously misrepresents the source of his strength. Beckett's *Waiting for Godot* throws aside all the paraphernalia of realism, and pares action and setting to the bone: two tramps in a bare landscape wait for the appearance of 'Godot,' whom they expect but of whom they know nothing. He never comes. The tramps are clowns, of vaudeville lineage, but central to the tragic, discomfiting effect of the play is language: Beckett employs a dazzling melange of styles which purposely never mesh, but create discontinuities, anti-climaxes, the bathos of misunderstanding and non-communication. Speech in Beckett is a sort of futile last resort, a gesture of assertion against a hostile universe, a scrap of self-comfort in a terrifying emptiness. Beckett's world, in this and his later plays, is permeated by the absence of God. The author struggles anew in each work to find some image for the loneliness, the horror, the degrading futility of life; in each of them the aim is reductive, achieving effects with the minimum of theatrical gestures. Yet all of them are permeated by a sort of poetry both visual and verbal, which adds its particular sense of loss and horror to the waste-land scenarios.

The plays of Harold Pinter are very different in feel. The settings in most of them are realistic enough; nor does Pinter aim at a virtuoso mixture of verbal styles, as in *Godot*. He makes, nevertheless, a sort of poetry out of the repetitions, banalities and non sequiturs of everyday conversation. A Pinter play, properly performed, both amuses and frightens us, forcing us to become aware of the fragmentary, insecure nature of our relations with others. The humour sharpens the fear that arises from the sense of inadequate comprehension (in translation this vital dimension, the humour, is often lost, due to the problem of finding equivalents in other languages for Pinter's comic exploitation of English demotic speech styles). Comedy and fear mingle in the action as well: menace is in the air, but it is not pinned down, or explained. A struggle is going on, as in *The Homecoming*, but the terms of the struggle and the precise nature of the goal is left undefined. Violence lurks below the surface of the language, hovers in the pauses. The language itself as often as not is sentimental cliché or advertisers' jargon – pulled up sharply by an eruption of genuine but not fully explained passion:

He was very fond of your mother Mac was. Very fond. He always had a good word for her. (*He pauses*) Mind you, she wasn't such a bad woman. Even though it made me sick just to look at her rotten stinking face she wasn't such a bad bitch . . .

Pinter opened up new vistas in drama by his dazzling exploitation of the inadequacies and flatnesses of present-day spoken language, by the unique mixture of the banal and the terrifying which is at the heart of his plays.

Pinter's influence on the whole gallery of sixties playwrights was enormous. One dramatist who early came under his influence, but went beyond it to forge his own highly individual style was Joe Orton (1933–1967). Orton's distinction was to recreate the comedy of manners, dragging it several rungs down the social ladder, adding a strong admixture of farce and fantasy. He learned from the great forerunners, such as Congreve and Wilde, but though, like theirs, his plays contain a poised wit, the poise in Orton comes not from a confident class superiority, but from a confident classlessness. In achieving this rare classlessness, Orton's homosexuality may have played its part: homosexuality has always penetrated determinedly through class barriers. Any Orton play contains a number of superb one-line witticisms, delivered with Wildean aplomb:

God is a gentleman. He prefers blondes.   (*Loot*)

or

MCCORQUODALE: It was my intention to represent – in a symbolic fashion – the Christian Church.
TESSA: A bird of prey carrying an olive branch. You've put the matter in a nutshell.   (*Funeral Games*)

But there is also, particularly in *Loot*, a farcical action which proclaims a faith in anarchy as a way of life, and points up the violence and intolerance inherent in social organisms, in the whole set-up of law and order. As with Wilde, one thinks while watching the play that one is in the realms of fantasy; yet reading the papers afterwards one is pulled up continually by post-echoes of the Orton world. His satire on the police in *Loot* – seemingly way-out farce – was in fact based on fascinated observations of actual police behaviour. Orton died, as he hoped, young – battered to death by his lover Kenneth Halliwell. Orton would never have wished to fill the role of the ageing *enfant terrible*.

The theatre of the sixties, both the commercial and the subsidized wings, was bursting with talent and invention, and it made London the theatre capital of the world. The years since have been slightly anticlimactic, with the big subsidized theatres becoming less exciting, and with the virtual collapse of the commercial theatre as a promoter of interesting new plays. Most things worth seeing in the West End became transfers from the subsidized theatres, often provincial ones. In the sixties the dazzling verbal displays of Tom Stoppard, or the painstakingly honest explorations of David Storey, could find at times a home in the commercial theatre. Things are less easy today: a dramatist of the younger generation may, if he is lucky, get the odd play put on in the subsidized theatre, but for the most part he is likely to have his plays staged by the burgeoning 'fringe' companies, playing in a variety of locales, from pubs to old warehouses.

This is appropriate enough, for the new generation of dramatists is nothing if not committed politically, and the fringe theatre aims at ridding the theatre of middle-class connotations and bringing plays to the people. This was also the aim of, for example, Arnold Wesker in the fifties, but the Socialism of the new writers has little in common with that of Wesker. Where his was humane, concerned about human dignity and the quality of life, theirs is more ideological, more committed to Marxism (whatever, these days, that is taken to mean). Their theatrical mentors are less likely to be Osborne or Wesker than Arden or Bond. John Arden (1930–   ) has had an erratic career in the theatre, but his *Serjeant Musgrave's Dance* (1959) was one of the key works of the dramatic revival: a dark fable, eclectic in technique, which preached a powerful message about war and the inhumanity of man to man within the capitalist system. Edward Bond (1934–   ) started his dramatic career in a blaze of controversy: his play *Saved* included a scene depicting a baby being stoned to death in its pram by a gang of yobbos, one of them its father. Many people found this distasteful, but the controversy obscured the fact that the play was a compassionate and even hopeful piece of social analysis. Bond has, since then, attracted disciples and publicisers as few others in the British theatre have, but his achievements are less impressive than his debut would have led one to hope. *Bingo* (1973) is a powerful play which links Shakespeare's last days to the thriving, ruthless world of Jacobean capitalism. On the other hand *Summer* (1981) takes a somewhat Rattiganish situation (a rich woman, formerly one of the ruling class in an East European country, revisits each year her home, now communist controlled, where she stays with one of her old servants), and tricks it out with some rather half-hearted stylization, and writing that falls all too easily into characters discussing abstractions. In all, Bond's talent has only intermittently realized its potential, and in his case one feels the political commitment has contributed to the lack of fulfilment.

This is certainly not the case with the younger writers. They have faced head on questions such as race, colonialism, the decline of capitalism. Sometimes, inevitably, their doctrinaire stance has seemed to the uncommitted to degenerate into wordiness or rant, but their theatrical flair and the eclectic techniques have equally often produced a hard-hitting theatre of debate. David Edgar's *Destiny* (1976), for example, centres on the legacy of colonialism – the racial tensions in a big industrial city, highlighted by a bye-election and the presence of the National Front. It is a play of great power and scope, and much of its impact comes from its commitment. Howard Brenton's early plays are affairs of disjointed vividness, though his *Revenge*, with its treatment of law and order, the affinity between police and criminals, has a real Ortonesque flair:

> P. C. GEORGE: Sweat. Your criminal sweats out of fear for his evil deeds. Your peace-loving citizen has no need to sweat. If you're questioning a man and he starts to sweat, book him. They didn't tell you that in Police College, did they? Didn't tell you about the armpits of the underworld, did they?

By the time he wrote *The Romans in Britain* (1980), a play which combines scenes from the beginning and end of the Roman occupation with present-day incidents in Northern Ireland, Brenton was showing a strong grasp of dramatic strategy, of the presentation of political viewpoint through *showing*. The play had the misfortune (or fortune) to be the subject of a ridiculous prosecution for indecency, one of the last examples, one hopes, of what Macaulay called that ridiculous spectacle, 'the British public in one of its periodical fits of morality.' Two other dramatists who have contributed powerfully to the politically committed theatre have been David Hare (with, for example, *Plenty*) and C. P. Taylor (with *Good*).

The years of Thatcher's prime ministership spawned one brilliant theatrical realization of yuppiedom, that brief and flashy phenomenon of the mid-eighties. Caryl Churchill (1938–   ) capitalized in *Serious Money* (1987) on the 'Big Bang,' the deregulation of City practices, when the markets were in effect thrown open. The hectic, hypnotic atmosphere of the City in those months is caught with thrilling dramatic impact: sums of money, impenetrable jargon, crude language used casually, all flood the stage at a high voltage in the dramatic equivalent of a punk rock concert. Embedded in the shouting is a story of takeovers, financial shenanigans and murder, but the audience is distanced from this through Churchill's decision to tell it in a rhymed verse which (deliberately) smacks of doggerel. The play catches in a wonderful way the flavour of a time and an ethos. It will be interesting to see whether it survives the passing of that time: it already, so much has history speeded up, has something of a period flavour.

A playwright whose work has, by contrast, a feel that is timeless is Brian Friel (1929–), who has been slowly and gloriously maturing over the last four decades of the century. The timeless quality of his work no doubt springs partly from the fact that it is rooted in Irish rural life, where change has come more slowly than anywhere in Western Europe. In *Philadelphia, Here I Come* (1964) he caught a sort of emotional constipation which prevents the generations in Ireland from communicating: emigration seems a matter less of economics than of a freezing of the feelings. In *Translations* (1981) he focuses on a different failure of communication, that between England and Ireland. Set in a small community in the 1830s we see a British team mapping the area and in the process obliterating the Irish names of places and landmarks. This subtle form of colonial take-over (part unthinking, part deliberate) is intensified by the inability of many of the characters to communicate with each other. This is brilliantly conveyed by Friel in scenes in which both characters speak in English, but in one case it is an English translated for the benefit of the audience. The apartness of the two races, neither side lacking entirely in good will, is emphasized by the fact that, as Friel unobtrusively makes clear, the horror of the potato famine is just around the corner.

Friel's masterpiece to date, and one of the great plays of our time, is *Dancing at Lughnasa* (1990). The play centres on a summer in the lives of five sisters living, together, lives of poverty and emotional stagnation in a rural Irish community. The eldest, a school-teacher, has a religion which is hardly more than shibboleths and prohibitions; one of the younger ones is retarded but eager for sexual fulfilment; one has a love-child and cannot still yearnings for his incurably irresponsible father. The child himself acts as occasional narrator, setting the people and events into a wider time context. One of the catalysts for change in the women's situation is the presence in the house of their elderly uncle, back in Ireland after decades as a missionary in Africa, where, as we gradually realize, he has taken in as much of the native religion as he has spread of his own. The pressures on the women take symbolic shape in the music – sometimes the primitive force of ceilidh dancing which erupts with passionate intensity to galvanize the household, sometimes the dreamy passions of thirties dance music, intruding into their lives and changing their perceptions of it through the newly acquired (but old and unreliable) wireless set.

The mood of the play is elegiac – even the dancing which periodically breaks out having a tinge of wild or sad desperation. Yet when the household breaks up at the end of the play we know that, without the frail bonds of affection and solidarity that have kept them together, the lives of these people will be poorer and sadder.

British theatre goes towards the new century with any amount of writing and acting skills that seem certain to ensure vitality for decades. With continuing recession there is much greater doubt about the futures of some of our companies and of the commercial theatre. In the eighties government parsimony towards the arts was to some extent offset by commercial sponsorship. As industry staggered through a second and more long-lasting recession in a dozen years that source very nearly dried up. Some companies, forced into a diet of sure-fire commercial successes, hardly fulfil the purpose of subsidized theatre. During the last decade, too, classical and challenging modern plays have more or less disappeared from the television screen, to be replaced by soaps and series programmes which employ actors but not minds. The first edition of this book found hope for the future in a sort of theatre that was less pretentious and more flexible – the pub theatres and travelling groups with energy and new material. But the masterpieces of the past and of our own century must find a place too, if our drama is not to be intolerably impoverished.

19

From the Fifties to the Nineties

The history of Britain's post-war fortunes is one of adaptation and adjustment. The euphoria of winning a war soon gave way to dissatisfaction with the austerities of post-war socialism. The succeeding decades brought Britain face to face with her altered position in the world: she was a post-Imperial power, whose importance was merely secondary – and in danger of declining into something less than that. The prosperity of the fifties went some way to disguising this unpalatable truth. It was a time of rising economic expectations, especially for the working class – a time for cars and televisions and all the paraphernalia of a consumer society; and if the pundits talked about 'private affluence and public squalor,' then it had to be admitted that private affluence went a good way towards mitigating public squalor. Even in the sixties, when the economic facts were being brought inexorably home, the vitality of British cultural and sub-cultural life – her theatre, her music, her pop and her clothes businesses – allowed moments of euphoria.

The seventies and eighties have been a hangover of reappraisal after a binge of illusion. Inflation has sapped the confidence of the middle classes, unemployment that of the working class. Even Britain's international adventures took on a different aspect, though foreigners seldom understood this. The Suez invasion, the military role in Cyprus, these were the last flings of a nation asserting a global role; the British army in Northern Ireland, the Falklands crisis, showed Britain reluctantly assuming burdens that were a hangover of imperial days, fighting to give people the right to remain British, but without conviction or enthusiasm. It has been a time of shrinking expectation, national cynicism; a time for pulling the bedclothes over one's head and having as good a time as possible underneath.

A great deal of the artistic activity of the period went, as we have seen, into the theatre. Post-war poetry has produced no figures of towering stature, has spoken mainly in a lowered tone of voice. The dominant mood of poets in the fifties was in sharp reaction to the bardic rhetoric and the (as it was seen) inflated romanticism of a Dylan Thomas or an Edith Sitwell. Many of the fifties poets were (as in the thirties) Oxbridge products, who shared common aims, and they were dubbed by literary editors The Movement. Whether there was anything as definite or as purposive as a movement remains a matter of debate, but if there was it was moderately clear where it was heading: it aimed at clarity, a level, unexcited tone of voice, a classical poise. It was heterosexual, rooted in English life; its poets tended to come from State schools, but any radicalism they may have professed in the fifties was skin deep. They were often in or on the fringes of academic life, and their subjects were often 'literary,' though they professed a John Bullish scepticism towards 'culture.'

Undoubtedly the most distinguished of the poets was Philip Larkin (1922–1985). His œuvre is tiny, almost as if poetry was for him, as it was for Housman, a morbid secretion, but it is finely judged and finely crafted. He commands, above all, a spendidly controlled tone of voice, which shapes our reactions to his subjects. After the hectoring tones of Dylan Thomas it was a relief to many readers to come upon a poem like 'Church Going,' where, initially, the voice addressing us is cool, conversational, even 'flip' in its treatment of a traditionally poetic subject:

> Mounting the lectern, I peruse a few
> Hectoring large-scale verses, and pronounce
> 'Here endeth' much more loudly than I'd meant.
> The echoes snigger briefly. Back at the door
> I sign the book, donate an Irish sixpence,
> Reflect the place was not worth stopping for.

As the poem progresses, the tone modulates, and it becomes a considered, unemotional meditation on the role the church retains in an age which has lost its faith. It is a Hardyesque theme, but Larkin has little of Hardy's agonized schizophrenia: he concludes that the church has been central to all the vital acts and decisions of men's lives for so long that it will retain some of its mystical power, since here 'all our compulsions meet, / Are recognised, and robed as destinies.'

Such a determinedly low-keyed, even jokey poetry as that of the Movement was bound to provoke a reaction. Ted Hughes (1930–) sees it as a matter of differing early experiences: what the Movement poets had in common, he said, was the 'post-war mood of having had enough . . . enough rhetoric, enough overweening push of any kind, enough of the dark gods.' He on the other hand came later: 'I hadn't had enough. I was all for opening negotiations with whatever happened to be out there.' Hughes's poetry is inevitably linked with that of his wife, the brilliant American poet Sylvia Plath, who since her death by suicide has become both a myth and an industry. But where her poetry is pure confession – naked, painful, self-absorbed, groping towards death – his is very different. His way of getting in touch with whatever is out there is through the natural world, and his poetry strains to convey both the otherness and the relatedness of animals and birds. There are inimitable pictures of natural things in his poetry – for example the parrots who 'shriek as if they were on fire, or strut / Like cheap tarts' – but the essential Hughes is the attempt to capture the essence, the being of the natural world, very much as Hopkins strained to:

> Terrifying are the attent sleek thrushes on the lawn,
> More coiled steel than living—a poised
> Dark deadly eye, those delicate legs
> Triggered to stirrings beyond sense . . .

Two poets who have stood outside the swings and counter-swings of poetic fashion, and who have been cried up by no coteries – such independence is not easy in British literary life – are R. S. Thomas (1913–) and Seamus Heaney (1939–), both of whose work is rooted in the Celtic fringes of the islands. Thomas's poems are sober, conventional in form, as befits a clergyman-poet, but are instinct with the history of the Wales he lives in, particularly the dark primitive eras:

> It is to be aware,
> Above the noisy tractor
> And hum of the machine
> Of strife in the strung woods,
> Vibrant with sped arrows.

Indeed, Thomas is obsessed with the gap between himself and his farm-labouring parishioners, but when he discusses the latter it is almost as if he is talking not of the workers in present-day, mechanized, prosperous Welsh farms, but of something infinitely old – dumb and unknowable:

> Don't be taken in
> By stinking garments or an aimless grin;
> He also is human, and the same small star,
> That lights you homeward, has inflamed his mind
> With the old hunger, born of his kind.

Heaney, from the Catholic minority in Northern Ireland, is equally taken up with rural routines, which at times become rituals, with timeless farming activities, and with animals – again, one is reminded of Hardy, who lies behind so much of recent poetry. Like Hardy Heaney seems at time to cling to timeless rituals as a refuge from the mess and uncertainty of modern life, which nevertheless intrudes and disrupts. In the early poem *Churning Day* the large earthenware pots containing buttermilk remind him of 'large pottery bombs.' It is inevitable that the situation in his native country overshadows his more recent work and gives it an urgency which the reading public has responded to. But the thirst for old certainties has also won him his public: there is an honesty and craftsmanship which shine through his work, and they ensure that it speaks directly to reader and listener, without glitter or showmanship.

V, the most famous poem of Tony Harrison (1937–), inhabits a more urban and still blacker world, though here too there is a hankering back to an ordered, settled world of working-class routines. On a brief, guilt-ridden visit, between trains, to his parents' graves in a Leeds cemetery Harrison finds them sprayed with obscenities by passing Leeds United supporters and the whole graveyard subsiding into the disused pit beneath. The tanner and organ-builder who lie nearby, the pit below, symbolize a way of life not pleasant necessarily, but stable and full of communal values that Harrison can relate to. The mindless graffiti-sprayer, possessed by disorderly hatreds represented by the 'v' of a football team's 'versus,' acts as a barely verbal spokesman for what has happened to the working class in recent decades. His life revolves around beer cans and minor acts of rebellion and vandalism, his prospects are endless unemployment, his vocabulary minimal and foul, and yet his imagined abuse of the poet and his attitudes acts as a challenge and a stimulus to Harrison's musings on society and those clinging around its bottom rung. When a television version was made the poem reached an immense audience and led to a predictably silly outcry in the tabloids about foul language (which is the heart and point of the poem). Ironically the weakest element in the poem is the use of tabloid language, including the sentimental shortenings of headline-writers, which sits uneasily in the sophisticated poet's meditations:

When I first came here 40 years ago
with my dad to 'see my grandma' I was 7.
I helped dad with the flowers. He let me know
she'd gone to join my grandad up in Heaven.

It is, in fact, doubts about the language and the poet's control of it that makes one hesitate to endorse descriptions of the poem as a late-twentieth-century Gray's *Elegy*. That it is a haunting and memorable achievement, however, is undeniable.

The painful reappraisal of Britain's position which was mentioned as one of the dominant characteristics of the period finds a more direct expression in the fiction than in the poetry of the last three decades. It might be salutary to begin our survey by putting ourselves in the position of a fiction critic of the early fifties, contemplating the fields of his labours. What did the state of the novel look like then? There were the older generation, of whom more could be expected, but probably more of the same: names that would have occurred to him would be Waugh, Greene, Elizabeth Bowen, Rosamund Lehmann. There was a slightly younger generation, or one that started later, which was just getting into its stride: C. P. Snow (1905–1980) and Anthony Powell (1905–   ), for example, started writing in the thirties, but their novel sequences *Strangers and Brothers* and *A Dance to the Music of Time* were mainly to come. Snow's is an impressive, slightly laborious chronicle of men who rise to positions of some power or influence – 'Establishment' men. Powell's is a wittier, more oblique chronicle of upper-class mores, a picture of a ruling class that is adapting and diversifying, but still very much in control.

And then – what of the younger writers? One that the critical talent-spotter would certainly have mentioned was Angus Wilson (1913–1991). His early short stories had aroused a good deal of attention, and they still read well today. Wilson had learnt from Katherine Mansfield, but his stories have a sharpness and a hint of the grotesque that is all their own, not to mention a considerable grasp of changing social patterns. 'Such Darling Dodos,' for example, is a biting sketch of an encounter between the generations – an older generation that is radical, caring, rather dowdy, a younger generation that is pushy, reactionary and ruthless. It is the sort of generation clash that is not unknown in our own times. By the early fifties Wilson had already branched off into the novel proper with *Hemlock and After*, another vivid picture of liberal values in decay – decaying, in fact, into grisly farce. Wilson's later career was varied: his production included serious socio-psychological studies such as *The Middle Age of Mrs Eliot*, 'state of the nation' novels such as *Anglo-Saxon Attitudes*, lively experiments such as *No Laughing Matter* (perhaps his best book), and horrendously inflated novels such as *As If By Magic*. He was undoubtedly one of our most distinguished novelists, but one chooses that adjective with care, to suggest that his work never quite added up to what people hoped of him, never came together to form a distinctive whole.

Another writer whom the talent spotter in the early fifties might have mentioned was William Golding (1911–1993), whose *Lord of the Flies* (1954) was deservedly an instant success. The novel is one in a long line of 'desert island' and 'children alone' books, of which examples earlier in the century had been Rose Macaulay's *Orphan Island* and Richard Hughes's *High Wind in Jamaica*. Golding's book tells in miniature the story of civilization, but in reverse. Wrecked on a desert island in some future nuclear war, the boys try at first to rule their lives by the sort of orderly, representative institutions they have some memory of from back home, but they regress step by step to tyranny, superstition, blood-lust and anarchy, with a horrifying man-hunt at the conclusion. It is a book with a firm, uncompromising and exceedingly uncomfortable vision of man: of his 'original sin,' of the violence submerged beneath his stable, tolerant life-style. It is, in fact, a very modern view, one understandable in a man of the generation which had to absorb the lessons of the Nazi extermination camps, and of the dropping of the atomic bombs on Japan. Golding has never tried to avert his eyes from such horrifying knowledge. All the novels of his first decade as a novelist, up to the superb *The Spire* (1964), are marked by a similar hard, unflinching view of human history and potential. For more than a decade thereafter Golding went through an arid period as a writer, but he suddenly re-emerged in top form with *Darkness Visible* (1979) and *Rites of Passage*

(1980). The latter is at first deceptively light, almost insouciant in tone: it narrates a voyage to Australia in the early nineteenth century, with the narrator a breezy, puppyish young man of breeding, gradually exploring the 'world' of the ship. Slowly that world gains larger resonances, enabling Golding to explore through it social and sexual mores of the larger world: the 'passage' of the title has sexual, precisely homosexual, significance, but it also signifies a passing to a state of wider compassion and fuller understanding. By any count Golding is a major figure in twentieth-century fiction, as was recognized by all but one of the Swedish committee that awarded him the Nobel prize for literature in 1983.

Our talent scout in the early fifties would then have looked across the sexual divide at the women novelists — for he would, inevitably, have compartmentalized writers and his line of women writers would have stemmed from Jane Austen and Virginia Woolf, rather than from Emily Brontë and George Eliot. One hopes he would have recognized the talents of Elizabeth Taylor (1912–1975), particularly as she had most of the virtues most praised in women writers at the time — charm, atmosphere, observant eye for domestic detail, an ironic wit. Actually she had a great deal more than that, and her production is extremely varied: *Angel*, for example, is a social conspectus with at its centre a literary monster — a late Victorian romantic novelist of the Ouida type: egocentric, outrageous, absurd, yet in the end earning a sort of respect. *A Game of Hide and Seek* is a tender, witty love story (one of the last, surely, in serious fiction). Her two final novels, *Mrs Palfrey at the Claremont* and *Blaming*, are both studies of growing old, and growing lonely, both done with unsparing realism, great wit, and a wonderful ear for the pretensions and insincerities of middle-class conversation. Elizabeth Taylor is a novelist's novelist: her virtues are not showy ones — perfect writing that never draws attention to itself, delicate themes that illuminate human relationships, low-keyed but devastating wit.

And then he might, too, have mentioned Barbara Pym (1913–1980). In fact, Barbara Pym provides an interesting point of entry to the later development of the novel. For she wrote, during the fifties, a series of novels of a kind that, still more than Taylor's, were the sort of fiction women were supposed to write. She kept rigidly within her own experience: middle-class, usually maiden ladies, their relations with men, usually the clergy, occasionally scholars; there were whiffs of romance that seldom got anywhere, frequent church-going, fêtes and bazaars. Pym seemed determined to outdo Jane Austen in the contraction of her focus. Then in the early sixties her publishers told her there was simply no market for her books. Middle-class maiden ladies were emphatically no longer a saleable commodity. It was not until the late seventies, when Philip Larkin and Lord David Cecil named her in a literary periodical as the most underrated writer in England, that she once more began to be published, and she came back with a superb novel, *Quartet in Autumn*, which justified all her deliberate restrictions of her range. It is, in fact, a study of four people who have *nothing* in their lives, whose existence is a mere flicker, pending extinction: they work together at a non-job that will be abolished when they retire; one plans holidays he will never take, another guiltily frequents Anglo-Catholic church services, another collects milk bottles. It is a very funny book, but frightening too, highlighting a sort of deprivation we try to turn a blind eye to. It began an immense revival of interest, which Barbara Pym only lived to see the beginnings of. Most of her fame, and doubtless all her financial rewards, have been posthumous.

So what had happened between 1950 and 1960 that suddenly made a writer like Barbara Pym unmarketable? According to journalistic formula it was the Angry Young Man – though in fact the only figure in literature who really embraced anger as a way of life was Jimmy Porter, a stage rather than a fictional figure. What actually happened was that in the mid-fifties a new generation of writers appeared (hardly surprising), who expressed discontent with the then organization of society (hardly very surprising either). More interestingly, they achieved a decisive re-orientation of the novel downwards socially, and they created a kind of novel that was light, freewheeling, with something of the zest of the old picaresque tradition. This generation of novelists continued the process of re-establishing the novel as a popular medium, and they were popular because they were accessible: at last the novel was not only saying things about contemporary life, but it was saying them to an audience wider than educated coteries in Hampstead and Golders Green.

All this did not happen at once. The first generation of the new wave, whose first novels seemed to reviewers to form some kind of group, were John Wain (with *Hurry On Down* in 1953), Kingsley Amis (with *Lucky Jim* in 1954), and Iris Murdoch (with *Under the Net* in the same year). The common factor was a cheerful desire to cock a snook at respectable society, at safe, middle-class professions, at dull provincial institutions. The typical hero is middle-class himself, but alienated from it, pricking its pretensions both social and cultural. Lucky Jim at the madrigal-singing party of his repulsive professor, Welch, is a typical fifties hero in a typical predicament. The tone of the books is anti-Establishment taking that word in its usual specific sense (the people who hold the reins of power, who occupy the influential, opinion-forming positions in the nation at large), and in its more general one (those who sit on any sort of plum job, and have a degree of patronage to dish out). Lucky Jim has to keep in well with his professor as well as pretend to write his all-too-typical thesis throwing 'pseudo-light . . . on non-problems;' inevitably, as a fifties hero, he proves inept at both tasks. Typically too, he walks off at the end of the novel with the pneumatic blonde from the metropolis, where a cushy job awaits him. Fantasy, obviously, is already entering in; what is more dangerous, the justified rebellion and snook-cocking seem to end in nothing more than rejecting the phoney and embracing the meretricious.

More interesting, perhaps, was what happened with the next wave of new novelists, in the later fifties. Representative debuts may be taken to be John Braine's, with the immensely popular *Room at the Top* (1957), Alan Sillitoe's with *Saturday Night and Sunday Morning* (1958) and *The Loneliness of the Long-Distance Runner* (1959) and Stan Barstow's with *A Kind of Loving* (1960). The heroes of these books are no more angry than their predecessors, but they are all, like their authors, born working-class. Braine's hero, type man for the fifties, claws his way up to glossy affluence; Barstow's settles reluctantly into dull job and dull marriage. The heroes of Sillitoe (1928–   ) are the most interesting, and his career has shown the most staying power. Arthur Seaton spends his Saturday nights drinking, fighting and sleeping with married women. He voices hatred and rebellion, of a joyously wholesale kind, hating the union foreman as much as the bosses, the woman next door as much as the army. He is a natural anarchist, but his anarchism is a form of egotism – a hatred of anything that interferes with his comfort, convenience and his male chauvinist code. That he is not going to find it too difficult to conform to the affluent society is shown by his joy in his pay-packet and his wardrobe full of sharp clothes. Smith, the long-distance runner in what is Sillitoe's most perfectly achieved piece of fiction to date, has a less ego-based, more philosophically worked out anarchism – indeed the image of the practice run, paralleling his working through to an understanding of his social credo, is brilliant and memorable.

Neither hero, it is important to emphasize, is an author-surrogate, neither code is fully endorsed, but the mixture of involvement and judgment is beautifully managed. Sillitoe is often thought of as an instinctive working-class tale-spinner whose work declined the further he got from his source of inspiration, but this is a condescending over-simplification. Certainly some of his later work is very disappointing, and he has proved to be a hit and miss writer who does not seem to be able to judge when he has a good subject (or even when he has a subject at all). But the late *Widower's Son* (1976), a mature and compassionate novel, is comparable in quality with his early work, and the title story of his collection *Guzman Go Home* is as brilliant a piece of virtuosity and ventriloquism as one has seen in the modern short story. A dreary English pair, from the fringes of the art world, are stranded in a Spanish village and forced to listen to the *apologia pro vita sua* of Guzman, an ex-Nazi who has taken refuge in Franco's Spain. It is an exercise comparable to a Browning dramatic monologue, where the indefensible is defended, and where the hopelessly tarnished character seems infinitely more alive and attractive than the upright and right-thinking. Sillitoe's working-class Nottingham tales, then, by no means represent the whole of him.

Most of the 'angry' or 'protest' novels of the fifties sat more or less comfortably in the realistic tradition. But dissatisfaction with the limits of realism was very evident before the decade was over. Already in her second novel, *The Flight from the Enchanter*, Iris Murdoch (1919–) was wriggling away from the Angry Young Man group (triply inaccurate, in her case), and flirting with the unexplained, the dimly-suggested supernatural. Many of her later novels were to explore the hinterland between the solid world of everyday and a mysterious, unknowable world that impinges on it. This trend culminates in *The Sea, the Sea* (1978), a long, sensuous, tantalizing novel of memory and quest, in which reality and illusion are delicately poised, and the supernatural at times assumes palpable form.

Murdoch was not the only novelist who tried to import into the novel the sort of freedom from realistic shackles that had hitherto been enjoyed mainly by the very special sub-genres of 'Gothic' or 'ghost' story. Many, if not most, of the novels of Muriel Spark (1918–) blithely mingle the real and the paranormal: in *Memento Mori* a mysterious voice, unexplained, warns the old people in the novel that they must die; in *The Ballad of Peckham Rye* the central catalyst of the story, Dougal Douglas, acquires the conventional attributes of the devil, including horns. Even when these novelists remain, apparently, within the real world they manage to import a flavour of mystery, of the unknown. In Murdoch's *A Severed Head*, a Restoration comedy-style sexual dance involving much changing of partners, the figure of Honor Klein acquires a sinister power much beyond what might be explained by her profession of Freudian psychiatrist. And in Spark's *The Prime of Miss Jean Brodie* (1961) the cavalier treatment of time, the constant shifting backwards and forwards in the lives of the Edinburgh schoolgirls and their form mistress, gives the novel a fluidity which is tantalizing, and endows the author with a more than usually God-like omniscience.

Jean Brodie is the teacher of every school-child's dream — fascinating in herself, cavalier towards school authorities and discipline, scornful of littleness, meanness and the duller institutions of childhood: 'For those who like that sort of thing,' she says disdainfully of the Girl Guides, 'that is the sort of thing they like.' As the novel progresses (if that is the word) we gradually see that Miss Brodie is a Fascist of private life, one whose apparently 'advanced' notions cover a very primitive form of power lust. She plays God with the lives of her 'set,' determining in her mind their futures, and she would be dangerous were it not for the fact that, in Spark's treatment of them, schooldays seem to be the most irrelevant days of our lives. At puberty the girls cast off her influence effortlessly, and take directions quite unsuspected by her. The sad, final picture of her is horrifying: querulous and broken she winges on about which of the girls 'betrayed' her and ruined her career. These books of the late fifties and early sixties are Spark's great achievement. It was only with *Loitering With Intent* (1981), when she ceased dealing with the hideously boring international super-rich and returned to an English setting and the period of her early writing days, that she regained some of her power to dazzle and to (the word is used advisedly) charm.

It was in the late sixties that Bernard Bergonzi, in *The Situation of the Novel*, complained about the plethora of safe, formula novels with unambitious themes: 'sensitive, rather neurotic girl, living in an Earls Court bedsitter and having sexual difficulties,' and so on. But in retrospect it seems in fact to have been precisely in the sixties that British fiction began to tackle again the larger themes and canvases: this was the period of Lessing's *Golden Notebook*, of Olivia Manning's first trilogy and of Paul Scott's Raj Quartet. To these may be added several of the works of Anthony Burgess (1917–1993), a rich, productive, idiosyncratic writer, who produced fictions that are like none of his contemporaries' fictions, and often like none of his own previous ones. He was incapable of playing safe. Through his books stride the figures of great men – Keats in *Abba, Abba*, Napoleon in *Napoleon Symphony*, practically every notable in twentieth-century cultural life in *Earthly Powers* (1980). He produced one of the best pictures of the British Empire in retreat in his Malayan Trilogy, and achieved an unlikely popular success with *A Clockwork Orange* (1962). Taking as his starting point the violence of modern Western society – and intellectuals' tolerance of violence was to be vividly exemplified in that very decade – Burgess projected a nightmare futuristic world of gang violence and institutionalized violence. He did so in a language invented for the purpose, a dazzling conflation of jargon and slang. The central character, a teenage thug, is both monster and victim, and, as in all good Utopian or Dystopian novels, the reader's emotions are disturbed, his preconceptions upset, in ways that no realistic novel can achieve.

Doris Lessing (1919–　) is no mean Dystopian writer herself, but her major achievement remains *The Golden Notebook* (1962) and the *Children of Violence* sequence, both solidly autobiographical. Lessing was taken up by the seventies feminist movement as some kind of guru (a process she resisted, and which must have been a great embarrassment), but this emphasis seriously distorted her achievement. Women's role and potential are always seen in Lessing in the largest possible social context, and are part, not the whole, of her analysis and vision. The *Children of Violence* sequence sometimes repels in its early stages by the petulant self-absorption of its central character, but there can be no doubt about its impressive scope, passing from racialism in a colonial possession, through post-war communism to (in the last volume) an age in which nuclear catastrophe is imminent, and the 'mad' are the seers and survivors (Lessing has been greatly influenced by the theories of R. D. Laing). The form of *The Golden Notebook* is fluid, experimental. The central character, Anna Wulf, is a novelist in a state of writer's block and a person near breakdown, ravaged and uncertain in her sexual, familial and social relationships, disillusioned in her political commitment. The literal progress of her crisis is interrupted by excerpts from her notebooks, which fictionalize her life, relate it to her political stance and to cataclysmic world events, and provide material for her course of psychoanalysis. The fragmentary, blocked life is righted in the final golden notebook (not, perhaps, the most satisfactory part of the novel). The whole provides a multi-dimensional portrait of this particular woman, and of the pressures on women, particularly feminists, in the later twentieth century – all seen in the context of world events which are both shaping our lives and taking away individual powers of decision. As Joan Didion observes, Lessing is a writer who has been drawn in different directions by her 'impulse to final solutions.' It seems irrelevant at this point to ask whether *The Golden Notebook* quite comes together to form a consistent artistic whole: it was – and remains thirty years on – an immensely important book for our times.

The dominant preoccupation of those novelists who attempted the larger canvas in the sixties and seventies was a re-examination of Britain's past, of her imperial greatness and her periods of moral authority. It was a re-examination prompted, obviously enough, by Britain's shrunken international role, her tatty and chaotic political life, her determined self-denigration throughout these decades. It was paralleled, in popular literature, by the immensely popular spy stories of John Le Carré, obsessed with *trahison des clercs*, betrayal from within – an obsession which has spilled over on to the stage, in such plays as Alan Bennett's *The Old Country* and Julian Mitchell's *Another Country* (1982). The novel sequences by Scott, Farrell and Olivia Manning take a larger view, and a more humane one.

Olivia Manning (1911–1980) deals in her Balkan and Levantine trilogies with historical events (the war, by then over for a quarter century or more), but also with the personal conflicts of her own early married life. Still less than Lessing does she disguise the autobiographical nature of her enterprise. The first trilogy centres on the lightly disguised pair. Guy and Harriet Pringle, he a British Council lecturer in a Rumanian university. By the end of the second volume the inexorable German stranglehold over Rumania has forced them to flee to Greece; by the end of the third, German invasion has meant a nightmare voyage to Egypt. In the second trilogy, they are closer to the theatre of war. Feeling, rightly, that she could not base a further series entirely on the marital ups and (mostly) downs of Guy and Harriet, Manning diversifies interest with another central character. Simon Boulderstone, a young British soldier fighting in North Africa. Though this presents some structural problems, what cannot be doubted is that Manning proves herself a brilliant military novelist. An interesting comparison here is with Evelyn Waugh, whose *Sword of Honour* trilogy (1952–61) covers some of the same ground, and was surely an inspiration to Manning. Waugh, himself a combatant presents a wonderful picture of the pressures and hysteria of battle but the overall strategic pattern eludes the reader.

Manning is also good on the blood and sweat, but she presents the larger pattern with great clarity, and with such simplicity of means that the non-combatant feels he has grasped the progress of a campaign.

The typical Manning situation is one of limbo: countries not quite at war and not quite at peace; characters who are married, but with none of the 'settled' qualities of the married state. Her characters are always 'between' states. The triumph of the two trilogies lies in the intersection of the personal with the larger movements of politics, war and world-shattering change. A recent reviewer called Guy 'a sort of secular saint' and Harriet a nagging, irritating body. To me Guy is a deluded egotist who, while seeming to be used by his friends, in fact uses them to bolster his self-love and his empty political idealism: Harriet is the inevitable marital victim. It is a tribute to the evenhandedness of Manning's narrative stance that two such judgments can be made. Around these two flows a continuously entertaining stream of minor characters – exiled Russians, academics, Jews, soldiers. Manning's admiration, unfashionably, is reserved for the soldiers: cheerful, earthy, doing their duty in the face of death and every kind of deprivation. Her contempt is for the odious British Council parasites who cluster round and betray Guy – feeble, blustering cowards who use pacifism and communism as a shield for personal inadequacy or turpitude. Always the characterization, even at its most devastating, is economical, as are her methods of conveying world events: ominous arrows on the maps of the British and German propaganda offices in Bucharest, pins on maps in Cairo, inform us of the progress of the war; the singing of *Capitanul* the Fascist anthem, sounds throughout the first trilogy, first distant and rather ridiculous, then progressively louder, closer and more menacing. No other book conveys quite as involvingly as Manning's just what it is like to live through a cataclysmic change in the world order.

Something of Manning's economy, one feels, would have benefited the *Raj Quartet* of Paul Scott (1920–1978), which is magisterial, solid, but which by the fourth volume undoubtedly has its longueurs. Its starting-point, in *The Jewel in the Crown*, is the apparent rape of a white girl in war-time India. Thus the Quartet begins in daring, for what author would not fear comparison with Forster's *A Passage to India*? In the course of the later novels the events open out, but the rape remains somewhere there at the back of things. In his reappraisal of the British imperial role, Scott has no time for the bull-headed, prejudiced stereotypes who represent British officialdom in Forster's book. The novel has a British villain, certainly, in Ronald Merrick, a repressed, perverted, disturbing creation. But the bulk of the British Raj are responsible, not unimaginative, and in some cases genuinely love India. But it is a love – and here we recall Forster's conclusion – that is frustrated by the positions of rulers and ruled. In his large cast of soldiers, missionaries, native princes and politicians, outcasts, there are many who are well-meaning, few who can translate good intentions into concrete results. Even the independence of India is a defeat for those who have loved and meant best by her, for the partition of the country into two seems a betrayal of those ideals of racial harmony which they tried to establish, a defeat for the view that differing people can live together in peace. It is a pessimistic vision that the central rape provides an image for, and only the child who is a result *not* of the rape, but of sex with the girl's Indian lover immediately before, provides some hope for the future. But the lover himself is the saddest figure in the books – an Indian brought up in England, where he feels accepted, but brought back to India where he is accepted neither by Indians nor by British expatriates. He is one of a line of dispatriated figures in our literature, a feature of our age of large-scale emigrations.

The career as a novelist of J. G. Farrell (1935–1979) was begun by poliomyelitis, in the years it forced him to spend in an iron lung, and ended by the same disease, when it prevented his saving himself from drowning. Farrell's examination of Britain's imperial past resulted in three completed novels – *Troubles* (1970), *The Siege of Krishnapur* (1973) and *The Singapore Grip* (1978). He writes, as he said, about people 'undergoing' history, and in the swirl of large events the individual is always central, as are the minutiæ of everyday life; when the siege of Krishnapur is lifted, we prepare for reunion between the besieged Victorian girl and her sentimental admirer among the relieving forces; when at last they approach each other he staggers back at her stench. Farrell, typically, does not forget what happens to the body after weeks in an Indian town practically without water. His most complete and beguiling achievement is *Troubles*, set in the Irish 'troubles' of the early twenties, and written presciently before their present recurrence. Set in a decaying hotel, once splendid, lively and prosperous, now rotting, with room after room, section after section, becoming dangerous and uninhabitable, the setting is an image of Empire, but without portentous underlining on Farrell's part. The tone is urbane, inconsequent, funny, and the 'troubles' at first seem a distant murmur, an irrelevance. Indeed, until the end Farrell keeps full-scale violence to a minimum, but violence is there: a scene in which a cat savagely attacks an old lady's feathered hat is a shocking, unnerving eruption in the genteelly decaying atmosphere. The novel conveys the way human beings determinedly go on living, cling to illusions, take refuge from reality, while around them events are changing the shape of their future lives.

The works I have been talking about, the re-examination of Britain's immediate past, were being written in the late sixties or early seventies – the years of political violence, student revolution and the mass chanting of fatuities from Mao. It is a period which now seems very distant and very dead. Its leavings, in literary terms, are not very impressive, but its end was hastened by one superb work of demolition, *The History Man* by Malcolm Bradbury (1932–). His earlier novels *Eating People is Wrong* (1959) and *Stepping Westward* (1965) were funny, farcical, overlong university novels which did not quite prepare one for the concentrated brilliance of his novel for the seventies. Howard Kirk, the 'history man,' is a sociologist, an opportunist wearing the mask of idealism, determined to ride ahead on the wave of history. His clothes, his ideas, his speech are the clothes, ideas and speech of today, certified acceptable by the radical journals and the trendy Sunday papers. The future, he knows, is his, and he merely manipulates things now and then to hurry the future on a little. If people – the tired old liberals with worn-out, muddled consciences, for example – get destroyed in the process, well, they really shouldn't stand in the way of History. Howard is a creation of his times: ten years before he was a mousey research student; ten years later he would vote for Margaret Thatcher. *Now* he is in the radical vanguard. 'Now' is the word the novel begins with, and it is narrated, densely and with constant use of fashionable cliché and the jargon of pop sociology, in the present tense – a present tense that, camera-like, records actions but never thoughts. The treatment of Howard's wife Barbara is especially brilliant: at first she seems to be the mirror image of Howard – tireless fighter for such causes as The Children's Crusade for Abortion and No Sex for Repression – but we soon see that she is sufficiently distanced from him to judge him cynically: 'Howard Kirk . . . what we have instead of faith.' In the middle of the book we come within an ace of getting into her mind, in a brief, tender episode with her lover in London. The novel ends as she repeats at a final party an incident that had happened to one of the decaying liberals at an earlier one: she breaks a window and draws her wrist across the jagged glass. Violence, like fashion, is imitative and cyclical. Nobody hears the noise.

The History Man single-mindedly, with great comic gusto, directs its fire on the one target, the fashionable, ruthless radicalism of the time, and, like Dryden's *Absalom and Achitophel*, it has all the urgency that comes from being written in the thick of the struggle.

The feminist movement coincided and coalesced with the radical excursions of the late sixties, but it survived longer; and its results – in practical and in literary terms – were infinitely more valuable. Britain produced few propagandist feminist novelists, high on ideology, analysis and 'solutions.' The feminist novelist in Britain tended to be allusive, satirical, needling their way under encrusted layers of prejudice and arrogant assumptions. The older generation of women novelists – Edna O'Brien, for example, or Penelope Mortimer – had in fact been doing this for years. The younger feminists did not very often depart from the traditional areas of women's writing: marriage, home, children, the fight to assert individuality. To that extent it may be said that Olivia Manning is a more hopeful portent for the future than any of them. But they deal with these areas in a spirit and tone that is widely different from that of the traditional 'sensitive' woman writer; and, without being ideologues, they are conscious that in the air there is an ideology that backs them up. The three younger woman writers I have chosen are very various, and perhaps all they have in common is that feminists have found them interesting.

Margaret Drabble (1939–) has been the most admired and popular of the younger generation. Her success has been attributed to all sorts of reasons but the right one, her immensely involving gift of narrative. It is very easy – one or two reviewers do it regularly – to take a chunk of Drabble prose and pull it to pieces, pointing to the loose syntax, the repetition, the tired vocabulary. In isolation the demonstration looks unanswerable, but put the chunk back into the novel and you find it works perfectly well. For what distinguishes Drabble is the button-holing, compulsive nature of her narrative voice. She is like a stranger telling you a story on a train, telling it with no apparent artifice, yet riveting your attention and establishing through her story a close and warm relation with you, the listener. Drabble's subjects have been traditional (*The Ice Age* was an unsuccessful exception), but in her treatments she has never gone in for easy options or the sentimental way out. In *Jerusalem the Golden* we sympathize with the heroine from an arid, love-starved Northern home, understand her enthusiastic embracing of swinging London and the glamorous chic of the Denham family. But we see through the fragile shell of this glamour, and we note the hardness she has acquired in her determination to cast off her childhood world. Drabble has never lost the backbone which is the relic of her Puritan upbringing, and it gives an unfashionable moral toughness to her books. It means, too, that she always makes things hard for herself artistically. The two central characters of *The Needle's Eye* are a 'poor little rich girl' figure who years before has featured in a scandalous elopement, and a lawyer specializing in defending Trade Unions involved in 'closed shop' disputes. It is difficult to think of two figures less likely to arouse sympathy or involvement, yet Drabble compels us into both. And in her treatment of them she never takes the expected line. Her heroine has given away her money to a poor African state, but done it so ineffectually that it has evaporated in corruption – yet her action is approved. Her ex-husband is trying to get their children away from her, so they can be 'better' educated, but he and his motives are treated with understanding. In the end, the heroine, who has acquired something approaching saintliness in the course of the narrative, goes back to her husband, knowing that she will be less happy, less good, a worse mother as a result. Her motives are complex, but among them certainly is a George Eliotish feeling that one does not dodge one's mistakes, that all real relationships involve hurt. Here, as in all her best books, Drabble combines a sharp eye for the contemporary scene with an almost Victorian insistence that a life without moral standards is meaningless, chaotic, degrading.

A moral imperative of any sort would hardly know what to do with itself in the world of Beryl Bainbridge (1933–   ). Her books are peopled with sloppy and slapdash women, half-hearted lovers, families that seem strangers to each other – all made funny by a style that is a most engaging deadpan, relating the outrageous as if it were the everyday. For into her world of muddling-on, of low expectations and lower achievements, there erupts, as often as not, violence. And the eruption is treated as if it were as normal as the milk delivery. If, for once, there is no one killed in one of her books, or no incursion of terrorists, there is nevertheless a feeling of violence simmering, implicit. *A Quiet Life*, the most autobiographical of her books, depicts a 'normal' suburban family, in a 'normal' home – but the very clutteredness of the middle-class household presents threats of danger and injury, and the impotent furies of 'father' become like the ravings of a Fascist dictator. Bainbridge is the poet of half-hearted relationships – querulous, unsatisfactory, teetering on the absurd. The first chapter of *Injury Time*, with the telephone conversation of the dyspeptic businessman and his two-evenings-a-week lover, is pure Bainbridge. Never was there a love affair that involved less passion, or that seemed so certain of imminent collapse: 'He knew at once it was Binny, because when he said Hello there was no reply, merely a sort of offended breathing.' Bainbridge characters, unlike Drabble's, never aspire to any sort of moral wholeness, or to ecstasy. If they have a moment of vision (as the central character in *Winter Garden* (1980) has a vision in Leningrad of the scene of Pushkin's death in a duel, hears the clashing of swords), we know that eventually, subterraneanly, the vision will be undercut (the duel was actually with pistols). Nor will Bainbridge's books ever have an ending as such: they are chunks of wry, funny, second-rate living, and what will go on after the novel finishes is more of the same.

Human relationships, especially male-female ones, are hardly more satisfactory in the novels of Fay Weldon (1933–   ), but the style of conveying them is very different. Realistic surface, reader identification, mean nothing to her: she goes all out to avoid them by the style of her story-telling – full of artifice, studded with repetitions that almost gain the status of ritual chants, an ostentatious balancing and patterning, and a constant addressing of the reader. Her novels are like tapestries or ikons, and they convey their message through their design. Her style is Jane Austenish irony, hardened, sharpened into a brutal cutting instrument. She is also very funny. Her novels are novels about the wrongs of women, but she inhabits a domain a hundred miles from Bleeding Heart Yard, and she does not demand empathy or compassion. She invites ridicule, anger, contempt. Only through them is there any hope of change. Her novels are battle-grounds of exploiters and exploited, but she asks no easy sympathy for the latter. In *Praxis* (1978) the most totally bitchy character becomes the feminist who changes Praxis's life. Weldon sees no future in shedding easy tears in the path of people like the narrator's dead mother in *Female Friends:*

> The soles of her poor slippers, which I took out from under the bed and threw away so as not to shame her in front of the undertaker, were quite worn through by dutiful shuffling. Flip-flop. Slipper-slop. Drifting and dusting a life away.

Weldon is a dazzling stylist, a mistress of brittle artifice, and perhaps the funniest writer of her generation.

So insistently did Margaret Thatcher claim to be the dominant force not just of her cabinet and party but of the decade itself, with tabloid talk of Thatcher*ism*, of her having put an end to this, created a new that, that it is tempting simply to say that under her leadership the British economy veered drunkenly from boom to bust and back again very much as it had done since the fifties, the main difference being that the busts were bigger and more dreadful in their social consequences. There is much truth in such reductivism, faced with journalistic myths of fairy-tale transformations. When she became Prime Minister unemployment had never since the war reached one million. In the mid-eighties it exceeded three million, and when she was toppled from office in 1990 after a party rebellion and a back-room coup it was headed that way again.

Nevertheless it is certainly true that Margaret Thatcher, if not her spurious 'ism,' had a great effect on many areas of British life. Though there was much talk about giving power back to the people the tendency of her governments was consistently centrist, with Whitehall taking powers at the expense of local government and regional authorities. A combination of mass unemployment and restrictive legislation left the trade unions a spent force, probably the most generally popular of the changes during her period of office. One after another the state industries were privatized, and if they were little regretted by the British public, the private monopolies that were their successors aroused little respect or affection, which is perhaps in the nature of monopolies. There were a series of shake-ups in state education and the health service, putting the emphasis on 'market forces,' leading to head-teachers who were as much managers as leaders, and medical decisions being taken by non-medical staff. The decade marked an ever-widening gap between rich and poor, with homelessness and vagrancy endemic and an apparently unstoppable crime wave. Though the racially-inspired riots of the early eighties were not repeated later on, the poll tax, a ludicrous replacement for the old rates system, united many sections of society in civil disobedience, and was a major cause of Thatcher's downfall.

There was a large degree of consensus among creative artists of all kinds (apart from a few self-consciously belligerent elderly figures such as Kingsley Amis) which opposed the government, in particular its policies in education and towards the arts. This opposition, in the midst of tabloid jubilation and celebration, sometimes gave writers the air of being voices crying in the wilderness.

Many of the novelists of the sixties and seventies were, by the eighties, running out of steam. From *The Ice Age* (1977) onwards Margaret Drabble's novels began to seem repetitive in their themes and narrowed in their range of characters. Similarly Fay Weldon, though never losing her bravura, began to give readers the feeling that this was a performance they had watched before. One of the most admired fiction writers of the seventies was Ian McEwan (1948–), particularly in his two short story collections *First Love, Last Rites* (1975) and *In Between the Sheets* (1978). These chronicled, in extraordinarily supple prose, episodes of sexual awakening, casual cruelty, social decay. His transition to the novel, like Angus Wilson's thirty years earlier, was an uneasy one. Too often he chose to write prose that was unemphatic to the point of dullness to recount events of a sensational or horrific nature. Perhaps the most successful of the novels is *The Comfort of Strangers* (1981). A young couple, in a loving but slightly stale relationship, walk the streets of Venice on a holiday that has lasted too long and become routine, even boring. The maze of streets – confusing, disorientating, full of dead ends – seems to mirror the point the relationship has reached. Their encounter with a Venetian who apparently wants to take them under his wing introduces them to a milieu worlds away from the tourist trails, a world where power and cruelty dominate, though this is conveyed for the most part through sinister hints. At first the encounter seems to stimulate their decaying love for each other, particularly in its sexual side, but as the sinister hints begin to harden into uncomfortable realities they find themselves headed inexorably towards disaster. This is an unnerving book in which atmosphere, setting and character fit together and hold the reader in a grip of claustrophobic tension.

A. N. Wilson (1950–) has been providing elegant and thoughtful fictional entertainments for nearly two decades now, while simultaneously developing a public persona as a 'young fogey' – a three-piece-suited man of unfashionably backward-looking views. The books are best read with the persona pushed firmly out of the mind, because the two do not coalesce. There are few more reliable performers, whether he is observing the contemporary scene or recreating a historical one. In *Gentlemen of England* (1985) he brings to life the sexual tensions of late-Victorian England in his portrait of an empty marriage and an ill-starred, slightly ludicrous love affair. One's only doubt is whether he brings to the telling much that is new or revelatory – much, that is, that the later-Victorian novelists, who dealt often enough with such subjects, would not also have brought to it. *The Healing Art* (1980) has a simple but striking central situation: a woman is diagnosed as suffering from cancer but refuses the modern treatments for it. As the novel progresses we realize that there has been a medical or clerical error, and she has been mixed up with a woman who has been mistakenly diagnosed as cancer-free. The subject is handled sympathetically, and Wilson, through his clear-eyed understanding of the predicament and issues, manages to build up some of the page-turning qualities of popular fiction.

Who was Oswald Fish? (1981) is a rumbustious, capacious novel in the comic Dickensian mode. It encompasses several worlds, but it hinges on Fanny Williams, an earthy, generous, loud woman who has had her five minutes of fame as a model and pop-star in the sixties, and who now runs a chain of boutiques merchandising pseudo-Victorian tat. She is altern-ately exhilarating and irritating, or both simultaneously. Her obsession with the one architectural masterpiece of Oswald Fish brings her first into conflict but rapidly into bed with a Birmingham civil servant. As the novel progresses we find that not only the civil servant and Fanny herself but almost everyone else of importance in the novel, including her black homosexual lodger, are related to the Fish family – a joyous and wholesale extension of Dickens's coincidental discovery of hidden relationships. Implied comments and comparisons abound in the book on the progression from Victorian faith and tormented sexuality to modern sexual licence and trivialization of the spiritual dimension. The novel sweeps one along with a generosity and verve not unlike that of its heroine. The climax is predictable and the conclusion perfunctory, and one sometimes has doubts whether Wilson is completely at home in all the worlds he deals with, but these are doubts for after the book has been put down. It ends appropriately with a comic epitaph for an era: Mrs Thatcher on the steps of Downing Street intoning in a voice 'the product of goodness knows how many elocution lessons' the words of St Francis of Assisi. Thus ends, he seems to say, the sexy, wayward, iconoclastic era of the sixties and seventies.

A decade later, as the Thatcher years drew to their close, A. N. Wilson discarded his Christian faith and became the provider of 'thoughts' for the popular press. Martin Amis (1949–   ), never a media figure, travelled in a very different direction, from stylized novels of sexual decadence such as *Dead Babies* (1975) to more ambitious and searching analyses of nuclear madness and global decay. *London Fields* (1989) was one of the most admired novels of the decade. It is set in a London of the near-future, one experiencing a growing breakdown of law and order, a climatological and environmental crisis and burgeoning sickness and deformity – familiar territory in seventies and eighties fiction, but used with a chilling casual mastery here. The central thrust of the plot traces Nicola Six as she progresses (like the central character in Muriel Spark's sixties novella *The Driver's Seat*) to her destined and desired fate as 'murderee,' each stage plotted with the meticulousness of a crime writer, and with a 'surprise' solution that will astonish no reader of Agatha Christie. The men in Nicola's life include the basically (or supposedly) decent Guy Clinch and the working-class yob Keith Talent. Observing the progress of the murder plot is the failed American writer Sam Young.

Keith Talent, with his obsession with darts and booze, his frequent and boasted-of copulations and his argot that ranges from semi-literate linguistic gestures to the prose of the tabloid sports reports is a monster. The cliché is 'authentic monster,' yet that seems here to be inapt. His speech is an intensely-willed literary confection which never quite convinces and coheres, as it needs to do if this mindless monster is to make his necessary impact. In fact, obsessively 'nasty' as they so often are, Martin Amis's novels always seem to be literary artifacts, pieces on the printed page, rather than convincing pictures of imagined worlds. Similarly his prose, often vivid and brilliant, seems willed, with an intensity that is self-regarding, almost self-congratulatory. It comes to seem almost an end in itself, which may partly explain why the book is so much longer than it needs to be – though this is a phenomenon of the eighties, possibly answering to a public demand, possibly a result of the word-processor.

One of the strongest elements in eighties fiction was the embracing of what came to be called 'magic realism.' The major influence here were the South American writers, particularly Gabriel García Marquéz – though it is worth reminding the reader that in Britain writers like Muriel Spark and Fay Weldon were making extensive use of the super-natural and other magic elements long before the South Americans were being widely read here. One of the foremost 'magical' writers was Angela Carter (1940–1992). Her all-too-brief career began with Swift-ian fables charged with sex, sadism and other marketable ingredients which made a high-gloss product irresistible to many, distasteful to some. The great advance came with *Nights at the Circus* (1984), a chronicle of the life and adventures, natural and supernatural, of the music-hall and circus performer Fevvers. The opening chapter, with an American journalist interviewing Fevvers in her dressing room, blends the realistic and the unaccountable with a brilliance none of her British contemporaries could match. But the success of magic realism depends crucially on the writer not using the suspension of natural laws as an excuse for indiscipline, and later in the book the reader's patience is tested by a surfeit of the irrational which has led to chaos.

Carter's masterpiece is her last novel *Wise Children* (1991). Once again we are in a theatrical setting, as we hear from one half of a song-and-dance team of twins the story of their life in the English theatre and music hall, a story which broadens in scope to include the legitimate theatre, through the twins' relationship with their (putative) father, Sir Melchior Hazard, a grand (if distinctly phoney) knight of the Shakespearean stage. On the day of his one hundredth birthday the memories of his elderly daughters range over their careers and his (some distinctly odd chronology may be put down to their defective memories by the charitable), and take in their brief encounters with the unacknowledging father and his three wives. The book is a celebration of the theatre, its generosity and egotism, its love and lust, its falsity and its quest for truth of a kind. It is also, as its title implies, a study of relationships – parental and filial, but ranging far beyond that and embracing real and imagined ones, which merge as the theatre itself merges the two. Though the plot is instinct with glorious improbabilities throughout, the magic element only really explodes in the birthday party which ends the book. Nora and Dora, earthy, open-hearted, seeking, bitchy, uproarious, are likely to remain Angela Carter's most memorable fictional legacy. She died of cancer at the age of 51.

'Magic' enters *Waterland* (1983) by Graham Swift (1949–) at times, and in particular in the episode of the miraculously potent and destructive Atkinson's Coronation Ale of 1911, but this is an all-embracing novel, totally sure in tone, that switches backwards and forwards in time, takes in episodes of wildly contradictory natures, yet welds them to a satisfying whole. The nodal points of the novel are two episodes: in the 1980s the history teacher Tom Crick is being eased out of his job after his wife has brought bad publicity on the school by stealing a baby; forty years earlier, when the same Tom Crick was an adolescent indulging his curiosity about sex, the body of a boy was found bobbing in the waters of the fenland where he lived. But these two events are only starting points for a novel that ranges over the history, geography and natural history of the fens, concentrating especially on two families, the Cricks and the Atkinsons, a family of brewers. As this subtle and various novel proceeds we become conscious that what we are learning is not just a series of past events that explain the crisis in an elderly teacher's life, but an evocation of a whole region – its atmosphere, its social life, its very essence. So flexible are Swift's writing skills that the most disparate materials coalesce into a moving, disturbing yet illuminating whole. None of Swift's other novels to date have anything like the same power. When writers are said always to have one good novel in them it is usually thought to be an autobiographical one. In Swift's case it seems to be geographical.

It was in *Midnight's Children* (1981) by Salman Rushdie (1947–   ) that the so-called 'magic realism' most confidently and joyously took its place in the English novel tradition. Its Booker Prize and large sales showed that subject matter and treatment far from mainstream realism could capture an audience here. Significantly the book is built around a strong and attractive central idea: the children born on the stroke of midnight as India gained its independence. This link, fortuitous yet significant, forms the basis for events that are gloriously subversive of the normal order of things. At times the central character, Salim Sinai, is in paranormal communication with his fellow 'midnight's children,' though the relationship is not always friendly or fruitful. The link is only a small part in the multifarious magic of the novel, which is handled with an inventiveness, confidence and style that set Rushdie apart from most other British practitioners. With the inventiveness goes discipline, so that the paranormal elements never become an end in themselves but are a part of a picture of India – an 'alternative India,' if you will. The book is never a 'condition of India' novel in the sense that late Dickens novels are 'condition of England' ones, yet one finishes the book with the vividest sense of the variety, energy and oddity of the country, as well as of its physical feel, its smells, its weathers, its warm, infuriating relationships.

The Satanic Verses is marginally less successful, perhaps because the framework is less strong, less able to sustain the immense comic inventiveness. The miraculous survival of two passengers from an air crash and their subsequent adventures and metamorphoses are nevertheless chronicled with Rushdie's unquenchable zest and stylistic grace. His confidence, scope and vitality lead one to hope that, if he is spared, a totally new and enchanting strand of fiction may be woven by him.

It is tempting to end this new edition of the history, as I ended the first edition, with a few names of younger writers who would thus be in a way 'tipped' to go on to greater things. The names are there, in plenty, though perhaps we lack the two or three front-runners that seemed to push their way forward then. As I said then: all writers coming to the end of a survey such as this must experience some feeling of hope and gratitude at the new sproutings already showing through the soil, and feel relief in the knowledge that – barring accidental disasters, or disasters engineered by the idiocy of politicians – the end of his account is in fact no end.

Index

Page numbers given in bold face are main references.

Abba Abba (Burgess) 212
Absalom and Achitophel (Dryden)
  58–61, 217
Absentee, The (Edgeworth) 105
ADDISON, Joseph (1672–1719) 69, 75
Adonais (Shelley) 101
Æneid (Virgil) 10
Aestheticism 134
Agnes Grey (A. Brontë) 119
Aids to Reflection (Coleridge) 93–4
AINSWORTH, Harrison (1805–1882)
  122
Alexander's Feast (Dryden) 62
All for Love (Dryden) 57
Amelia (Fielding) 82
AMIS, Kingsley (1922–) 208, 220
AMIS, Martin (1949–) 222–3
Ancient Mariner, The Rime of (Coleridge)
  87, **94–6**, 98, 124
Andrea del Sarto (Browning) 127
Angel (E. Taylor) 207
Angel Pavement (Priestley) 178
Anglo-Saxon Attitudes (Angus Wilson) 206
Animal Farm (Orwell) 181–2
ANNE, Queen (1665–1714) (Reigned
  1702–1714) 64, 66
Annus Mirabilis (Dryden) 62
Another Country (Mitchell) 213
Antony and Cleopatra (Shakespeare) 17,
  33, 151

Apology for Poetry, The (Sidney) 11
Arcadia, The (Sidney) 11
ARDEN, John (1930–) 197
ARNOLD, Matthew (1822–1888)
  112, **129–30**, 145
As If By Magic (Angus Wilson) 206
As You Like It (Shakespeare) 26, 42
ASCHAM, Roger (1515–1568) 7, 10
Astrophel and Stella (Sidney) 11
AUBREY, John (1626–1697) 62
AUDEN, W. H. (1907–1973) 152,
  171, **173–4**, 183, 192
AUSTEN, Jane (1775–1817) 90,
  107–9, 119, 140, 157, 207, 219

Bagpipe Music (MacNeice) 174
BAINBRIDGE, Beryl (1933–)
  218–19
BALDWIN, Stanley (1867–1947) 23
BALE, John (1495–1563) 16
Balkan Trilogy, The (Manning) 213–14
Ballad of Peckham Rye, The (Spark) 210
Ballad of Reading Gaol (Wilde) **134–5**
Barchester Novels, The (Trollope) 120
BARSTOW, Stan (1928–) 209
Bartholomew Fair (Jonson) 37
'Beach at Falesa, The' (Stevenson) 143
BEAUMARCHAIS, Pierre Augustin
  Caron de (1732–1799) 71
BEAUMONT, Francis (1584–1616) **38**

Beaux' Stratagem, The (Farquhar) 58
BECKETT, Samuel (1906–1991) 194–5
BEHN, Aphra (1640–1689) 63, 74
BENNETT, Alan 213
BENNETT, Arnold (1867–1931) 156
Benthamism 111, 112, 113
Beppo (Byron) 99
Bermudas, The (Marvell) 51
Bingo (Bond) 197
BINYON, Laurence (1869–1943) 147
Biographia Literaria (Coleridge) 89,
    93–4
Bishop Orders his Tomb, The (Browning)
    128
BLAKE, William (1757–1827) 70, 73,
    88
Blaming (E. Taylor) 207
Bleak House (Dickens) 113–14, 165
'Bliss' (Mansfield) 170
BOLEYN, Anne (1504?–1536) 9
BOND, Edward (1934–) 197
BOSWELL, James (1740–1795) 71–2,
    86
BOWDLER, Dr Thomas (1754–1825)
    110
BOWEN, Elizabeth (1899–1973) 205
BRADBURY, Malcolm (1932–) 216
BRAINE, John (1922–)209
BRENTON, Howard 198
Bride of Lammermoor, The (W. Scott) 106
Brideshead Revisited (Waugh) 150, 176
Brief Lives (Aubrey) 62
Brighton Rock (Greene) 178–9
BRITTAIN, Vera (1893–1970) 147
BRONTE, Anne (1820–1849) 119
BRONTË, Charlotte (1816–1855) 75,
    117–18, 119
BRONTË, Emily (1818–1848) 111,
    118–19, 130, 160, 207
BRONTË Sisters 114, 116
BROOKE, Rupert (1887–1915) 146,
    147
BROWNING, Elizabeth Barrett
    (1806–1861) 129
BROWNING, Robert (1812–1889)
    125, 126–9, 210

BUCHAN, John (1875–1940) 175
BUNYAN, John (1628–1688) 5, 45,
    62–3
BURGESS, Anthony (1917–1993)
    211–12
BURNEY, Frances ('Fanny')
    (1752–1840) 83–4
BURNS, Robert (1759–1796)   72–3
BUTLER, Samuel (1835–1902) 132,
    134, 187
BYRON, Lord (1788–1824) 33, 85,
    87, 89, 98–100, 101, 105, 106, 109,
    117, 130
Byzantium (Yeats) 154, 155

Calisto and Melebea (Rastell) 15
CAMPBELL, Roy (1902–1957) 174
Canterbury Tales, The (Chaucer) 2–4
CARLYLE, Thomas (1795–1881) 129
CARTER, Angela (1940–1992) 223–4
CARY, Joyce, (1888–1957) 179–80
Caste (Robertson) 185
CASTIGLIONE, Baldassare
    (1478–1529) 7, 10
Castle Rackrent (Edgeworth) 105
CAXTON, William (1422?–1491) 5
CECIL, Lord David (1902–) 49, 208
Changeling, The (Middleton) 40
CHARLES I, King (1600–1649)
    (Reigned 1625–1649) 46, 51
CHARLES II, King (1630–1685)
    (Reigned 1660–1685) 40, 46, 52–3,
    54, 59–62
CHAUCER, Geoffrey (1340?–1400) 1,
    2–4, 5, 6, 7, 8, 11, 12, 33, 45, 62,
    74, 85
CHEKHOV, Anton (1860–1904) 9
CHESTERFIELD, Lord (1694–1773)
    66, 72
CHETTLE, Henry 22
Childe Harold (Byron) 98–9
Children of Violence (Lessing) 212
Christabel (Coleridge) 94, 97, 103
CHRISTIE, Agatha (1891–1976) 175,
    223
Church Going (Larkin) 202

CHURCHILL, Caryl (1938–) **198–9**
CHURCHILL, Sir Winston
(1874–1965) 11
Churning Day (Heaney) 204
Civil War, The (1642) 40, 46, 58, 64
Clarissa Harlowe (Richardson) **79**
Clockwork Orange, A (Burgess) 212
Cloud, The (Shelley) 101
CLOUGH, Arthur Hugh (1819–1861)
130–1
Cocktail Party, The (T. S. Eliot) 192
COLERIDGE, Samuel Taylor
(1772–1834) 87, 89, **93–7**, 98, 100,
103, 106
COLET, John (1467?–1519) 7
COLLIER, Jeremy (1650–1726) 57–8
COLLINS, Wilkie (1824–1889) 122
Comfort of Strangers, The (McEwan) 221
Communist to Others, A (Auden) 173
Comus (Milton) 47, 49
CONGREVE, William (1670–1729)
56–7, 196
CONRAD, Joseph (1857–1924) 145,
158–62
CORNFORD, John (1915–1936) 172
Corsair, The (Byron) 99
Country Wife, The (Wycherley) **54–6**
Courtier, The (Castiglione) 7, 10
COWARD, Noel (1899–1973) 187, **191**
COWPER, William (1731–1800) 70
Cranford (Gaskell) 120
CRASHAW, Richard (1612?–1649) 46
CRAWFORD, Thomas 105
Crime and Punishment (Dostoevsky) 143
CROMWELL, Oliver (1599–1658) 40,
50, 51, 52, 58
Culture and Anarchy (Arnold) 129
CUNARD, Nancy (1896–1965) 174

Dance to the Music of Time, A (Powell) 205
Dancing at Lughnasa (Friel) **199–200**
Darkness Visible (Golding) 206
DARWIN, Charles (1809–1882) 111,
132
'Daughters of the Late Colonel, The'
(Mansfield) 170

David Copperfield (Dickens) 113
DAY LEWIS, Cecil (1904–1972) 171,
173
Dead Babies (M. Amis) 222
Decline and Fall (Waugh) 176
DEFOE, Daniel (1660?–1731) 63,
76–8, 80
DEKKER, Thomas (1570?–1632) 38
DELANEY, Shelagh (1939–) **194**
Deserted Village, The (Goldsmith) 70–1
Destiny (Edgar) 198
DICKENS, Charles (1812–1870) 23,
38, 81, **112–14**, 118, 121, 122,
132, 143, 157, 165, 175, 180, 222,
225
Dictionary of the English Language, A
(Johnson) 64, 72
DIDION, Joan 213
'Dill Pickle, A' (Mansfield) 169
DISRAELI, Benjamin (1804–1881)
120, 122
Doctor Faustus (Marlowe) 19, 21
Don Juan (Byron) 80, **99–100**
DONNE, John (1572–1631) 12,
41–5, 46, 51
Dover Beach (Arnold) 130
DOYLE, Sir Arthur Conan
(1859–1930) 144
DRABBLE, Margaret (1939–) 180,
217–18, 219, 221
Driver's Seat, The (Spark) 223
DRYDEN, John (1631–1700) 44, 57,
58–62, 65, 68, 217
Dubliners, The (Joyce) 169
Duchess of Malfi, The (Webster) **38–40**
DUNBAR, William (1460?–1520?) 6
Dunciad, The (Pope) 69

Earthly Powers (Burgess) 212
Easter 1916 (Yeats) 154
Easter Rising, The (1916) 153
Eating People is Wrong (Bradbury) 216
EDGAR, David (1948–) **198**
EDGEWORTH, Maria (1767–1849)
105
Edward II (Marlowe) 20, 21, 24

EDWARD III, King (1312–1377)
(Reigned 1327–1377) 1, 5
'Elegie: Going to Bed' (Donne) 43
Elegy Written in a Country Churchyard
(T. Gray) 70, 71, 205
Elementary School Classroom in a Slum
(Spender) 172
ELIOT, George (1819–1880) 62, 112,
120–2, 131, 137, 140, 207, 218
ELIOT, Thomas Stearns (1888–1965)
130, 140, 142, 145, 146, 148–52,
168, 174, 191–2
ELIZABETH I, Queen (1533–1603)
(Reigned 1558–1603) 7, 8, 10, 16,
18, 35, 41, 42
Eloisa to Abelard (Pope) 68–9
ELYOT, Sir Thomas (1499?–1546) 10
Emma (Austen) 90, 108–9
Enemy of the People, An (Ibsen) 190
England in 1819 (Shelley) 89, 102
England Made Me (Greene) 178
Epistle to Dr Arbuthnot, An (Pope) 69
ERASMUS, Desiderius (1466–1536) 7
Erewhon (Butler) 187
Essay on Criticism (Pope) 68
Essay on Man (Pope) 68
ETHEREGE, Sir George
(1634?–1691?) 56, 57
Europeans, The (James) 141
Eve of St Agnes, The (Keats) 103–4
Evelina (Burney) 83
EVELYN, John (1620–1706) 62
Every Man in His Humour (Johnson)
36, 37
Everyman (Anon) 15
Expostulation and Reply (Wordsworth)
92

Facade (Sitwell) 182
Faerie Queene, The (Spenser) 12, 47
FARQUHAR, George (1678–1707) 58
FARRELL, J. G. (1935–1979) 213,
215–16
Faustus see *Doctor Faustus*
Female Friends (Weldon) 219
Fern Hill (D. Thomas) 184

FIELDING, Henry (1707–1754) 79,
80–3, 84, 110
Finnegans Wake (Joyce) 84
First Love, Last Rites (McEwan) 221
FLETCHER, John (1579–1625) 38
Flight from the Enchanter (Murdoch) 210
FORSTER, E. M. (1879–1970) 157–8,
180, 214
Four Quartets (T. S. Eliot) 152
Fra Lippo Lippi (Browning) 128
FREUD, Sigmund (1856–1939) 145,
163, 183
FRIEL, Brian (1929–) 199–200
FRY, Christopher (1907–) 192, 193
Funeral Games (Orton) 196

GALSWORTHY, John (1867–1933)
156, 189
Game of Hide and Seek, A (E. Taylor) 207
Gammer Gurton's Needle 16
Garden, The (Marvell) 51
GASKELL, Mrs Elizabeth
(1810–1865) 114, 119–20
Gawain and the Green Knight, Sir
(Anon) 1, 4–5
GAY, John (1685–1732) 68
Gentlemen of England (A. N. Wilson) 221
GEORGE I, King (1660–1727)
(Reigned 1714–1727) 64
GEORGE III, King (1738–1820)
(Reigned 1760–1820) 65, 84, 99
Getting Married (Shaw) 188
Giaour, The (Byron) 99
Globe Theatre, The 26, 34
GODWIN, William (1756–1836) 89
Golden Notebook, The (Lessing) 211, 12–13
GOLDING, William (1911–1993)
206–7
GOLDSMITH, Oliver (1730?–1774)
70–1
Good (C. P. Taylor) 198
Goodbye to Berlin (Isherwood) 177
Gorboduc (Norton & Sackville) 16
Governor, The (Elyot) 10
GRANVILLE-BARKER, Harley
(1877–1946) 189

GRAY, Simon (1936–) 161
GRAY, Thomas (1716–1771) 70, 71, 205
Great Expectations (Dickens) 113, 143
GREEN, Henry (1905–1973) 180–1
GREENE, Graham (1904–1991) 45, 178–9, 205
GREENE, Robert (1558–1592) 22
GRENFELL, Julian (1888–1915) 147
Gulliver's Travels (Swift) 67–8, 75
Guy Mannering (W. Scott) 106
Guzman Go Home (Sillitoe) 210

HAGGARD, Rider (1856–1925) 144
HALLAM, Arthur (1811–1833) 126
Hamlet (Shakespeare) 28–9, 38, 65, 150
Hard Times (Dickens) 113
HARDY, Thomas (1840–1928) 119, 134, 137–40, 146, 147, 202, 204
HARE, David (1947–) 198
HARRISON, Tony (1937–) 204–5
HATHAWAY, Anne 22
Healing Art, The (A. N. Wilson) 222
HEANEY, Seamus (1939–) 203, 204
Heart of Darkness (Conrad) 159–61
Heart of Midlothian, The (W. Scott) 105–6
Heartbreak House (Shaw) 188
Helen (Edgeworth) 105
Hemlock and After (Angus Wilson) 206
Henry IV (Shakespeare) 25
Henry VI (Shakespeare) 23
HENRY VII, King (1457–1509) (Reigned 1485–1509) 7
HENRY VIII, King (1491–1547) (Reigned 1509–1547) 8
Henry Esmond (Thackeray) 116
HENRYSON, Robert (1425?–1500?) 6
HERBERT, George (1593–1633) 45, 46
Heroic Stanzas to the Glorious Memory of Cromwell (Dryden) 58
Herself Surprised (Cary) 179–80
HEYWOOD, John (1497?–1580?) 15
HEYWOOD, Thomas (1570?–1641) 40
High Wind in Jamaica (R. Hughes) 206

History Man, The (Bradbury) 216–17
History of King Richard III (More) 10
History of Mr Polly, The (Wells) 157
HOLTBY, Winifred (1898–1935) 178
Holy Sonnets, The (Donne) 43, 44
Homage to Catalonia (Orwell) 181
Homecoming, The (Pinter) 195
HOPKINS, Gerard Manley (1844–1889) 136–7, 203
Horatian Ode Upon Cromwell's Return from Ireland (Marvell) 50–1
HORNUNG, E. W. (1866–1921) 144
Horse's Mouth, The (Cary) 179–80
"House of Eld, The" (Stevenson) 143
HOUSMAN, A. E. (1859–1936) 50, 70, 134, 135–6, 138, 202
Howard's End (Forster) 180
HUGHES, Richard (1900–1976) 206
HUGHES, Ted (1930–) 203
Humphrey Clinker (Smollett) 83
HUNT, Leigh (1784–1859) 103, 124
Hurry on Down (Wain) 208
HUXLEY, Aldous (1894–1963) 87
Hymn to Proserpine (Swinburne) 134
Hyperion (Keats) 102

IBSEN, Henrik (1828–1906) 56, 185, 186, 187, 188, 189, 190
Ice Age, The (Drabble) 180, 217, 221
Ideal Husband, An (Wilde) 186
Idylls of the King, The (Tennyson) 125
Importance of Being Earnest, The (Wilde) 186–7
In Between the Sheets (McEwan) 221
In Memoriam (Tennyson) 125–6
Injury Time (Bainbridge) 218–19
Interludes 15
Irene (Johnson) 71
Isabella (Keats) 103
ISHERWOOD, Christopher (1904–1986) 172, 177–8, 192

JAMES I, King (1566–1625) (Reigned 1603–1625) 31, 35, 39, 40
JAMES II, King (1633–1701) (Reigned 1685–1688) 58

JAMES, Henry (1843–1916) 140,
141–3, 157
Jane Eyre (C. Brontë) 117–18
"Je ne Parle Pas Français" (Mansfield) 170
JELLICOE, Ann (1927–) 194
Jerusalem the Golden (Drabble) 217–18
Jewel in the Crown, The (P. Scott) 214
JOHN, King (1167–1216) (Reigned
1199–1216) 16
JOHNSON, Samuel (1709–1784) 64,
71–2, 84, 86
JONES, Inigo (1573–1651) 35
JONSON, Ben (1572–1637) 11–12,
23, 36–8, 65
Joseph Andrews (Fielding) 80–1
Journals (D. Wordsworth) 86–7
Journey of the Magi, The (T. S. Eliot)
130, 151–2
JOYCE, James (1882–1941) 3, 165–8,
169
Jude the Obscure (Hardy) 139–40
Julius Caesar (Shakespeare) 28
Juno and the Paycock (O'Casey) 190
Justice (Galsworthy) 189

KEATS, John (1795–1821) 38, 87, 97,
101, 102–4, 124, 130, 133, 147, 212
Kind of Loving, A (Barstow) 209
King of Henry IV (Shakespeare) 25
King Lear (Shakespeare) 23, 33
KING, Edward (1612–1637) 47
KIPLING, Rudyard (1865–1936)
143–4
Knight of the Burning Pestle, The
(Beaumont & Fletcher) 38
KORZENIOWSKI, Josef *see*
CONRAD, Joseph
Kubla Khan (Coleridge) 94, 96–7
KYD, Thomas (1558–1595) 18, 29
Kyng Johan (Bale) 16

Lady of Shalott, The (Tennyson) 124
Lady Windermere's Fan (Wilde) 186
Lady's Not For Burning, The (Fry) 192
L'Allegro (Milton) 47
"Lament for the Makaris" (Dunbar) 6

Lamia (Keats) 103
LANGLAND, William (1330?–1400?)
1, 5, 45
LARKIN, Philip (1922–1985) **202**, 208
Latest Decalogue, The (Clough) 131
LAWRENCE, D. H. (1885–1930) 81,
156, 162–5, 169, 175
LE CARRE, John (1931–) 213
LEHMANN, Rosamund (1903–) 205
LESSING, Doris (1919–) 211,
212–13
Levantine Trilogy (Manning) 213–14
LEWIS, C. Day *see* DAY LEWIS, Cecil
LEWIS, Matthew Gregory
(1775–1818) 88
*Life and Opinions of Tristram Shandy,
Gent* (Sterne) 84
Life of Samuel Johnson (Boswell) 71–2
*Lines Composed a Few Miles Above Tintern
Abbey* (Wordsworth) 91–2
Little Dorrit (Dickens) 133
Lives of the Poets, The (Johnson) 72
Living (Green) 180–1
Loitering with Intent (Spark) 211
London Fields (M. Amis) 222–3
*Loneliness of the Long-Distance Runner,
The* (Sillitoe) 209
Look Back in Anger (Osborne) 192–3
Look! We Have Come Through!
(Lawrence) 163
Loot (Orton) 196
Lord of the Flies (Golding) 206
Love Song of J. Alfred Prufrock, The (T. S.
Eliot) 148–50, 168
Love's Labours Lost (Shakespeare) 25–6
LOVELACE, Richard (1618–1658) 46
Loving (Green) 180, 181
Lucky Jim (K. Amis) 208–9
Lullaby (Auden) 173
Lycidas (Milton) 5, 47, 101
Lyrical Ballads (Wordsworth &
Coleridge) 89, 94

MACAULAY, Rose (1889–1958) 206
MACAULAY, Thomas (1800–1859)
189, 198

Macbeth (Shakespeare) 17, 23, **31–3**

McEWAN, Ian (1948–) 221

MacFlecknoe (Dryden) 61

MacNEICE, Louis (1907–1963) 171, 174

Madras House, The (Granville-Barker) 189

Magistrate, The (Pinero) 186

Maid's Tragedy, The (Beaumont & Fletcher) **38**

Malayan Trilogy (Burgess) 212

MALORY, Sir Thomas (d. 1471) **5**

Man of Mode, The (Etherege) **56**

MANNING, Olivia (1911–1980) 211, 213–14, 217

MANSFIELD, Katherine (1888–1923) 169–70, 205

"Markheim" (Stevenson) 143

MARLOWE, Christopher (1564–1593) 7, 16, **19–21**, 22, 23, 24

Marriage of Figaro, The (Beaumarchais) 71

MARVELL, Andrew (1621–1678) **50–1**

MARX, Karl (1818–1883) 145

MARY I, Queen (1516–1558) (Reigned 1553–1558) 8

Mary Barton (Gaskell) **119–20**

Masques 35, 47

Massacre at Paris, The (Marlowe) 20

Master Builder, The (Ibsen) 190

Maud (Tennyson) **125**

MAUGHAM, Somerset (1874–1965) 193

Mayor of Casterbridge, The (Hardy) 140

Measure for Measure (Shakespeare) **33**

MELBOURNE, Lord (1779–1848) 36, 189

Memento Mori (Spark) 210

Merchant of Venice, The (Shakespeare) 27

MERES, Francis (1565–1647) 22

Merry Wives of Windsor, The (Shakespeare) 37

Metaphysical Poetry **41–6**, 50, 137

Middle Age of Mrs Eliot, The (Angus Wilson) 206

Middlemarch (G. Eliot) **121–2**

MIDDLETON, Thomas (1570–1627) 40

Midnight's Children (Rushdie) 225

MILL, John Stuart (1806–1873) 112, 129

Mill on the Floss, The (G. Eliot) 62, 121

MILLER, Arthur (1915–) 192

MILTON, John (1608–1674) 5, 10, 13, 33, 41, **42–6**, 50, 51, 80, 101, 102, 103

Miracle Plays *see* Mystery Plays

Miss Gee (Auden) 173

MITCHELL, Julian (1935–) 213

Modest Proposal, A (Swift) 67

Moll Flanders (Defoe) 74, **77–8**

Monk, The (Lewis) 88

Moral Essays (Pope) **69**

Morality Plays 15

MORE, Sir Thomas (1478–1535) 7, 10, 15

Morte D'Arthur (Malory) **5–6**

MORTIMER, Penelope (1918–) 217

Mousetrap, The (Christie) 192

Mr Norris Changes Trains (Isherwood) 177

Mr Sludge, 'The Medium' (Browning) 129

Mrs Dalloway (Woolf) **168–9**

Mrs Palfrey at the Claremont (E. Taylor) 207

Mrs Warren's Profession (Shaw) **187–8**

Much Ado About Nothing (Shakespeare) **26**

Murder in the Cathedral (T. S. Eliot) **191–2**

MURDOCH, Iris (1919–) 208, **210**, 211

My Last Duchess (Browning) **127–8**

Mystery Plays **14–15**

NAPOLEON I (1769–1821) 89, 212

NAPOLEON III (1808–1873) 129

Napoleon Symphony (Burgess) 212

Needle's Eye, The (Drabble) 218

NEWBOLT, Sir Henry (1862–1938) 146

Newcomes, The (Thackeray) 116

Nightmare Abbey (Peacock) 106
Nights at the Circus (Carter) 223–4
No Laughing Matter (Angus Wilson) 206
North and South (Gaskell) 120
Nostromo (Conrad) 161–2
Notorious Mrs Ebbsmith, The (Pinero) 186
"Nowaks, The" (Isherwood) 177–8

O'BRIEN, Edna (1932–) 217
O'CASEY, Sean (1884–1964) 190, 190–1
Ode on a Grecian Urn (Keats) 104
Ode on Melancholy (Keats) 104
Ode to a Nightingale (Keats) 104
Ode to the West Wind (Shelley) 102
Odes to St Cecilia (Dryden) 62
Old Country, The (Alan Bennett) 213
OLIPHANT, Mrs Margaret (1828–1897) 122
Oliver Twist (Dickens) 112–13
"On Reugen Island" (Isherwood) 177
On the Constitution of Church and State (Coleridge) 93–4
Origin of Species (Darwin) 111, 132
Oroonoko (Behn) 63
Orphan Island (R. Macaulay) 206
ORTON, Joe (1933–1967) 187, 196, 198
ORWELL, George (1903–1950) 145, 181–2
OSBORNE, John (1929–) 192–3, 194, 197
OSSIAN 73
Othello (Shakespeare) 29–31
OTWAY, Thomas (1652–1685) 57
OUIDA (1839–1908) 144, 207
Our Mutual Friend (Dickens) 165
OWEN, Wilfred (1893–1918) 147–8
Ozymandias (Shelley) 101–2

Pamela (Richardson) 75, 78–9, 80, 81
Paradise Lost (Milton) 46, 47–50, 61
Paradise Regained (Milton) 46, 50
Passage to India, A (Forster) 158, 214
PATER, Walter (1839–1894) 152

PEACOCK, Thomas Love (1785–1866) 106
Pearl (Anon) 5
Pendennis (Thackeray) 116
Penseroso, Il (Milton) 47
PEPYS, Samuel (1633–1703) 53, 62
Peregrine Pickle, The Adventures of (Smollett) 83
Philadelphia, Here I Come (Friel) 199
Picaresque Novels 81, 83
Pickwick Papers (Dickens) 112
Picture of Dorian Gray, The (Wilde) 134
Piers Plowman (Langland) 5
Pilgrim's Progress (Bunyan) 62–3, 116
PINERO, Arthur Wing (1855–1934) 186
PINTER, Harold (1930–1) 194–6
Pippa Passes (Browning) 126
PLATH, Sylvia (1932–1963) 203
PLATTER, Thomas 17
Play of the Wether, The (Heywood) 15
Playboy of the Western World, The (Synge) 190
Plenty (Hare) 198
Plough and the Stars, The (O'Casey) 190
POPE, Alexander (1688–1744) 65, 68–70
Porphyria's Lover (Browning) 127
Portrait of a Lady (James) 141–2
Portrait of the Artist as a Young Man, A (Joyce) 166–7
POUND, Ezra (1885–1972) 146, 152, 174
POWELL, Anthony (1905–) 205
Power and the Glory, The (Greene) 179
Praxis (Weldon) 219
Pre-Raphaelites 134
Prelude, The (Wordsworth) 91, 93
Pride and Prejudice (Austen) 107
PRIESTLEY, J. B. (1894–1984) 178
Prime of Miss Jean Brodie, The (Spark) 211
Prince Hohenstiel-Schwangau (Browning) 129
Prometheus Unbound (Shelley) 101
Prophetic Books (Blake) 73
Prothalamion (Spenser) 13

Prufrock see *The Love Song of J. Alfred Prufrock*
Pygmalion (Shaw) 188
Pylons, The (Spender) 173
PYM, Barbara (1913–1980) 207–8

Quartet in Autumn (Pym) 208
Quiet Life, A (Bainbridge) 218

RADCLIFFE, Mrs Ann (1764–1823) 88
Rainbow, The (Lawrence) 164
Raj Quartet (P. Scott) 211, 214–15
Ralph Roister Doister (Udall) 16
Rape of the Lock (Pope) 69
Rasselas (Johnson) 71
RASTELL, John (1475–1536) 15
RATTIGAN, Terence (1911–1977) 192, 197
Recessional (Kipling) 143
Recruiting Officer, The (Farquhar) 58
Reform Bill, The (1832) 121, 122
Refusal to Mourn the Death, by Fire, of a Child in London, A (D. Thomas) 184
Return of the Native, The (Hardy) 138
Revenge (Brenton) 198
Revenge Tragedy 18, 29
Revenger's Tragedy, The (Tourneur) 40
Richard II (Shakespeare) 18, 24–5
RICHARD III, King (1452–1485) (Reigned 1483–1485) 23
Richard III (Shakespeare) 23–4
RICHARDSON, Dorothy (1873–1957) 167
RICHARDSON, Samuel (1689–1761) 75, 78–80, 81, 83
Riders to the Sea (Synge) 190
Ring and the Book, The (Browning) 129
Rites of Passage (Golding) 206–7
Rivals, The (Sheridan) 71
Road to Wigan Pier, The (Orwell) 181
ROBERTSON, T. W. (1829–1871) 185
Robinson Crusoe (Defoe) 75, 76–7
ROCHESTER, John Earl of (1647–1680) 62
Roderick Random, the Adventures of (Smollett) 83

Romans in Britain (Brenton) 198
Romanticism 84–98, 123, 149, 155
Romeo and Juliet (Shakespeare) 17, 27–8
Room at the Top (Braine) 209
Roots (Wesker) 194
ROSENBERG, Isaac (1890–1918) 147
RUSHDIE, Salman (1947–) 225
RUSKIN, John (1819–1900) 129

Sailing to Byzantium (Yeats) 154–5
Saint Joan (Shaw) 188–9
Samson Agonistes (Milton) 46, 50
Satanic Verses, The (Rushdie) 225
Saturday Night and Sunday Morning (Sillitoe) 209
Saved (Bond) 197
SAYERS, Dorothy L. (1893–1957) 175
School for Scandal, The (Sheridan) 71
SCOTT, Paul (1920–1978) 211, 213, 214–15
SCOTT, Sir Walter (1771–1832) 88, 97, 105–6, 107, 117, 137
Sea and Sardinia (Lawrence) 164–5
Sea, the Sea, The (Murdoch) 210
Seascape (Auden) 173–4
Second Coming, The (Yeats) 154
Secret Agent, The (Conrad) 145
Serious Money (C. Churchill) 198–9
Serjeant Musgrave's Dance (Arden) 197
Severed Head, A (Murdoch) 211
SHADWELL, Thomas (1642?–1692) 61
SHAKESPEARE, William (1564–1616) 17, 18, 19, **22–34**, 36, 37, 38, 42, 50, 65, 72, 85, 102, 103, 110, 114, 130, 150, 185, 192
Shamela (Fielding) **80**
SHAW, George Bernard (1856–1950) 186, 187–9, 193
She Dwelt Among the Untrodden Ways (Wordsworth) 90–1
She Stoops to Conquer (Goldsmith) 71
SHELLEY, Percy Bysshe (1792–1822) 13, 87, 89, **100–2**, 106, 123, 134
Shepheardes Calender, The (Spenser) 12–13

SHERIDAN, Richard Brinsley
(1751–1816) 56, 71, 186
Shoemaker's Holiday, The (Dekker) 38
*Short View of the Immorality and
Profaneness of the English Stage*
(Collier) 57
Shropshire Lad, The (Housman) 50, 135
SIDNEY, Sir Philip (1554–1586) 11
Siege of Krishnapur, The (Farrell) 215
SILLITOE, Alan (1928–) **209–10**
Silver Tassie, The (O'Casey) 190
Singapore Grip, The (Farrell) **215**
Sir Gawain and the Green Knight see
Gawain and the Green Knight
SITWELL, Edith (1887–1964) **182–3**,
184, 202
SITWELL, Osbert (1892–1969) 182
SITWELL, Sacheverell (1897–) 182
SKELTON, John (1460?–1529) 8
SMART, Christopher (1722–1771) 70,
73
SMOLLETT, Tobias (1721–1771) **83**
SNOW, C. P. (1905–1980) 205
Society (Robertson) 185
Soldier, The (Brooke) 147
Solitary Reaper, The (Wordsworth) 90
Songs of Experience (Blake) 73
Songs of Innocence (Blake) 73
Sons and Lovers (Lawrence) **162–3**, 166
SORLEY, Charles (1895–1915) 147
South Riding (Holtby) 178
SOUTHEY, Robert (1774–1843) 88,
89
Spanish Civil War 172, 173, 174, 181
Spanish Tragedy, The (Kyd) **18**
SPARK, Muriel (1918–) **210–11**, 223
Spectator, The (Addison & Steele) 75
SPENDER, Stephen (1909–) 171,
172–3
SPENSER, Edmund (1552?–1599) 7,
9, 11–13, 38, 42, 85, 98, 103
Spire, The (Golding) 206
St Joan (Shaw) **188–9**
Stanzas from the Grande Chartreuse
(Arnold) 130
STEELE, Richard (1672–1729) 75

Stepping Westward (Bradbury) 216
STERNE, Laurence (1713–1768) 84
STEVENSON, Robert Louis
(1850–1894) 143, 144
Still Falls the Rain (Sitwell) 183
STOPPARD, Tom (1937–) 197
STOREY, David (1933–) 197
Strangers and Brothers (Snow) 205
Strife (Galsworthy) 189
"Such Darling Dodos" (Angus Wilson)
206
SUCKLING, Sir John (1609–1642) 46
Summer (Bond) 197
Sun Rising, The (Donne) 43–4
SURREY, Henry Earl of (1517?–1547)
8, 9–10
SWIFT, Graham (1949–) **224–5**
SWIFT, Jonathan (1667–1745) **66–8**,
70, 110, 223
SWINBURNE, Algernon
(1837–1909) **133–4**
Sword of Honour (Waugh) 176, 213
SYNGE, John Millington
(1871–1909) 190

Tables Turned, The (Wordsworth) 92
Tale of a Tub, The (Swift) 66
Tamburlaine the Great (Marlowe) 19, 21
Taming of the Shrew, The (Shakespeare)
25
Taste of Honey, A (Delaney) 194
Tatler, The (Steele) 75
TAYLOR, C. P. (1929–1982) 198
TAYLOR, Elizabeth (1912–1975) **207**
Tempest, The (Shakespeare) 34
TENNYSON, Alfred (1809–1892) 10,
12, 97, 112, **123–6**, 127, 129–30,
183
Tess of the D'Urbervilles (Hardy) **138–9**,
140
Testament of Cresseid (Henryson) 6
THACKERAY, William Makepeace
(1811–1863) 66, **114–16**, 121
THOMAS, Dylan (1914–1953) 155,
183–4, 202
THOMAS, Edward (1878–1917) 147

THOMAS, R. S. (1913–) **203–4**
THOMSON, James (1700–1748) 70
Tintern Abbey (Wordsworth) **91–2**
Tithonus (Tennyson) 125
Titus Andronicus (Shakespeare) 19, 23
To a Skylark (Shelley) 101
To Be a Pilgrim (Cary) **179–80**
To His Coy Mistress (Marvell) 51
To the Lighthouse (Woolf) 169
To the Memory of Mr Oldham (Dryden) 62
Tom Jones (Fielding) 74, 75, **81–2**
TOURNEUR, Cyril (1575?–1626?) 40
Towneley Cycle 15
Toxophilus (Ascham) 10
Translations (Friel) 199
Treasure Island (Stevenson) 143
Trelawny of the Wells (Pinero) 186
Trilogy (Wesker) 194
Tristram Shandy (Sterne) 84
Troilus and Cressida (Shakespeare) 33
Troilus and Criseyde (Chaucer) (6)
TROLLOPE, Anthony (1815–1882)
  45, 74–5, 114, **120–1**, 137
TROLLOPE, Frances (1780–1863) 122
Troubles (Farrell) **215–16**
TURGENEV, Ivan (1818–1883) 140
Twelfth Night (Shakespeare) **26–7**

UDALL, Nicholas (1505–1556) 16
Ulysses (Joyce) 84, 165, **167–8**
Ulysses (Tennyson) **124–5**
Under the Net (Murdoch) 208
Utopia (More) 10

V (Harrison) **204–5**
Vanity Fair (Thackeray) **115–16**, 121
Vanity of Human Wishes, The (Johnson)
  71
VAUGHAN, Henry (1622–1695) 46
Venice Preserved (Otway) **57–8**
VICTORIA, Queen (1819–1901)
  (Reigned 1837–1901) 36, 110, 112,
  123, 124, 132, 137
Vile Bodies (Waugh) **175–6**
Villette (C. Brontë) 117
Vision, A (Yeats) 154

Vision of Judgment, The (Byron) 99
Vision of Piers Plowman, The see *Piers
  Plowman*
Volpone (Jonson) **36–7**
Vortex, The (Coward) 191

WAIN, John (1925–) 56, 208
Waiting for Godot (Beckett) **194–5**
WALPOLE, Sir Robert (1676–1745)
  64, 65
Wars of the Roses 5, 7
Waste (Granville-Barker) 189
Waste Land, The (T. S. Eliot) **150–1**
Waterland (G. Swift) **224–5**
WAUGH, Evelyn (1903–1966) 150,
  169, 171, 174–7, 179, 182, 187,
  201, 205, 213
Way of the World, The (Congreve) **56–7**
Way We Live Now, The (Trollope) **120–1**
WEBSTER, John (1580?–1625?)
  38–40, 151
Weir of Hermiston (Stevenson) 143
WELDON, Fay (1933–) **219**, 223
WELLS, H. G. (1866–1946) 156
WESKER, Arnold (1932–) **194**, 197
Where Angels Fear to Tread (Forster) 157
Who was Oswald Fish? (A. N. Wilson)
  222
Widower's Son (Sillitoe) 210
WILDE, Oscar (1854–1900) 57, 132,
  134–5, 152, **186–7**, 196
WILLIAMS, Tennessee (1912–1982) 192
WILSON, A. N. (1950–) **221–2**
WILSON, Angus (1913–1991) **205–6**,
  221
Windhover (Hopkins) 137
Winter Garden (Bainbridge) 219
Wise Children (Carter) 224
Wives and Daughters (Gaskell) 120
Woman Killed With Kindness, A
  (Heywood) 40
Women in Love (Lawrence) 164
WOOLF, Virginia (1882–1941) 156,
  168–9, 175, 207
WORDSWORTH, Dorothy
  (1771–1855) **86–7**

WORDSWORTH, William
(1770–1850) 10, 70, 85, 86, 87, 88,
89–93, 94, 98, 100, 102, 130, 137,
183
World War I 145, 147, 171
World War II 176, 181
Wuthering Heights (E. Brontë) 27,
118–19

WYATT, Sir Thomas (1503?–1542)
8–9, 10
WYCHERLEY, William (1640–1716)
54–6, 57

YEATS, William Butler (1865–1939)
152–5, 190
York Cycle 14

Farm Dog Martha

Adaptation by Karen Barss
Based on a TV series teleplay written by Peter K. Hirsch
Based on the characters created by Susan Meddaugh

HOUGHTON MIFFLIN HARCOURT
Boston • New York • 2009

Green Light Readers and its logo are trademarks of Houghton Mifflin Harcourt Publishing Company.

For information about permission to reproduce selections from this book, write to Permissions, Houghton Mifflin Harcourt Publishing Company, 215 Park Avenue South, New York, New York 10003.

Library of Congress Cataloging-in-Publication data is on file.

ISBN: 978-0-547-36893-1

Design by Stephanie Cooper

www.hmhbooks.com
www.marthathetalkingdog.com

Manufactured in China
LEO 10 9 8 7 6 5 4 3 2 1

Martha is going to a farm for the first time. The farm belongs to a man named C.K. "I'm going to love the farm," Martha says. "I think."

Martha asks, "Can I do some farm chores?"
"Sure! We herd the sheep, feed the
chickens, and milk the cows," says C.K.
Martha cannot wait to begin in the morning.
Those chores sound like fun.

It is late when they arrive.
Wooo-rooo!
"What is that sound?" asks Martha.
C.K. tells her not to be afraid.

"A hound dog lives next door," C.K. says.
Martha wonders.
Dog howls are not so scary.

The next morning C.K.
wakes Martha.
He says, "Rise and shine."
"But it is still dark out!"
Martha cries.
C.K. says farm chores begin
before the sun rises.

Here is their task:
First, they will herd the sheep.
The sheep must be moved from
the pen into the pasture.

C.K. tells Martha that the sheep
are stubborn.
But Martha tells the sheep what to do.
The sheep go out the gate!
No problem.

"Good job, Martha," C.K. says.
"Now you keep the sheep in the pasture.
I will milk the cows."
C.K. leaves Martha alone with the sheep.

Martha talks to the sheep.
"Eat as much as you want.
But stay in the pasture."
The sheep walk into
the woods.

"Baaaaa!" say the sheep.
They say the woods are part
of the pasture.
Martha believes them.
She goes to see what other
jobs she can do.

Martha enters the hen house.
"Any chores for me here?" Martha asks.
The hens say, "Cluck!"
"You want me to sit on your eggs?"
Martha asks.

No problem.
Martha sits.
"Oooh, nice and toasty," Martha says.
She sees a photo on the floor.
What a mean-looking dog, she thinks.

Soon C.K. goes into the house.
He finds a surprise.
Sheep and chickens
are everywhere.
This is a problem.
"The chickens belong in the
hen house."

"And the sheep belong in the pasture," C.K. says. "The pasture is the grassy area where they can eat." "They tricked me!" says Martha.

Late that night, Martha
hears the sheep.
They are trying to trick me
again, she thinks.
But the sheep sound scared.
Martha runs to the pasture.

Martha sees a mean-looking
dog in the pen.
The sheep are trapped!

Martha opens the gate for the sheep.
But Martha gets locked in the pen!
The mean-looking dog comes closer.
It is a coyote!

Martha is brave.
She barks.
She growls.
The coyote runs away.
The sheep are safe.

"Thank you for saving the sheep," C.K. says. "You are a great farm dog, Martha."
Martha beams.
"It was no problem!"

Don't miss these
MARTHA SPEAKS
adventures:

Chapter books

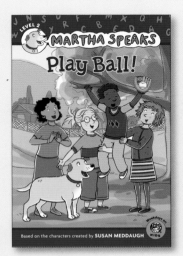

Early reader

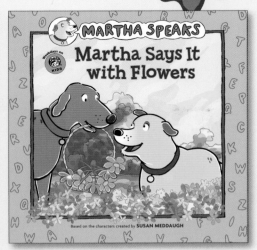

Picture book